23 SWEET FAs

23 SWEET FAs

Round the World With a Football Table

by Andy Sloan

First published in Great Britain in 2006 by
Virgin Books Ltd
Thames Wharf Studios
Rainville Road
London
W6 9HA

A catalogue record for this book is available
from the British Library.

ISBN 0 7535 1125 8
ISBN 9 780 753 511251

Typeset by Phoenix Photosetting, Chatham, Kent
Printed and bound in Great Britain by
Clays Ltd, Bungay, Suffolk

CONTENTS

To everybody who believed in me, you know who you are.
Thank you.

'Whatever you do, or dream you can, begin it. Boldness has genius, power and magic.'

Goethe

IN THE NAME OF GOD

**FOOTBALL FEDERATION
ISLAMIC REPUBLIC OF IRAN**

1. 23 SWEET FAs

Email from Stephen Spence to Andy Sloan, 7 April 2001:

> Alright mate, how you doing ... you nearly had me with your email, sounds great, what an idea, carrying a football table overland to the world cup! But then I saw the date, 1st April, nice one, maybe next time. I'm not that gullible!
> Steve

The telephone rang. It was my mum. 'Errr ... Andrew ... you have a letter at home from the Football Federation of the Islamic Republic of Iran ... what are you up to?'

Officially I was slaving away revising for my university finals. However, between library sessions, the impeccable timing of three housemates turning 21 within four days, and a nasty elbow in the face that involved two operations and a piece of metal screwing my eye back together, I was dreaming about, and planning, the year ahead: an adventure the size of which I could never have believed.

It was a beautiful, crisp morning as Matt and I dragged ourselves from the depths of our beds to begin the painful journey home. We were returning after a night of New

1

Year's festivities, and the English tradition of drinking too much had sprung another cunning attack on us. The inevitable train delay gave us time to converse. I was planning to travel after university and, having never backpacked alone, I had been trying to talk Matt into joining me on an overland trip from England to Korea, which, tantalisingly, was hosting the World Cup in partnership with Japan in June 2002; a perfect end to a yearlong adventure.

Naturally, he baulked at the idea of travelling for a year. To backpack and be constantly on the move for so long would surely get tiresome. Although our senses would be taking in new and wonderful splendours, we feared a monotonous routine of arriving, unpacking, seeing the sights, then moving on. So, our minds loosened by hangovers that replaced common sense with a tendency to ramble, we started joking about how to make it more exciting.

The World Cup is a magical event, an important part of the social make up of the majority of Englishmen, if not the human race. Proposing to end the trip with such a football spectacle, we had toyed with the idea of turning it into a football pilgrimage. It would give us direction. We would aim for the great stadiums en route, follow a trail of foreign fixtures and hunt down the bizarre and the beautiful of the world game. I then got a bit carried away and something slipped out about a football table 'we could challenge all the Football Associations on the way . . . can you imagine!' That was it. The idea was out.

When friends at university asked what I was going to do after exams I would joke that I was going to travel overland to the World Cup. After a few beers I would joke that I was going to carry a table-football table with me. It was a mixture of telling too many people, combined with their reactions of disbelief, and the inherent Britishness of doing something adventurous for absolutely no reason, that sealed my fate.

It was a ridiculous challenge. Could we sneak into stadiums? Would the Football Associations of the world accept the challenge? Could two fans really get behind the scenes of world football, pace the corridors and pitches of power, with a smile and a football table? Did world minnows like Laos or Bangladesh even have football teams?

Napoleon once said, 'I was full of dreams, I saw myself founding a new religion, marching into Asia riding an elephant, a turban on my head and in my hands the new Koran I would have written to suit my needs.' Just what exactly would the world outside our safe haven of Europe make of two Englishmen striding around their country with a table-football table? Would they embrace our football religion? Would the billion-strong cricketing nation of India drive us from their shores? Would the brutal Russian winter finish us off as it did the Germans and Napoleon himself? Wasn't Iran next to Iraq? And could we cope with the prospect of squat toilets for at least eight months?

A plan was needed. Having pushed my revision joyfully to one side, I drew a rough route on a world map then wrote 23 letters to the Football Associations of the 23 countries through which it passed. The addresses were on the FIFA website. Even military regimes like Burma (now Myanmar) keep up their football. By the time I came to post them I had been persuaded to carry a camera and make a film, which might even cover the cost of the trip. The letters suddenly took on a more official feel.

> Horsham
> England
> tablefootball@hotmail.com

Football Association
Random nation

Dear Sirs

My name is Andy Sloan. Later on this year I will be making a television programme about world football in the run up to the World Cup in 2002 and am looking to secure interviews with personnel in each country, hopefully national managers, players and FA presidents. There is a slight difference from conventional interviews.

In short a friend and I are carrying a table-football

table overland from London to Korea with the aim of challenging the Football Associations of each country and as many famous footballers or people connected with football as we can track down on our journey through the country.

We hope to uncover the footballing history of each country we pass through and visit the places and the people who made that history. We want to convey the rich past and future of football around the world, from the top nations to the minnows of the game, whose national teams may not share such a celebrated history but whose people live and breathe the same passion for what is arguably the greatest game on earth.

If you would be able to grant us an interview, even for a few minutes, to share some memories, views, and a quick game of tablefootball, or if you could supply us with some useful addresses that would be fantastic. Please feel free to email me at the above address if you can help in any way.

Yours hopefully

Andy Sloan

In reflection I wince at the innocence of the letter, but 23 of them went out and I was bowled over by the response . . . nothing.

Then the phone rang: 'Mum!' We were in business.

2. 'OJOGO BONITO' (THE BEAUTIFUL GAME)

Every little boy dreams of playing in the World Cup final. At school I used to run around the playground pretending I was Gary Lineker or Bobby Charlton. With the football came the mandatory commentary as I dribbled towards goal. Sadly it would more often end in a bloody knee and torn trouser than 'Sloan wins the World Cup for England!'

When you did score, which for me, being placed at left back for the school team, was rarely, it was the most fantastic feeling on this planet. It may only be a muddy field with a packed crowd of seven dutiful parents in their wellies, but at that moment you are transported onto the biggest stage your imagination can deliver.

There is a certain infectious magic to football. Although this feeling is not shared by everyone all of the time, football has the power to draw in and captivate even the most sceptical critics with its flashes of brilliance, triumphs of teamwork and, most of all, its emotion. Just consider that the 1994 World Cup in America had a cumulative audience of thirty billion. Either everybody on the planet watched five games or a lot of people watched a lot of football.

Its magic stems from its universality. It lacks the brutality of rugby, it demands not the expenses of golf and it does without the pernickety rules of cricket. It can be played with anything vaguely spherical of any size on any surface. Anyone, any-where, can emulate their heroes just as we did on our play-grounds and do now in our lunch breaks. Anybody can become a footballer, be they fat, skinny, tall or short – the dream is always alive. And when the heroes of the present day are doing badly, then there is always next year, next season, the next World Cup to look forward to and cheer.

The prospect of travelling overland across the globe using the international language of football as a passport was mouthwatering. We had heard on the news about the fanatical support in Asia for the English Premiership and now the Far East was hosting its first-ever World Cup. Amid Asia's great feeling of pride and celebration our adventure should be well received, the medium of football proving the perfect introduction.

It was also a chance for us to challenge the conventions of the modern age. Football has taken off commercially over the past decade or so and its working heart has become increasingly inaccessible to the man on the street. More available than ever on our screens, with enough channels now to cover every competition, the game has distanced itself from the very fans that support it. The players have become well protected, heavily contracted possessions of wealthy media empires, and the clubs are neurotic over their prized turf. Would it be possible to talk our way into these corridors of the famous, to break down the barriers, to walk the hallowed pitches of the world's great stadiums, and all with a football table?

Two things were missing and a third was starting to scare me. First, it does not take a genius to work out that for a tablefootball adventure one needs a table-football table. A hunt around various toy stores drew an alarming blank. The internet produced only eighty-kilogram beasts designed to withstand a riot in a pub. Eighty kilos seemed a bit much for my eleven-stone physique. I was at a loss until a friend pointed out the Toys 'Я' Us superstore on the outskirts of town.

A tired but colourfully clad Toys 'Я' Us worker took my docket and found the football table that I was requesting. It looked perfect: a cartable size (as far as football tables go) and with a wealth of features. There were electronic scoreboards at each end, crowds painted all the way round and cheering when someone scored. It was fantastic.

The assistant looked bemused when I asked him to pass it over the counter so I could gauge its weight. It was heavy: about fifteen kilograms. With a rucksack and video camera to worry about, carrying fifteen kilos of football table was just too much. After several minutes balancing it in turn on each shoulder I passed it back asking, 'I don't suppose you've got a lighter one?' Blankness met me. 'I'm thinking about carrying it up to Everest so the weight is kind of important.'

'Eh? Oh . . . err . . . I'll go look,' came the reply. The mention of the highest mountain on earth had sparked something behind his glum exterior but he hid it well. Along with those sinister people on computer helplines, superstore helpers are masters in the art of withholding information. Eventually he returned. 'No, we don't.' It was back to the drawing board.

Someone was looking down on me though; the very next day I had a call from a friend whose flatmates had a table-football table. It was going to be homeless after exams when they all moved out. The perfect size, with screw-in metal legs and all up weighing about seven kilos, we had found our companion. Lovingly placed in the centre of their living room, it was used to attention and was deserving of our journey. What is more, it was the exact replica of a football table I had had at home many moons before. It was ideal: loved for years and now off on one last adventure. As we left, its former owner tapped me on the shoulder, shook my hand, gave one last, longing look and said, 'Take care of her'.

The second missing item was tickets to the World Cup. As the crowning glory at the end of the long road they were rather key to our adventure. How sickening would it be to travel all that way, experience all the excitement and anticipation and not see a game? They proved far easier to obtain than I could have imagined.

For the first time in the competition's history, tickets were available over the internet. The sale would be in three stages: a ballot, a first-come-first-served allocation and a final ballot of the remainder. You could select a team-specific ticket (TST) as far through the tournament as you felt your team would go. Being an English football fan, i.e. naïve and hopeful, I put down to go all the way.

A month later I got the rejection email. I was devastated but remained determined. I watched the dates like a hawk, and when the hour came for the first-come-first-served stage I was ready. Sadly, so were millions of others, from England to Shanghai, all logging on chasing the ultimate pot of gold. The site crashed, unable to cope with such overwhelming numbers. It became the most 'hit' site in internet history.

Patience is a virtue and, after hours of trying over several days, mine was rewarded. As we were restricted to one set of tickets per person I had alerted Matt to give me his passport details. An availability chart appeared. For England a TST-7 (all the way to the final) was 'low availability'. A TST-6 (up to and including the semi-final) was 'good availability'. Resisting the urge to go for the final tickets, I sensibly selected the greater chance of any tickets at all. A bird in the hand is worth two in the bush, as the saying goes. And it was true, as all those who gambled on trying to get the TST-7 and ended up with nothing will no doubt vouch for. Greed, however, is a bastard. It took me a long time to hit that TST-6 button.

To glorious delight, days after my last exam, I learned that Matt and I had tickets to the World Cup; more precisely, we had tickets for every England game bar the final. I had emailed everyone to let them know that World Cup tickets were on sale and was sure there would be a stampede to join me. I was wrong. No one believed England would qualify.

Personally, the thought of England not qualifying had never even crossed my mind. I was about to embark on a crazy adventure across the world to far-flung foreign shores and had tickets to the World Cup, the mightiest competition on Earth. We were invincible. I must admit that it did subsequently cross my mind, frequently. But after a few drinks there was never any doubt about it, and I let everybody know.

The third thing, the potentially scary one, was that Matt had not yet agreed to come. He kept putting his decision off. 'Probably, but ...' Travelling on my own would be something new and somewhat daunting, but setting out alone doing something as conspicuous as lugging a football table with me was downright terrifying. I was quite happy to try my luck rocking up to FAs and stadiums with someone else to laugh with afterwards, but on my own the highs and lows would be much more personal. So I pestered him. In fact I pestered everyone: anyone who I knew would love a year on the road and many more who would be wholly unsuited. Most did not believe I would be able to pull off such a venture. Some, as evidenced by Steve's email at the start of this book, simply did not believe me.

Eventually Matt said yes. My excitement had rubbed off on him. Travel talk is infectious and it is almost impossible not to get itchy feet, especially when a trip is served on a plate. We both spoke to the bank the very next day.

Lacking a job offer for his return, Matt found that his bank was not quite as forthcoming as my own. He was forced to work over the summer and would join me at the end of September. I would be on my own for the most worrying part of the journey, the start.

A knight in shining armour appeared: Mike, a friend from university. It could not have been easier. 'Yeah mate, love to, sounds mad.' A sound and jovial Yorkshireman, Mike could only join the trip for the summer as he still had another year in Bristol, but as it was his former flatmates who had provided the table it was fitting that he should escort it on its first forays. Everything was falling into place.

The planned route was simple; simple because we only had three set points. First was the crucial World Cup qualifier, Germany v England, in Munich on 1 September 2001; second, revealed courtesy of the FIFA website, was the jaw-dropping prospect of Iran v Iraq in Tehran on 12 October 2001; and third, the start of the World Cup itself on

31 May 2002 in Korea and Japan. With only three dates to remember there was plenty of room for one more and it was to be the most important. The start of our journey, kick-off: 21 July 2001.

3. FRANCE

The 21st of July came around brutally fast. So we left on the 23rd. A journey of a thousand miles must begin with a single step, but often that step is the hardest to take. It was my girlfriend's birthday on 19 July so I was under orders not to leave before then. Of course I could not leave on the 20th either as that would mean she would be sad on her birthday. This left the 21st. But that enabled me to have a farewell bash. This bash knocked out the 21st and eliminated the 22nd through a combination of hangovers and last-minute panics. Mike and I finally jumped on a train on the morning of the 23rd.

With a metal plate now holding my cheekbone together, I had scraped through my exams and embarked on sorting visas for Russia and Iran. Before you ask, no, I do not beep in airports, you cannot adorn me with fridge magnets and I cannot pick up Radio One.

Funnily enough, Russia and Iran will not let you simply stroll in and say hello. This is part of the reason I wanted to go there. It transpired that to obtain both visas simply involved enrolling for fake tours and parting with plenty of US dollars. The Russian Embassy website even had a link to the '*buy* an invitation to Russia' site.

Visas sorted, Lonely Planets bought, fears banished,

England shirts washed; we were ready for action. Mike's mum had even sewn a fantastic, giant, waterproof, purple bag to carry the table in. Yet we were still lacking a video camera to capture our exploits. A few months earlier I had contacted a production company. They had replied instantly with promise after promise, but delayed and delayed until I was forced to say sorry, we have to leave, we'll film it ourselves.

A few calls to the Beeb revealed the quality of camera needed to realise any aspirations of securing a documentary and out we bowled to hunt one down. Such an investment was a mighty risk, but I had a strange confidence in our plans and a big enough loan to be able to cover it.

The catch was that I had never used a video camera before in my life. The first film we shot heavily featured the inside of the lens cap. That said, the last film, at the end of the trip, also has lots of shots of the inside of the lens cap. I like to think that the latter are slightly better composed.

Having hyped ourselves up for our grand adventure, we had no plane ticket, no set date for departure; it was all rather strange. It was a fine morning, however, when finally, bags on backs, we staggered out of the front door, set the camera up on its tripod and, unable to take the moment seriously, declared, 'We're off to carry this little baby overland to the World Cup. See you in Japan.' We turned and set off down the drive to let the dream begin. In the quiet summer morning, chins held high, we slipped off gracefully into the big unknown. Months of talk were now reality, and reality shortly reminded us that we had forgotten the camera.

The train from Horsham station took us down through the rolling Sussex countryside to Portsmouth. It was a glorious, sunny day, England in full bloom, as if tempting us to stay. It was an uneventful but exciting journey, full of the elation that we had lived up to our word and were finally on our way. From Portsmouth station it is a three-mile walk round to the ferry terminal. Somebody chose cunningly to place a naval dockyard between the two. Until now, the weight of the table, the camera and the various maps and guidebooks

I had packed seemed perfectly reasonable. That was before I had to walk three miles. A sweaty mess and muttering less-than-sweet nothings, I struggled into the ferry terminal. Being male, we naturally had not booked any tickets in advance, but knew that the night ferry was the cheapest option. Mike was instantly into the swing of things. 'Come on. We'll blag it.'

Up we sauntered to the desk for Brittany Ferries, smiled innocently and told them we were making a film for Channel 4 trying to get overland to the World Cup without spending any money. Could they help us? At the first blank stares we pointed to the table as proof of our madness. The reply was swift and simple: 'No.' So we went to the next counter, P&O. The female assistant was enthralled, giggled with delight and went to ask her manager. 'No.' Bugger. But the pretty Scots girl with peroxide hair on the Brittany Ferries counter waved us back shortly afterwards. She and her inventive sidekick, Richard, had hatched a cunning plan that enabled us to jump in on a ticket that had just been cancelled without refund. All we would have to pay for was the name change. £2.30 for two £47 tickets. It was fate. Her name was Miss Hope.

At 11 p.m. we set sail for the continent.

Nelson once called a midshipman to his cabin to instruct him in three essentials to survive at sea in the Royal Navy. One, implicitly obey orders. Two, consider every man your enemy who speaks ill of your King and, three, hate a Frenchman as you do the devil. Times have obviously changed since those hard words but rivalry still remains and yesterday's wars are today played out on the football pitch. We have two opportunities to clash with the French: internationally against the nation of France and domestically against Arsenal.

The English have had a mixed relationship with the French over the centuries. Although not technically French, William the Conqueror set out from Normandy and gave our Harold a hiding in 1066. This was revenged with crushing English victories at Agincourt and Waterloo

(Belgium, not the London Borough of Lambeth) before we fought side by side to save Europe from Germany's grand plans.

Nowadays we are joined in the European Union and bicker about beef while they stride to footballing victory after footballing victory. France won the World Cup in 1998 and then the European Championships in 2000, only the second team to hold both titles at the same time, and their players have swarmed into the wealthy English leagues. It is good for our players to play against the best in the world, but why do the best in the world have to be French? Vengeance was to be had, however, in our epic year: the French would swallow beaucoup de pride.

To our horror, in our first official match on the table, aboard the ferry, the French scored the first goal. Minutes later they scored a second. I glanced nervously at Mike. His look reflected exactly my thoughts. We could not lose our first game, especially not to the French. We were two goals down though and not looking good.

At Agincourt the English had also fought against the odds – a force of six thousand against some forty thousand French. But they held firm and King Henry bravely declared (with a helping hand from Shakespeare) that 'he which hath no stomach to this fight' may leave at once, and return to England, for he would prefer not to risk his life in that man's company, and that those who remained would acquire a shared dignity: anyone shedding his blood with the King would become the King's brother. A famous victory ensued.

The French had arrogantly threatened to cut off the trigger fingers of all captured English archers, but it was a promise that was to prove their downfall. Legend has it that the English archers taunted the French into charging into a bottleneck by waving their threatened, and now extended, first and second fingers in a V-sign at the French front lines (supposedly the origin of today's gesture); and then rained down a ceaseless torrent of arrows on their hapless foes. As so often happens on the field of play, the French were let down by their indiscipline – in three hours it was all over.

We rallied. A cheeky flick of the fingers in memory of his ancestors and Mike scored a cracker to make it 2–1. Suddenly we were level. The smell of victory was in the air and we sent them crashing to an almighty 10–5 defeat. A rematch was called by our startled opponents for whom 'babyfoot' (table football) is actually a national hobby. 10–4 to Her Majesty's loyal subjects! The words of the poet Petrarch, albeit from a different age, summed up the moment: 'In my youth the English were regarded as the most timid of the uncouth races, but today they are the supreme warriors; they have destroyed the reputation of France in a series of startling victories and the men who were once lower even than the wretched Scots themselves have crushed the realm of France with fire and steel.' The adventure had begun.

The ferry docked in Caen under the orange glow of the early morning sky. We killed time lounging around outside the castle in the centre of town until the sun was high enough for an English café called 'Dollies' to open. William the Conqueror had lived there before he came to England. The castle that is, not 'Dollies'.

Mike had studied for the past year in Caen. He had been to watch the local side, Caen FC, in the second division and at noon led the way to nobble our first stadium, the 'Stade Malherbe'. As we were nervously debating how to get onto the pitch, Mike miraculously recognised the head of the Caen FC supporters club, Christophe, sitting just two tables and an umbrella away in the club café. Needless to say Christophe was rather baffled at first by our tale but quickly warmed to it and ended up giving us a tour of the stadium. We had stumbled across the right man: he had a set of keys.

The reason Christophe had a set of keys is that the fan club makes giant replica shirts that are pulled down over the crowd before the games. He claims he was the first in Europe to have the idea. We spent the afternoon helping him put the finishing touches to a giant Caen shirt for the next home game, before taking our table onto the pitch. The stadium was the pride of the town but, despite the club colours being red and blue, the management had bought green seats.

Apparently they were cheaper. Not that boardrooms ever put money ahead of fans, of course.

Even with an audience of precisely one lone groundsman, walking out onto the pitch of a major stadium is childishly magical. Your imagination has more to work with. It is a place full of emotion, brimming every week with passion, victory, despair and thousands of eager, hope-filled eyes. For the moment the star of the show was our football table. Pitch invasion number one had been successful.

Our first night in France was spent culturally with two Irish lasses in an Irish pub owned by a Turk. Caen is a lovely town with some impressive buildings, but the capital was calling. The Eiffel tower, the Champs-Elysées, the cafés filled with lovers and, of course, the mighty Stade de France, where, for the first time, France had lifted the World Cup in 1998.

Both Mike and I had been to Paris before, so we skipped the sights and, still chuffed with our success in Caen, headed straight out to the Parc des Princes, home of the top French side Paris Saint-Germain (PSG). The receptionist looked bemused by the presence of two guys in England shirts, carrying a football table. She was even more bemused when, in faulty French, we tried to explain our plans. Nevertheless she called up the relevant PR man to fend us off officially. She spoke to him briefly, then covered the phone and asked which company we worked for. After a moment's hesitation Mike replied, 'us' with a big smile on his face. She chuckled and went back to the phone. Even my French was good enough to hear her say that we were simple crazy people.

Eventually a short, friendly PR man with dark hair came down. He told us that on Monday PSG were having an open training session and that we could come along and meet the players. After training the players pass through a number of rooms for separate media interviews; entertained by our tale, he was prepared to let us set up the table in a room at the end. He could not force the players to stop, but saw no reason why they would snub us. PSG also happened to be kicking off the French football season with a match against

Lille that Saturday. Two tickets, a baguette and a bottle of vin later and we were toasting our good fortune.

Before the match we made a dash out to the Stade de France to try our luck. The officials there had other plans. The entire building is one giant trademark. They photocopied our passports, made us sign a statement saying we would not use any of our footage and said the only access we could get would be on the hourly tour. Walking down the tunnel and out into the stadium, however, was on a whole new level compared to Caen. The Stade de France seats sixty thousand people, and you can hire it for five-a-side.

The PSG match was notable for its lack of burger vans and the high number of police in riot gear. Back in Caen, Christophe had told us that for some matches no fans are allowed because of past troubles and that the teams play in empty stadiums. The English are not alone in their reputation for hooliganism. Thankfully, the fans seemed in good spirits and good voice for the start of the season, and the boom, boom, boom of drums resounded through the humid, sticky air.

On the trip so far, we had been told that English football was too physical, so it was a surprise to see PSG spend ninety minutes kicking Lille off the park. Even Nicolas Anelka, formerly the sullen young star of Arsenal, was getting stuck in. He went down twice, looking for a penalty, but was denied by the referee despite the amazed cries of the home crowd and the fact that, for once, the frenzied masses were probably right. Anelka's endless frustration with life was compounded moments later when the referee disallowed his goal for offside. The crowd started a searing chant of *'arbitre enculé'*. No prizes for guessing the translation. It finished 0–0, but it was a 0–0 with plenty of French dramatics.

The day before the PSG match we had hunted down the FFF (Fédération Française de Football), situated just off the Place de l'Étoile, the world's biggest roundabout. At its centre is the Arc de Triomphe, commissioned by Napoleon to commemorate his imperial victories, but not completed until after his two great hidings.

Initially we were told simply to come back in a few hours, but after Mike had called someone upstairs in his best French, it was confirmed that everyone had hit the beach. It was August. Nobody in Europe works in August, especially the French.

Now, our respective law degrees had taught us that you are never wrong; you simply move the goalposts until you are right. Thus the lack of a game against the French FA, who denied having received my letter, did not constitute failure as it was out of our hands. Admittedly, we could have waited, but the adventure was about a journey. We did not have time doggedly to hunt down each FA, although we did our darnedest in the days we had. By regarding each conquest as a bonus rather than a notch off a list, our trip grew rather than diminished, and there were to be many bonuses on the way to the grand prize, the World Cup.

Ups and downs seem to be part and parcel of a plot on this earth. How you view those ups and downs greatly determines how much you enjoy life. We had failed to nobble the French FA, our first FA, which was a bugger considering that we had started out by aiming to nobble all the FAs en route. But we had got there, we had been accepted and thus had succeeded in the hard part and done what we said we were going to do. With an unlimited budget perhaps we could have chased them down and fought them on the beaches, but sadly reality has certain limits, even in the world of travels with a football table.

These limits, though, as we were to learn, could be pushed back extensively. This was only FA number one, there were many more to go. Had we honestly thought the French would do us a favour? No chance. They are almost as arrogant as we are.

Walking away to set up the table under the Arc de Triomphe, we met an English guy, accompanied by his son, who showed great confidence in his home country by sporting an Italian football shirt. He was amazed by our plans and launched into an animated flow about how football is so much more than just ninety minutes on a Saturday afternoon. For example, his brother-in-law had been cycling around Ireland and, 'just in the middle of nowhere came across a wall with a green and white Glasgow Celtic scarf nailed to it and a plate that said, "This is where the first sod [turf not fan] for the new Celtic stadium came from." A shrine, in the middle of nowhere. I think most football people understand that. It is a far greater world ... anyway, come on lads, let's have a photo.'

He was a firm believer that exciting things just pop up when you least expect them. We were his prime example today. If you expect the unexpected, sport an open mind and a welcoming smile you will be amazed by the adventures and the 'luck' that comes your way. We were delighted to bolster this theory and watch his surprise on learning that the French football season was kicking off the following day and that tickets were still available. In turn he revealed that the Tour de France was finishing by the Arc de Triomphe the day after. Our chance meeting had served us both well.

I had never seen the Tour de France, once missing it by a day when I got my dates wrong. So come Sunday morning I was first up and dragged Mike from his sleep. I was like a five-year-old waiting for Father Christmas. Having caught a metro to the Place de la Concorde and followed the barriers up the Champs-Elysées, we found that the race did not finish at the Arc de Triomphe at all. It went up one side of the Champs-Elysées and came down the other. Perched at the top by the turn, however, meant you had a long view of the cyclists coming up towards you, turning tightly and racing away down to the finish; a perfect viewpoint.

We were in place by 10 a.m. The riders were due at 2 p.m. As the crowds grew so did the anticipation. Many of the fans had been there since 7 a.m. to ensure a view. An hour before the riders were due a TV2 van pulled up and assembled a giant advertising balloon completely blocking the view of one half of the crowd at our precious turn-point. Not surprisingly it caused uproar. The sun was merciless and people had travelled a long way for this final stage of the Tour. The TV2 workers refused to take it down but were too scared to put up the second one. Maddened Frenchmen are not to be messed with. When the French public gets upset, heads start to roll.

It was an utterly ridiculous but most enjoyable moment to set up the table, enjoyable because it was so completely unexpected by the people around us. We managed to clear a small space within the crowd and, immediately, had a number of keen players, mainly in the form of an English family from Charlton. Mike later heard an American telling his mate, 'Everyone's really bored and hot and all and there's these two crazy English guys with a foosball table . . .' We were already famous.

By the time the bikes came round we had quite an international tournament going and it was amazing how worked up previously sceptical people had become. Roars of 'you beauty!' and various Dutch, French and German equivalents cut through the air, drawing the attention of a by now heavily sunburned crowd.

The Tour finally appeared two hours later than planned at 4 p.m. My neck was a nice shade of red but the roar of the crowd and the sight of the pack charging up towards us was quite something. Lance Armstrong was shepherded home by his team to win his third Tour de France. This was a sensational achievement by itself but was even more dramatic given that he had nearly lost his life to cancer. It is completely eclipsed by the fact that he has since gone on to win an unprecedented seventh Tour de France. The sheer spectacle, the speed, the colours, the gleaming rims reflecting the sunshine, the many support cars charging round behind the riders and the table's first taste of fame made it a day to remember.

With Monday morning came the prospect of luring Nicolas Anelka onto the table. The talented Frenchman shot to world stardom via his antics at Arsenal, where he demanded a big money transfer and refused to play for the club. Aged only 22 he had played for Arsenal, Real Madrid and PSG (now add Liverpool, Manchester City and Turkish side Fenerbahçe). His brothers are infamous for their demands and Anelka's pout has done little to aid relations with the world media or his team-mates. He was, however, a talented striker and a French international. We did not have wads of cash but we did have the promise of PSG's PR assistant.

PSG train at Camp des Loges, just outside Saint-Germain-en-Laye, a beautiful little town on the edge of Paris that used to be a summer retreat for the French aristocracy. A large garden by the station runs along the top of a terrace that grants magnificent views back over Paris. After a long walk round the town that had us bickering about directions and struggling to cope with the heat, we were saved by a delightful patisserie. Several currant buns and a sandwich later, all of life's little problems were resolved.

Ronaldinho, however, was an unforeseen problem that we could do nothing about. PSG's new Brazilian signing rocked up to training in an open-topped, chauffeur-driven Cadillac. There was already a small crowd watching the players turn up for training, cheering at the slightest glimpses of their nonchalant heroes. The biggest cheer was reserved for the new boy, Ronaldinho. I had never heard of him before, but, sadly, his name was to become all too familiar.

Once let in to a carefully controlled corner of the training field we were able to watch the players warm-up and then witness Ronaldinho being put through his paces in front of us. He was a cheeky little guy with funny teeth and crazy hair. The petty looking sprint exercise he was being made to do seemed beyond the needs of a young Brazilian star and, rising to the mantle, he joked his way through it, much to the annoyance of the two seriously meticulous French coaches. Ronaldinho was far more concerned with rearranging his pants at every opportunity.

Anelka was tucked well away in the far corner. As he was not one to smile much and, as usual, was struggling to build a rapport with the fans, it was probably a sensible decision. Having not yet seen any actual football, we turned our attention to finding our PR assistant, Mathias Barbera. This involved having to walk out and round to the leafy main entrance where, naturally, we hit security. Eventually, after trying to brush us off, they radioed for Mr Barbera. A Mr Bussiere appeared. He was the boss, probably the same age as Mr Barbera but more snappily dressed and with the air of someone very good at saying 'non'. He was not amused and did not see the funny, quaint, or any, side of our trip. Our attempts to talk him round ended in abject failure despite his assistant's enthusiasm earlier in the week. '*Pas ce soir*' was his curt reply, hands on hips, to all of Mike's well-phrased protestations in French. '*Pas ce soir*.'

Our only hope to get to Anelka now lay at the car park, after training, along with half of Paris. We had to wait a long time and the crowd swelled behind the barriers. We managed to explain to quite a few of them about the table and the trip and talked them into helping us upon the imminent arrival of Monsieur Anelka. A spitting image of Patrick Vieira launched into a long tale of admiration for the young Liverpool and England midfielder Steven Gerrard. 'He is very, very good ... but obviously he will lose against the French [in the World Cup].' In a flash we had forgotten about the wait and were on the table, defending Gerrard's reputation. The English record remained unbeaten.

A van pulled into the compound. Out hopped Anelka in a black sleeveless top, with his usual dour expression, alongside Dehu, the PSG centre-back and sometime French international. Dehu dropped his boots off in his car before immediately strolling out to the fans. Anelka did the opposite and skulked off to the far corner of the compound to speak to someone through the fence. As Dehu, sporting a rather French outfit of tight camo top and three-quarter-length trousers, dutifully repaid the fans for their long wait in the sun, Anelka finished his chat and jumped straight in his car. Several of the guys we had been talking to ran around the side of the enclosure to share a piece of their mind with him. Regrettably their insults do not really translate into English. But when Anelka opened his door, pointed his finger and allegedly said to them 'I'm going to hunt you down', things got heated.

The fans went nuts, banging the fence and screaming abuse at him. Anelka got out of his car and squared up to the fence in a ridiculous show before being hastily put back in his car by watchful security. 'You're only good enough for babyfoot,' they quipped. Quickly driving out and away, Anelka was loudly booed and whistled at as, head down, he sped off, monkey noises chasing his ego.

Dehu did take up the challenge. He was still doing the rounds signing every bit of paper and posing for photo after photo. It probably only took ten minutes of his time but the fans obviously loved it. When he got round to our table the fans championed him onto it. A young guy jumped in next to me, a look of absolute joy on his face as Dehu bent down to play. The table was on a hideous slope, the ball running into our goal almost immediately. Wisely he took advantage of the huge cheer and quit at the top. He carried on round the fence and signed everything before heading home.

'Anelka will pay' was the message left scribbled on the crash barrier for the troubled striker by the irate fans. Within a couple of months he had left PSG and was on loan at Liverpool. The pen is mightier than the sword indeed.

Our experiences in Caen and Paris served as a perfect introduction to the adventures that lay ahead. We had tasted success, clashed with officialdom and been denied by events beyond our control. We had also encountered our first, chance meetings and were gradually perfecting a polished introduction about ourselves, our trip and, most important of all, the table.

FUTBOL CLUB BARCELONA

Avgda. Aristides Maillol, s/n. - Tel. 93 496 36 00* - Telex 51804 FCBXE
08028 BARCELONA   Fax 93 411 22 19   www.fcbarcelona.com

4. SPAIN

'*¿Quiere usted jugar un partido de futbolín?*' Would you like to play a game of tablefootball?

Antoni Closa, a wonderful, enthusiastic, curly-haired man in his forties greeted me with a smile and a handshake and led me in. Hoping to get someone on camera talking about Barca, I had visited the offices of *Sport Barcelona. Sport* is a daily newspaper purely devoted to football and 95 per cent filled with news on their beloved Barca.

Spanish football is entrenched in history. Real Madrid and FC Barcelona are two of the most celebrated teams in world football and their rivalry is one of the fiercest. Barcelona lies in Catalonia, a historically distinct region with its own people and its own language. Madrid is the home of the King of Spain, their oppressor.

The mighty Spanish empire once stretched across the world. Its gradual disintegration spelled the end of its plundering of the New World territories discovered by Columbus in 1492. Columbus had claimed the Americas for Spain – not bad work for a bungled trip to India. Of all the bits he could have hit first, he hit Barbados. He must have thought all his Christmases had come at once.

By the twentieth century Spain had crumbled into civil

war, with General Franco leading the Spanish Nationalists to victory on Nazi money, bombers and football. The latter was carefully used as an instrument of unification to consolidate his control. Franco was no fool; he knew how to manipulate the attentions of the people.

Catalonia put up the most resistance to Franco's dictatorship and he exacted a heavy price for their opposition when the region finally fell under his control. But he held back from crushing Barcelona football club, arguably an emblem and focusing spirit of the region, at whose games the partisans voiced their hatred of his regime. Like many politicians he played populist politics and turned a blind eye to this harmless vent of emotions, which worked to distract and use up the energies of his opposition.

In 1986 Gary Lineker transferred from Everton to Barcelona for £2.2 million after winning the golden boot at the World Cup in Mexico. In his first game in the famous claret-and-blue stripes he scored two goals but was unimpressed with the atmosphere. Then he experienced the derby against Real Madrid at the Nou Camp, Barcelona's sensational 120,000-seater stadium. Lineker scored a hat-trick in a mighty 3–2 victory for 'Barca', the region's love and joy. 'In the Nou Camp I felt something extra when I scored . . . if there had been a roof on the stadium it would have been blown off. The sound was unbelievable, an explosion of noise.'

Having been at *Sport Barcelona* since its inception 22 years before and having written three books on Barca, Antoni Closa was something of an expert. I told him about the trip and that I would like to record an interview about Barca and Spanish football in general. I explained that we did not have time to go to Madrid and hit the Spanish FA but that I had always wanted to come to Barcelona, both the city and the club. Claiming his English was not good enough, Antoni insisted on passing the buck to a colleague of his, Santi, who would be free shortly. While I waited, sitting next to Antoni at his computer in the hubbub of the main room, he talked lovingly about Barca and Catalonia, sharing his great wealth of knowledge and revealing his passion for the club.

A subject evoking particular emotion was Luis Figo, the Portuguese international who sold his soul by switching from Barca to Real Madrid. Waving his arms, cursing and gesticulating, Antoni raged, 'Figo is the mother of all sons of bitches.' His broken English added to the moment as he struggled to translate his disgust. 'Real Madrid are like the nouveau riche, they have no respect for history or tradition. They just buy whoever they want, arrogantly, such as Figo and Zidane.

'When the Tour de Spain cycle race finished in Madrid the authorities made the winner's jersey white (the colours of the king) rather than the usual yellow. A Catalan rider won and was made to wear the white of Madrid.' Antoni was by now in full swing, his blood pressure saved only by the arrival of Santi, a Steve McManaman lookalike (formerly of Liverpool, England and, ironically, Real Madrid), with wavy ginger locks and a lanky stride. We were able to sit in the directors' room away from the buzz of the paper's computers and adorned with a replica of the European Cup.

Santi smiled. 'Barca's special. It's history, Catalonia; it's a sign of identity for the people. It's a sensation, a feeling. It is the opposite of Madrid. You can not support both, it is opposite ideas.' Started by two Englishmen, the Witty brothers, football has grown to extreme heights in Barcelona. To many it seems the region's sole remaining force with which to strike the rest of Spain and show support for the history and culture of Catalonia. 'Most Spanish people support their local team *and* Real Madrid. It is the great team of Spain. Barca is not part of this . . . it's an old thing.'

To finish, I asked why he thought that football is the biggest sport in the world. 'Because it's easy, it's only a few rules and so easy for everybody. Everyone can play it. When you watch a match of football you are sure that you can play like these people. I think you never can feel like a Pete Sampras, an Agassi or a Lance Armstrong. But you can feel like a Sol Campbell or Beckham when you play in the park with your friends.' It's funny that while the names of some of the greatest sportsmen ever are highlighted as unrecognised words by the computer upon which this book was written, it is quite at home with Beckham and Campbell. Point proved.

As soon as Santi had left and Antoni thought the camera was off he colourfully launched into his worries. It seemed he had worried that Santi would not come across emotive enough and repeated his 'Figo, son of a bitches' line to demonstrate the true feeling. We parted some three hours after my arrival with him apologising that he was unable to put the true sentiment of Barca into words. 'It is very hard to say in English. It is very hard to say in Spanish too.'

In Spain things had started to crumble. Mike and I, despite being good friends, were getting ratty with each other on the road. It is almost comedy how backpacking with someone can generate the most stupid of arguments. To be fair, in the extreme heat and with the number of rejections we got with each call to various football officials or redirections to further offices, it was easy to begin to question our cause. In our case I was too laid-back and optimistic for Mike and Mike seemed to be posing too many negative (albeit necessary) questions for me. Solution? Get away from it all.

Barcelona has a fantastic harbour and at 6 a.m. the next day I walked the planks trying to hitch a lift to Italy. Funnily enough, with the exception of a mad Frenchman who had just bought a new yacht and was willing to let me helm it on the basis of my limited experience of dinghies, there were no takers for two lads and a football table. On hearing that the Frenchman had even less sailing experience than I had, common sense got the better of me. I am sure the Spanish coastguard has enough work as it is.

'I hear your film's shit,' said the bloke opposite me in a Manchester accent as I took my seat. 'Pardon?' I exclaimed, taken aback.

'I've been hearing about your trip and apparently it's never going to work,' he continued bluntly to my astonishment. Mike, who was sitting opposite me on the train, looked equally stunned.

Unable to find takers at the harbour, that afternoon Mike

and I had resolved to travel out of Barcelona to the mountains, where, perched high on a rock face, was the breathtaking Benedictine Monastery of Montserrat. Pilgrims come from all over Christendom to pay homage to its Black Virgin (La Moreneta), a twelfth-century wooden sculpture of Mary, regarded as Catalonia's patroness. Barca's trophies are dedicated to her and in return the monks pray for the success of the team.

Before we had left I had been faffing around and trying Mike's patience as he waited in the searing sunshine. Eventually it became too much; he rightly lost the plot and headed for the train to Montserrat by himself. An hour later, after finally getting organised, I headed for the station hoping I might find him at Montserrat and apologise. Compounding his rage, but hopefully to his amusement in hindsight, I found him still waiting for the train at the platform. He had been venting his frustrations to a guy he had met from Manchester. He proved to be the least discreet guy from Manchester he would ever meet.

In the main tourist season around one thousand people a day visit Monserrat. Eighteen thousand people a day visit the Nou Camp, Barcelona's mighty cauldron. I doubt that figure includes the guy we saw on our return from Montserrat who wore a T-shirt reading: 'I feel better when I'm alone'.

Considering that for Barca's first-ever match the club were only able to field ten men and subsequently had to advertise in the newspapers for players, they have come a long way. The Nou Camp was built to accommodate the masses of fans and extended under Club President Nunez to generate more money. *'Con el socio todo, sin el socio nada'* (with the fan, everything; without the fan, nothing).

Barcelona has a great footballing record and the fans' expectations are high. Former Ipswich, Newcastle and England manager Sir Bobby Robson was replaced as coach of Barcelona after winning the UEFA Cup Winners' Cup, a domestic cup and finishing second in the league by three points. In recent years Barca's successes have been fewer, last winning the European Cup in 1992. The then vice president

Joan Gaspart had promised that if Barca won the final, which was being played at Wembley, he would throw himself in the Thames. He did so shortly before dawn and, miraculously, survived.

The club is associated with many greats: Pepe Samitier, 'El Sami', whose first contract at the age of seventeen in 1919 was for a watch with a dial that glowed in the dark and a three-piece suit; Kubala whose legendary strength ensured a quick recovery from drinking bouts that he saw, not as a personal weakness, but as part of the process of team bonding (he lost his captaincy in 1953 when, two days before a European tie against Copenhagen, he led a group of team-mates away from training on a drinking spree that ended up in a brothel); Diego Maradona, for whom the club originally refused to pay a million dollars because he was a mere teenager (and a few years later paid five million); Johan Cruyff, both as player and manager (who won the league three times in a row), Ronaldo, Rivaldo, Romario and, from England, Terry Venables, who brought the La Liga title back to Barca, with the help of Gary Lineker and Mark Hughes.

You can therefore imagine that the FC Barcelona officialdom were not interested in two jollies, wearing England shirts, who were trying to get onto their pitch. We went to the club offices next to the stadium but were stumped by a combination of summer holidays, siestas and a club tour to Poland. The sullen but impeccably suited front man eventually gave me the card of the person we needed to get permission from, but refused to let us use the office phone. We were forced to traipse out and round the perimeter fences to find a phone box in the midday sun; not conducive to staying fresh when carrying a football table. Having been put through to various numbers in the glass oven of the first phone box we found, we drew a blank and walked back to the main desk for help. 'Call the number I gave you' was the only help offered. 'And no, you can not use this phone.' Back at our plate-glass sauna we finally got through. 'Sorry, please call back in an hour.' An hour went by. We called again. 'Qué?' was the reply. Manuel from *Fawlty Towers* now has a job at FC Barcelona.

It was, to put it mildly, exasperating. Exhausted, Mike gave up hope and decided to go home. At the end of the day he was on holiday and this was not part of the package. My predicament was slightly different though. I was in it for the duration, whether I liked it or not. I needed to ensure that we stepped up a level from the success of Caen and Paris; that we kept up the momentum of the trip; and I had hoped that Barcelona and the Nou Camp would provide that opportunity. So it bugged me.

Struggling in the heat and still unable to get through to the phone numbers, I opted simply to sign up to the official stadium tour. It meant the table graced the edge of the pitch and that I got back at a reasonable hour to meet Mike, as, adventure or no, it was not worth spoiling a friendship over. The table got plenty of funny looks from my tour party and it eats me up inside that we did not try harder. It was, however, to prove a good lesson for the rest of the trip. If you are not completely committed to seeing something through or don't believe it is going to happen, then it never will. I still have the card.

Boom! 'What the hell was that?' exclaimed Mike.

'Sounded like scaffolding,' I replied, more concerned with the progress of my beer.

'No way, that, there it is again.'

'Probably workmen or something.'

'Right.' He turned back to his pint.

We were in San Sebastian on the Atlantic seaboard to chill out, having escaped along the length of the Pyrenees on another overnight bus from the heat and tensions of Barcelona. Like Paris it had got its claws into us for longer than we had anticipated.

San Sebastian is famed as a ritzy resort for wealthy Spaniards. Those who live there consider themselves the luckiest people in Spain. With two perfect crescent-shaped beaches, surf, Mounts overlooking the town, old, new and stylish buildings and a wild nightlife it is easy to see why. Unbeknown to us it had also been a stronghold of Basque nationalist feeling since well before Franco.

Boom! Boom! We finished our pints and ventured out into the narrow street of the old quarter to investigate. Walking along this pedestrianised area we reached a narrow cross-roads. Looking down to the right there was a wire mesh fence drawn across the street and funny characters in red and black costumes ... riot police. They had big guns and gas masks. A wheelie-bin was belching flames and the fence had been drawn across as a barricade by ... looking left quickly ... by the fleeing petrol bombers who were still launching the profits of their pastimes. I ran. Quickly. I was not alone. It will take a very special lady to get Mike to move that fast again.

Earlier in the day we had watched the end of a 'Freedom for the Basque Country' parade but had failed to realise it was the anniversary of the death of a Basque terrorist who blew herself up handling dynamite. Trouble had been expected. Trouble had hit.

The Basque people, who have their own ancient language called Euskara, have upped their campaign for independence since Franco's death in 1975. According to a Reuter's journalist, whom we found lurking in the half-darkness taking photos of the drama, Basque nationalism spills over onto the football pitch in much the same way as Catalan nationalism. In 1998 a supporter was stabbed to death at a match between Atletico Madrid and Real Sociedad in reaction to the stoning of an Atletico Madrid supporters' bus during a cup-tie in San Sebastian.

The end of the first part of the trip came after a much less exciting, but far more relaxing, second day on the beaches. The christening of Mike's godson had been arranged for a few days' time and he had decided to return home. Despite some of the inevitable tensions on the road he had been an excellent travelling companion and I was sad to see him go.

There was one last score to settle before we got on our respective buses, mine to Bordeaux, and his to Barcelona for his flight home. We had played many games on the table and were pretty even. It was time for a champion. The cheeky git stole the first game and then to my horror won the second as well. We had agreed on the first to three and I was seeing my honour as sole bearer of the table from now on being torn away. I am, however, a very lucky man.

I forget the exact result of the final game. On occasions we both just wanted someone to score so we could stop and stretch our backs. At other times, not that men are competitive of course, our concentration was so intense that nervous energy spurred us through the pain. Fittingly perhaps, as the continuing bearer of the table, I just managed to sneak it. We were both so relieved it was over that the result could have been anything by the finish, but we were simply too stubborn to call it an honourable draw.

Leaving Mike was a horrible yet exciting moment. It was the end of his adventure and it meant I was on my own. The bus to Bordeaux would arrive late at night. As it pulled away and Mike waved goodbye the doubts set in. We had had success in Caen at his instigation but had not truly graced another pitch since. The burden was now on my shoulders alone and I knew that a stadium awaited me in Bordeaux. I took a big breath, closed my eyes and dreamed of the adventures that would lie on the long road ahead. Of course there were fears, but at the end of the day what was the worst that could happen?

5. FRANCE (ENCORE UNE FOIS)

Bordeaux impressed me. It lacked the tourist-crazed pack that can spoil trips to Paris and Barcelona, yet had the same pretty buildings, wide avenues and beautiful parks. And of course there is the wine. In one of the parks, slumped on a bench was an extremely fat, pot-bellied, fifty-year-old man, his stubbly double chin collapsed on his chest, and his dirty white vest drawn up over his belly. His trousers were held up by string. I could not help but smile. Welcome back to France.

Bordeaux does not have a great footballing history. It was a random town to go to, chosen because it was the only bus destination in France on the day I wanted to leave Spain. Missing Mike's chatty company and having mulled through the prospective terrors of being on my own I decided to crack on with the tablefootball challenge with what Bordeaux had to offer. If I wimped out now, in Bordeaux, what hope was there for the rest of the trip?

It may be hard to believe but I am quite a shy individual. That was half the reason why I took up the table challenge. It would force me to be more forward and, in theory, gain confidence from the successes. I worry about consequences and people's reactions and, concerned with not making a tit of myself, I sometimes forget that the people I am approaching are just like me, be they important, famous, attractive or heavily armed, and could well be more nervous or apprehensive than me. Afterwards I look back and cannot understand why I worried. Regardless, there was still an inexplicable terror that seized me at the prospect of what I was about to do.

Finding Stade Chaban Delmas, home of Bordeaux FC, on the map, I set off, butterflies in stomach, for official pitch invasion number two. This was the important one. Was Caen just a flash in the pan? Lady Luck had smiled down on Mike and me by placing Christophe next to us at the café. Could I pluck up the courage to talk confidently and enthusiastically enough? Maybe my underlying belief that people would melt on seeing the table was simply naïve? Would the humour translate? What about the Germans?

It was a different world from the hive of the Nou Camp. Walking around the edge of the stadium I managed to track down an office. Three short, podgy, middle-aged men in short-sleeved shirts and shorts were hanging around what I guessed was the reception. They looked harmless but unamused by a stranger, appearing at the door in an England shirt and flowery surf shorts with a giant purple bag swinging from his shoulder, interrupting their lazy afternoon. '*Bonjour*,' I ventured.

In faulty French, brandishing my camera, I attempted to explain the purpose of my visit. They stared at me and started muttering, '*C'est impossible*. Where are you from? Who do you work for? Do you have permission? If so, where is it?' Dramatic hand gestures accompanied the interrogation.

'Well, I'm from England, the work thing is a long story and a matter of debate and no, I don't have permission,' I replied. It was not a promising start. 'I'm carrying a table-football table overland from England to the World Cup in Japan. It's *un défi*, a grand challenge, a bet to set it up on all the great pitches en route' (didn't somebody once say flattery will get you everywhere?). They didn't swallow it.

I had nothing left to lose so I persisted. I asked again and simply kept up the chat, finding ways round every excuse they threw at me until they addressed my request by trying to contact the Bordeaux press officer, albeit in an aimless and half-hearted fashion. Trying a different tack I put away my camera and emphasised that I was not from the press. 'The trip is simply *un défi de humour*, set by friends from home. See, look, it is a football table; look at it. *Je ne suis pas presse*. It is just a foolish adventure. I can leave the video camera and resort to photos. I just need some evidence that I succeeded. Come on, how about it?'

'Ahh,' they cried, poring over the table bag, finally taking a good look and chuckling. The transformation was remarkable. 'Sure, follow us, why didn't you say?' I felt like a long lost friend. '*On y va!* Let's go!'

Bernard, the caretaker, showed me onto the pitch, helped me set up the table on the centre circle and waited patiently while I ran up into the stands to take a couple of cracking photos. He also filled me in on Bordeaux's greatest moment. Despite being a top division French side, it came back in 1996 when they reached the UEFA Cup Final and lost, to Bayern Munich. Champions of Europe they might not have been, but pitch invasion number two was a much-needed title for the table.

'A gentleman would be ashamed should his deeds not match his words,' wrote Confucius. My words had been many and my deeds were yet to match them. Three days of beach life on Cap Ferret, just west of Bordeaux, allowed me to relax and collect my thoughts ahead of setting off, alone, into the unknown. The table was set up and left in the beach hostel for the duration of my stay. To my amazement nobody touched it with the exception of a small child who played by herself. One day I walked past as she was toying with it. I carelessly spun one of the men on whom the ball was resting, accidentally scored, laughed and smiled. She burst into tears and ran off.

There is an old story that when Marseille was founded 2,600-odd years ago the first building to be raised was the football stadium and the rest of the city was constructed around it. The fact that the majority of Marseille's inhabitants are immigrants and 70 per cent of those are male means a far greater than average following of football. If you think Manchester United are big, go to Marseille. Olympique Marseille, or 'OM' as it is more affectionately known, is not just a football club there, it is an institution.

My arrival in Marseille was well timed. Marseille was also the temporary home of Hadley, an English lad whom we had met in Barcelona, and Franck Leboeuf, a French international footballer who had just transferred to Marseille from Chelsea. I stayed with the former and amused myself by putting in a written request to challenge the latter at the offices of Olympique Marseille FC. I met Hadley and as we walked to his rented flat off Rue de Lodi, the streets were full of people gathered around TVs both in bars and on the street. OM were playing.

I set out the next morning to invade the Marseille pitch. Hadley thought I was talking nonsense and opted to stay in bed. My confidence was high after my success in Bordeaux, and it was that buoyant enthusiasm that helped me succeed in Marseille. I found the tour office and set about achieving my goal in rapidly improving French. I stressed that I was not from the press, that it was a bit of fun and how about it? The answer at first was a straight '*non*', but my large purple bag had caught the eye of a lady in the corner of the room. '*Qu'est-ce que c'est?*' she asked, pointing inquisitively.

'It's the table,' I replied, opening the bag further so she could see clearly. A huge grin broke across her face.

She turned out to be the wife of the stadium manager. Interrupting the official who had rebuked me, she said, 'That's amazing, sure, we would love to help, you will have to wait until the stadium tours finish at 5 p.m. as we can't have anyone else seeing you, but come back then and we'll let you in.' In French it took me a little longer to comprehend my achievement.

At just before five I was in place in the car park by the small Portakabin, from where the tours were led. True to her word the lady was there. She introduced me to her husband who held a big set of keys. Perfect. I told them I had been round to the OM offices while I'd been waiting and requested official permission to get onto the pitch (without revealing I was already unofficially primed to do so). The official rejection would look good next to shots of me on the pitch. They all grinned. It was a fantastic feeling to see their smiles. It was recognition of what the trip was all about: attempting to bypass the bureaucracy and security that separates the fan from the action, and all through the laughable medium of a football table.

Being led out onto the pitch I felt like I had cracked the system. Instead of wasting time trawling round offices for official permission, you find the man with the keys. The table was set up in the middle of the Marseille pitch, where England played Tunisia in the 1998 World Cup, and I ran up into the stands to take a photo and some camera footage. But then, to my horror, the sprinkler system started.

By the time I arrived breathless and dripping at the centre circle there was a good inch of water on the table. The plastic players were now all scuba qualified. Fortunately the thin plywood base did not warp too much. It was to take far greater wounds later on in the trip.

With every success my smile broadened and my ambitions grew. Throughout the trip the worry that nothing would come off, despite my massive optimism, was tiring. To have already talked my way onto the pitches of three major stadiums and to have got footage of an Anelka strop was a massive boost to morale.

Europe was always going to be hard. The sheer wealth and size of European football means not only a distancing from you and me (we are hidden behind agents, security, spokesmen and fences) but also far less inclination on the part of the authorities to take in random people with football tables. Could the success continue? Perhaps I was being too optimistic in believing that it would be easier outside Europe? Plenty of fears, questions and obstacles raced through my mind each evening as I closed my eyes.

Travelling by myself was enlightening. It was so easy to meet people and, being alone, I was far more open to saying hello and making new friends. Even if you just swapped notes about a place with a fellow backpacker over a quick beer then never saw them again, that brief contact was immensely comforting. The table, of course, was a dream icebreaker in the various dorm rooms I was to grace. I would walk in, drop my stuff, sleep and wake up to questions and stories, smiles and laughter, suggestions and new companions.

The next day the alarm went at 3.48 a.m. and, sod's law, could I find the bastard in the darkness? It was farewell to a bleary-eyed Hadley and a sleepy Marseille. Both had been good to me. Uphill in the warm night air, it was a hard half-hour walk to the train station. Waddling, overburdened, through one of the most notoriously crime-ridden cities in Europe, I was the perfect sitting duck. With every passing car my imagination accelerated my heart rate but I made the train bound for Italy with minutes to spare and readied myself for pizza, pasta and plenty more adventure. I never did hear from Franck Leboeuf.

6. ITALY

I meant to go to Milan, home of AC Milan and Inter Milan, two of the big guns in Serie A, Italy's equivalent of the Premiership, and the renowned San Siro Stadium. As a target for the table it was almost on the same scale as Barcelona. 'When people think of Italy, after the Mafia and pizza, they think of AC Milan,' said Silvio Berlusconi, AC Milan's president and Italian Prime Minister. Although the Italian FA was based in Rome I had not planned to go there. Halfway down Italy's boot, it was just too far and I had a timetable to keep to. England's 1 September 2001 World Cup qualifying clash against Germany in Munich was looming.

However, all roads lead to Rome. Everybody knows that. So, twelve hours later, after winding its way along the classy, yacht-strewn, bikini-clad Mediterranean coastline of France and diving down into Italy, my train pulled into Rome central.

I had opted to take the 4.30 a.m. train so as to arrive early enough the next evening to catch England's friendly against Holland. On arrival I found an expat bar and, tired, but glad to have made it, settled down on a stool and watched England's first loss under Sven-Goran Eriksson. Two goals in two minutes secured our demise. I am still not quite sure what Eriksson was playing at. As I was embarking on a mammoth journey to the World Cup, which England had not yet qualified for, this result was something of a blow. I was not a happy bunny.

Pessimistic thoughts were swarming my mind and as I left the bar I felt very alone. I wished for a moment that I could forget all about football. Getting back to the hostel I was subjected to camp, drunken Americans animatedly discussing their love of Ally McBeal. It was all a bit too much. Be careful what you wish for.

I had made a contact, though. At the bar I met an English guy. He was now living and working in Rome for a TV company and knew an American girl who worked for the American sports network ESPN in Rome. In fact, it was the girl who had stood him up that very night. He happily gave me her number. Naturally I called as soon as I could. She replied, with a voice like velvet, that she was enthralled by my tale and tried to arrange for me to attend a Roma training session.

Sadly, despite a number of further calls, nothing materialised. I was running between the FA and various parts of Rome and she was up to her eyes in work and moving house. Her avid interest, however, was a demonstration of the fixation that the table enticed. It was something the public could champion, a people's cause, as such. Everybody has a heart and most are especially willing to help anybody who is doing something out of the ordinary. It was this inherent goodness that I was banking on. I would have to work hard at this contacts thing. With officialdom being official, the back-door route was calling once more.

I woke late and found I was not the only one taking advantage of a long lie-in. Tomasz was from Poland. He had a large round face with shaved short blond hair, a big cheeky grin and glasses. When I explained to him what was in the purple bag under my bed, I thought he was going to wet himself. He was in stitches. 'No way!' he cried, 'that's crazy, I mean, you just can't do that, wow, you're crazy!' He was an instant new best friend. Teaming up, we set out to explore the heart of the Roman Empire.

Rome is on a par with Paris in terms of awe, but whereas

Paris is magical, Rome is majestic. Many relics symbolising the might of the former Empire and the power of Rome remain throughout the city. Rome wasn't built in a day, and its longevity is testament to that. Ian Rush, prolific striker for Wales and Liverpool in the 80s, was not so impressed. 'I couldn't settle in Italy,' he said. 'It was like living in a foreign country.'

Foreigners like to think of Italy as a land of passionate, animated people who gesticulate wildly when speaking, love to eat, drive like maniacs and have a healthy aversion to work. Certainly when they had slaves to do the work for them they created some magnificent buildings. Nowadays, expanded urban industry and poor urban planning make the outskirts of cities such as Rome rather less appealing. But the foreigners are right. Italy *is* a land of passionate, animated people who gesticulate wildly when speaking, love to eat, drive like maniacs and have a healthy aversion to work. There are also the overhanging myths, legends and realities of the Italian Mafia. Fuelled by Hollywood and substantiated by newspaper reports of dead judges, public interest outside Italy is massive. Public interest inside Italy is, well, bought.

'Welcome to Italia!' Arms raised, Italian football shirt on, the native we had collared obliged our request beautifully in front of the camera. He had found our attempts to speak to him in stuttering Italian most amusing, and waited some time before telling us that he was in fact Brazilian.

We walked humbly around the mighty Colosseum where thousands of good men, women, animals and 'northern barbarians' met their end in grizzly gladiatorial combat. Part of the floor of the Colosseum has been rebuilt and all too well succeeds in helping you to imagine walking out into the mighty arena, a walk that meant almost certain death. Rome's ruins hold many, many stories and can be brought to life by joining any of the many 'free' tours. Did you know that the Romans used piss to remove red wine from their togas? Apparently it is rich in ammonia. Next time you spill red wine on the carpet at a party, you know what to do.

'The Romans had a lot of time on their hands,' our

Geordie tour guide informed us. 'They had 178 holidays a year. As the Empire expanded the citizens of Rome became richer and richer as treasures and slaves were brought back from abroad. So it worked out as one day work, one day have a party, one day play games.' He paused, smiled and asked, 'Any Australians here?'

The gladiators of today who command audiences in the tens of thousands are footballers. If they have a bad day then they might be subjected to a few boos before stepping into their luxury cars to hurry back to their luxury mansions to greet their luxury wives beside their luxury pools. I'm sure the threat of being torn limb from limb by wild beasts did more to focus the minds of performers than the pen of modern journalism does today.

Rome is home to Lazio, who won the Scudetto (the Italian Serie A title) in 2000; Roma, who to the utter delight of their fans won it in 2001; and the Italian FA. There is no trophy for the Scudetto. The winning team simply get to wear the tricolour badge of Italy on their breasts for the following season. The newspapers were thus full of cartoons of Totti (the Roma captain) cutting the heart out of his Lazio compatriot. Both teams share the atmospheric Olympic Stadium, making each derby match between them something special. The Italian FA and this stadium were next on my list.

The policeman was sweating. His hand edged nervously towards the holster resting at his side. He was a big man but there were three of us and we looked like we were going to make a break for it. His eyes roamed in turn across ours as we stepped forward slowly making gentle gestures.

Football is very important to the Italians and the thought of our running around with a football table on his team's pitch was pushing this particular policeman to the limit. He had guided us in without much fuss, but as we neared the pitch he had become shaky. There was no precedent for this and a standoff ensued, before I went for it.

It had taken me two days to get to this point. I first caught the bus out to the stadium the day after my attempt to nobble the Italian FA. The FA was found in a little square block in a pleasant, residential area of apartments not too far out from the centre. Holidays struck again, along with the awkward question: 'Do you have an appointment?'

Security in the entrance hall handed me a telephone and I dialled the press officer. After about ten minutes of warbling on it was decided I should 'Come back on Monday. Maybe we can help you then.' At least it wasn't a rejection. Come Monday I would be there.

The Olympic stadium was a further twenty minutes out past the FA. From where the bus dropped me I had to walk through a small park, where a charming local tramp decided to spit at me, and cross a bridge before, there in front of me, was a monument to Mussolini. Alarmingly, his name guards the approach to Rome's present-day Colosseum. It was surprising to see a monument still bearing his name. It was also, however, an insight into the right-wing tendencies of Italian society.

According to a survey by UEFA (European football's governing body), Italian fans are some of the most right-wing in Europe. Verona allegedly had to abort the signing of their first-ever black player in the 2000/01 season because the fans revolted. Fair Verona indeed. At a derby match between Roma and Lazio, the Roma fans unfurled a banner saying all Lazio players were black bastards and their fans were shit. Those concerned were fined and banned from the stadium for – wait for it – two matches.

Once past the Mussolini monument I reached the tree-lined sides of the stadium and the swastika graffiti. Circling its perimeter, I found an open gate and in I walked with my table. Out I walked ten seconds later with the aid of security. Undeterred, I tried again at another gate. Out I was walked once more, but this time I had got to within about ten metres of the stadium itself. I tried to explain to my minder my desire to get in. He pointed at his gun then pointed at the gate. He knew he had the upper hand.

The league winners, Roma, were playing the Cup winners, Fiorentina, in the Italian equivalent of our 'Charity Shield' two days later, hence the increased security. The man who told me this then tried to sell me a ticket. When I said I would buy one from the stadium ticket office he was most insistent that they were all sold out and that, as a friend of the English, he would let me have his last ticket, for nearly double face value. Funnily enough he was nowhere to be seen when I returned after successfully buying a ticket from the office. As I had been evicted twice, it looked like the only route onto the pitch itself would also be by legitimate means. The French and Spanish authorities had not ratified any of my three pitch invasions with the table so far. Could the table go official?

It turned out I was at an advantage in this particular case as the stadium was owned by the council and leased out for matches. I did not have to go through the clubs who, in their haughtiness, were far more likely to reject me, as had Marseille. A few questions to a slightly friendlier security man later and I was on my way to the offices of the Olympic Association near the stadium, surrounded by sculptures of nude Greek Olympians.

With a deep breath and carefully composed smile, in I went. '*Buon giorno. Ce qualcuno che parla inglese per favore?*' Immediate success. A man looked up from his desk. It took him a long time to tell me that he did not speak good English. It is the thought that counts but it was a painful process. A lady was eventually found who gave me a welcoming smile and stopped to listen to my request.

The best thing about my attempted explanations to people was the look in their eyes. They glazed then sparkled then glazed again. You can see the questions rise and fall behind their pupils, despite the bland, often drawn out reply of 'riight'. Again a colleague of the beleaguered person in front of me saved the day and again it was by stressing that I was not from the press that made the difference. 'Is that a football table?' inquired a passing receptionist laughing and looking closer. We were in a large marble hallway and the sound echoed off the high ceiling, breaking the nervousness and launching me into a renewed, more enthusiastic explanation to which I had a far better response. 'You want to get inside the stadium?'

'Yes.'

'With that thing?' She pointed at the table.

'Of course.' This made her smile. She was starting to ease up and see the funny side.

'I can't grant you that permission, but if you wait here I can make a few calls and get the head of the press office to fax the man who can. There is a game on Sunday so it's a bit more complicated.'

Within half an hour I had a faxed reply to my helper, Pietro Carboni, granting, 'the student with the furniture access to the stadium'. Game on. It was not possible that afternoon as tests were taking place for the match on Sunday but she said that if I would like to turn up the next morning I could go in. I hopped back on the bus a happy man. This was potentially the fourth success. It was working. I did not even get spat at on my way back through the park.

Armed with the faxed authorisation, I descended on the Olympic stadium come daylight, as planned, but with two suitably football-mad French lads from my hostel who had excitedly agreed to come along during beers the night before. Fate had lined them up. Hakim was wearing a Roma shirt and Michel a Fiorentina shirt, the very teams that were competing the next day.

The guards kicked up as much fuss as they could when we handed them the fax. It must have been checked at least three or four times as they tried to fob us off but, eventually, begrudgingly, they let us in with a few grunts from their paunches and stares from behind their fighter pilot sunglasses.

So there we were inside the Olympic stadium in Rome, an armed policeman blocking the pitch. After a tense standoff the French double act created a diversion and within seconds the table was streaking across the hallowed turf.

We had been unable to get into a fancy nightclub the night before but had strolled into one of the biggest stadiums in ... 'in Rome,' interjected Hakim, laughing. 'One of the biggest stadiums in Rome.' I was getting a bit carried away. But it was an achievement nonetheless. My CV was getting more entertaining by the day.

The policeman was momentarily undermined as one of the groundsmen ran over to join in. When we sent Hakim far up into the stands with the camera to take a shot down from on high of the table on the pitch the policeman lost his rag and started marching Michel and me out. He was not amused but visibly relaxed once we were out of the stadium and out of his care. We trundled off congratulating ourselves in front of our own imaginary crowds.

'Roma, Roma, Roma' was the anthem as the Italian football season kicked off in style the following night. The fans had been arriving four hours before the game and sang their hearts out. The lyrics might have been simple, but the tune raised the hairs on the back of my neck. With the exception of two thousand heavily guarded and clearly segregated Fiorentina fans, the entire stadium belted out the song with all their might, creating a rousing atmosphere and a fitting start to the footballing calendar.

The champions lived up to their proud support, scoring two cracking goals in a game that started with ferocious fluidity. Not one long ball was even considered and the first goal came when the left back, whose equivalent in most English clubs could not hit a barn door, went past two players and let fly from 25 yards.

The Roma fans were equally accurate from the same distance. In an outrageous display of behaviour, flares were being lit and hurled into the small number of away fans. One flare landed spectacularly in the middle of the Fiorentina section, setting fire to their flag and sparking stadium-wide applause.

It is a special moment being in a stadium after a victory, the sound system blaring out a song that thousands of ecstatic fans add their voice to. While I was not a Roma supporter, I was swept up in the jubilation when they won and the anthem tingled my spine once more. I could not begin to imagine what the World Cup final must be like, so many joyous faces and such inexplicable wonder.

Looking back, recalling our successful attempts to get onto pitches, I remember the embarrassment and trepidation I sometimes felt. Seeing the same Olympic stadium that I had been walking around the day before filled with thousands and thousands of enchanted eyes, however, reinforced all my hopes for the trip's success. I had a grand feeling that England would be there on 30 June in the World Cup final, and I would have a ticket, somehow.

'I'm sorry but there is nobody here who can help you.' The Italian FA was not being forthcoming. It was Monday. 'What about yourselves,' I asked, scraping the barrel. 'You have to make an appointment at least three days in advance; most appointments are made months in advance.' I could feel it slipping away.

'Well, I was here on Friday, three days ago, and I wrote you a letter about it back in March,' I said.

'We have not received a letter,' was the reply that came a little too quickly.

'I definitely sent you a letter. I sent a letter to all the FAs on my route.' I was adamant.

'I'm sorry but . . .'

'Come on, just a quick spin, or a brief interview for the camera, a consolation prize for losing the letter.' Thinking they had taken the bait, I was led upstairs and introduced to a scruffy man in his office surrounded by football memorabilia of every kind.

'There was no letter,' he reiterated. 'I'm sorry but we aren't allowed to do anything involving the press without authorisation. Here are some posters and pin badges, I hope the rest of the trip is a success.' Bugger. My progress had been cut short. The flip side was that the table did grace the corridors of the Italian FA; they were just not man enough to take up the challenge. I was sure I had sent them a letter, though.

After a few beers for his birthday, Tomasz helped me carry my bags to the station for the overnight train to Switzerland via Milan. I had carefully put a couple of bottles of water in the hostel freezer that morning in preparation for the journey but had forgotten them. Leaving Tomasz at the station with the table and the bags I jogged back to fetch them.

What I saw when I returned almost brought a lump into my throat. I stopped and just grinned with amazement: the first, real, genuine display of unprovoked enthusiasm. There was Tomasz standing behind the table, which he had just managed to assemble, grinning back at me. 'Come on,' he said, 'had to give you a game before you left and you had to set it up in here. Look at all these people, and the setting. I love it, this is going to be legendary!'

I was tired, very tired, and for somebody else to show such belief, such camaraderie, was the finest thing that could have happened to me at that moment. We played and played until the tout from our hostel saw us and demanded a game, and then random people from the crowd asked to play. People watched, smiled, shook their heads as they trundled past and laughed. It was fantastic.

Unfortunately though, I have to confess that, as I had not originally planned to visit Rome, I never had written a letter to the Italian FA.

7. SWITZERLAND

Switzerland is a magical country with some staggering scenery nestled in the heart of Europe. The sky just seems bluer there. I headed straight for Basel as a good friend from university was working there. Her company would provide a timely break from my mission, though her boyfriend has a bizarre link with the world of tablefootball that deserves a mention. He once won an award for the fastest own goal in a tablefootball competition for Comic Relief. It was really quite spectacular. The ball had not even hit the table when he spun his player, connected perfectly with the ball and lobbed it over the rest of his team and into his own net.

Amazingly you can swim in the river Rhine which runs through the heart of this relatively large industrial city. The water is clear, warm and your clothes are safe on the river-bank as you float off with the current. But any thoughts of lazy days drifting downstream were dashed. Basel football club, I learned, had just built a brand new stadium, and their current manager was none other than Christian Gross, the doomed former manager of Spurs, the team whose weekly outings determine my level of song. I got my table ready and headed off to find him, unaware that he and the Basel team were actually in England playing Aston Villa.

Within hours I was sitting inside the Basel stadium as a

friendly English builder pointed to the fat guy on the lawn mower. 'You can film when he's got his back to you. He's the groundsman, so he's a bit of an idiot.' Approaching the seemingly bubble-wrapped ground earlier in the day I had heard him speaking English on his mobile and said hello. A handshake and a fantastically short explanation later he gave me a tour around the brand new complex and even up onto the roof.

The stadium itself was finished but the shopping centre underneath and the old folks' home attached to the side were still under way. Having had an unofficial tour and shared a beer in the club bar, I tried the official route to get onto the pitch. Almost in direct correlation to the club being smaller and less successful, the staff were far more patient and accommodating than those I had encountered in France and Spain. Within minutes I had lined up a meeting with the man who, metaphorically, held the keys.

It was very, very tense. Jan took me all the way to a sweaty-palmed 9–9 match of tablefootball on the pitch of the new Basel stadium. Originally from Denmark, he was to be the stadium manager until the following summer when, like me, he was heading for the World Cup. He had greeted me in a loose white shirt and chinos with a big friendly handshake, his easy-going manner shining through. I explained about the journey, which made him chuckle, and he readily agreed to do an interview in the stands before challenging me to a game on the pitch. If everybody was as friendly as he was life would be that much easier; but then I would have less of a story to tell.

'Why do you like football?' I asked. He visibly relaxed, shrugged and a smile crept irresistibly across his face. 'I grew up with football, my father was a football player and I've been playing and coaching teams, I still play now, and it's day and night football if I can have it. It's everything: it's passion, it's fight, it's spirit. I just love it. I go to every match that I can.'

When asked about the nature of the Swiss, he explained: 'The fighting spirit that the English have, Swiss people will never have it; they would like to play Italian style but they don't have the same type of players.' Ironically it was Basel who dumped Liverpool out of the Champions League the following season.

A noticeable change from Italy was the complete lack of fences, trenches and obstacles of warfare separating fans from the pitch. 'We learn from the English,' said Jan. 'We don't like fences, and the way it's done now in England, we like that. We have the stewards in front of the people and 39 video surveillance cameras and we are very happy with that.'

On England's chances for the World Cup he said he hoped that they would beat the Germans (in the 1 September qualifier), 'but I saw the match against Holland and I believe the Germans will beat the English. They [England] can make it to second place, but if they draw Holland in the playoffs it could be difficult.'

Jan's sentiment betrayed his Danish origins. I love the Danish. They are eternal optimists. It is not just the way they translate into English. Nothing is ever impossible. Rather, it 'could be difficult' or might involve 'having to work very hard to succeed'.

It was 9–9. As we played on the table Jan had been gleefully talking me through his greatest Danish footballing moments. '1984 European Championship quarter-final, Belgium v Denmark, Belgium lead after thirty minutes 2–0 but miss a penalty and Denmark win 3–2 to reach their first-ever international semi-final. World Cup qualifying, 1983, winning 1–0 against England at Wembley stadium through a penalty from Allan Simonsen . . .' I changed the subject. But he continued, delightedly questioning, 'When is England ever going to win something again?!' Fortunately this proved to be the cue for me to slap in the tenth goal and maintain the unbeaten run. Not only did I win, I scored the winning goal with my goalkeeper.

Gracious in defeat, he offered me a ticket for Basel's match on Saturday night against Lugano and, to my amazement, revealed he might be working for the German national team in Korea. 'We'll have to meet up. I want a rematch,' he said. A rematch inside the German team hotel in my England shirt ... My mind was already racing with the possibilities.

His girlfriend did not quite share our joy. 'Coming back from a fortnight's holiday in Scotland and having every night since Sunday at the football ground, my girlfriend is back to "why, why, why, we had such a wonderful time, two weeks without almost no football except a little bit on the television and now standing on the ground every day again,"' explained Jan. 'But it's like a virus, there's no way round it.' Good lad.

True to his word he met me on Saturday night with a choice of tickets. He had also primed security so that I would be allowed to use my video camera and film the crowd. I took it a bit further and by flashing his business card I was able to get past a number of security points, down in front of the Kop end, all over the rest of the stadium, and gained an excellent feel for the ground and its various supporters.

After conceding a shocking first goal, Basel made a ferocious comeback, knocking five past their hapless opponents. I bade farewell to Jan at full time but our paths were to cross again. He made it to the World Cup ten months later but I could never have imagined the circumstances in which we were to meet.

Priding itself on its neutrality, Switzerland is the perfect home for FIFA, football's world governing body. But even Switzerland hides a dark past, having allegedly harboured Nazi gold and absconded with the deposits of Jewish holocaust victims, and now FIFA was riding its own scandal. Sepp Blatter, the President, was challenged over the state of FIFA's finances and accused of dodgy dealing.

Dodgy dealing or no, Blatter was too good a target to pass up. With spare time on my hands while my friend Hil was working, I telephoned both FIFA (in Zurich) and the German FA (in Frankfurt). The plan so far had been just to turn up, knock on a door and wing it, but with 1 September getting closer by the day I could not afford a detour to

Frankfurt unless something was set in stone. If I had to hang around for several days I would be late for Munich. Zurich was en route but I felt that I would never be able to pull something off simply by turning up.

Unable to get through to FIFA by telephone, I resorted to sending a fax: '. . . our film would not be complete, nor our challenge successful without the inclusion of your organisation . . .' It was rather official but I figured I should start at the top before working my way down to loutish behaviour and begging. FIFA is after all the pinnacle of world football. I did not get a reply.

The German FA had actually contacted me before Mike and I left England with a belated email reply to my initial batch of letters. In it they gave the usual spiel about being inundated but suggested that if I gave a more specific request in terms of dates and people I would like to speak to, they would get back to me. I did; they didn't.

My subsequent telephone call to the German FA from Basel did not go well. I explained my cause to a rather severe man whose reply was curt and without good grace. On no terms would I be able to get anywhere near the German FA who would not be greeting anyone in the run-up to the qualifier against England, least of all the English. 'But I . . .' I began to venture.

'But you won't,' was the sharp, efficient reply.

Mulling this seemingly harsh and unmerited rejection, I managed to get through to FIFA. Slipping into the routine of things, I requested the press officer and waited. *'Guten Tag,'* he said.

'Guten Tag,' I replied. 'Errr, *sprechen sie Englisch?'* Once we had established he could speak it perfectly he listened politely to my ever-improving spiel. 'Look,' he replied, 'the World Cup kicks off in ten months. We're organising it. The President is rarely here and the other staff are exceptionally busy. I'm sorry, but no.' I was gutted. The house was empty so there was nothing to do but wallow in this double blow to my plans. I slouched my way back upstairs and fell into bed.

Later I threw myself in the river, then soaked up some

sunshine and life felt better. It was never going to be that easy. Did I honestly expect them just to say, 'Yes, sure, you sound like a loon but hey, come on up.' Where was my fight? Robert the Bruce, spider's cobwebs and all that. I pulled myself together and booked a train to Zurich for Sunday night. On Monday morning I would go a-knocking on FIFA's door.

It was at this moment that I got my first taste of India. An Indian palm reader appeared from nowhere and told me I was very lucky. Here we go, I thought. He pulled off a couple of simple prediction tricks before the inevitable demand for money. He then moved on to trying to read my palm, explaining to me the money and love lines. In exchange for my 'donation', jungle masters from his homeland would pray for me for 21 days, bringing me good luck on the 22nd day. He left rather sheepishly, however, when I pointed out the exceptionally deep money line on his own hand.

With a train ticket to Zurich and jungle masters from a remote village near Delhi praying for me, I gathered my things and set off to conquer.

Although it is Switzerland's most populous city, Zurich has a small-town feel nurtured by an ambience of affluence. Based around the northern end of Lake Zurich, with hills on both sides and the Limmat river flowing down the middle, it is another world compared to places like Marseille and Barcelona. It is home to over ten thousand millionaires and the streets are full of fancy boutiques, jewellery stores, banks and wine bars. The mountains hang in the distance at the far end of the lake for the more adventurous, while pedalos are on hire closer to home for the less motivated.

Despite the veneer of clean living, one finds, with amusement, that the tourist map touting fine restaurants, watch shops and fashion stores contains almost five pages of escorts and cabaret clubs. Money, it seems, cannot buy you love.

FIFA has carefully perched itself up on a hill overlooking the lake. It is a marvellous location, an idyllic work place and a bitch to get to if you are on foot carrying a football table. I had no idea that the signposts were diversions for traffic and hence zigzagged my way in mighty loops up the hillside before reaching my goal just after 9 a.m. on Monday morning.

Hoping my jungle masters were with me, I walked boldly into the FIFA headquarters. Wearing my England top, flowery shorts and with my big purple friend pulling on my shoulder, I approached the receptionist. 'Hi, could I please speak to the press officer?'

The lobby was filled with all sorts of tantalising paraphernalia including a 'Heroes of 1988' section that included Mark Hateley in an England shirt, a rack of every national kit and a spine-tingling teaser video for the World Cup in Korea and Japan, with a young Michael Owen rampaging through the Argentine defence at the 1998 World Cup in France.

'Which press officer?' came the reply. I was not prepared for this and it threw me. I did not know the name of the guy I had spoken to on the phone. He must have told me it. Now I had to explain. 'Erm, I can't remember his name. I phoned up on Friday to challenge the President to a game on this little beauty' (I pointed to the table) 'and he's the one who picked up the phone. He said no, so I just thought I'd try my luck, come along in person and have another go.'

'Right.' She was chuckling and shaking her head as she picked up the phone. It was a beautiful day, the sun was shining, the birds were yodelling and she expertly informed the guy on the other end of the phone that there was a young chap with a football table waiting to see him.

As he walked across the lobby to greet me, a broad smile crept across his face. He extended his hand and shook mine warmly. 'I take it you're the lad I said no to on Friday. Good on you for turning up.' He was a completely different man from the one I had previously encountered. On the phone he was just doing his job. There, then, at FIFA HQ, I was able to engage his personality and his own sense of adventure, eye to eye. It taught me a lot.

'I can't promise anything,' he said. 'The President is a busy man, but I'll go and ask seeing as you made the effort to come all this way and climb that hill.' It is inspiring how often people will go out of their way to help you if they feel you have made an effort.

He returned a few minutes later shaking his head. The smile was broader than before. 'You are extremely lucky. Most of the time he isn't even here, when he is he's always exceptionally busy and even when he's free you've got to appeal to his good humour. But he said he'd come down.' The Indian jungle masters were working overtime.

With a devilish sparkle in his eye Sepp Blatter appeared slowly but jovially. Not as sprightly as he once was, and separated from the table by a few more lunches than I was, he still bent down to play with a zest that showed he does not like to be beaten. In a light-coloured jacket and dark trousers he commanded a certain air and had an attentive grace. He is a man who, like Adam Crozier (now *former* head of the English FA), lets his eyes do a lot of the talking.

He carefully dodged most of my questions, a speciality I hear, but when pushed about the Germany v England match the following week, said he thought England would win. 'They are the better side at the moment I think.' And then he was gone.

Ecstatic that I had managed, against the odds, to pull off a meeting with the President, I bounced back down the hill in the glorious sunshine. The birds were, by now, doing cartwheels and Mother Nature herself had taken over the yodelling. Back at my hostel a Scottish couple were disbelievingly enchanted by my tale. Stuart, to the embarrassment of his girlfriend, Laura, rushed off to don his kilt and Scotland shirt for the camera; a crunch match down beside the emerald river ensued.

In one of Alex Ferguson's autobiographies he says, 'a few years back, when Paul Ince was involved in an incident at Wembley, I asked him why he got so upset when someone called him black. After all, he frequently referred to me as a Scottish ******. What was the difference? He told me the Scots aren't a race. I reminded him that we are the master race.'

Stuart lost 10–0, twice. He later finished his trip around Europe in Belgium where he had hoped to see his native Scotland crush the Belgians and qualify for the World Cup. Maybe next time.

The FIFA press officer who had helped me was called Andreas Herren. I learned this when, a week later, I received an email reply to my wayward fax. It was from a guy called Keith Cooper. He had been away but had since heard that I had called in and met Andreas and the President. 'He wishes you all the best, and so do I,' he finished. Although a fleeting touch of communication it was to prove one of the most important of the trip. Saying thank you and goodbye to Andreas I had joked that I might see him in Korea from high up in the stands. He smiled, shook my hand and said, 'Life has so many twists and turns that I wouldn't discount that we will run into one another again personally.'

8. THE GERMANS

I knew it was going to happen. It always does to England. We lost the ball and Jancker, the huge German striker, scored. Our heads fell. The Germans had done it to us again. England's qualification and thus my entire trip was in jeopardy. I could feel my dreams slipping away right there in the stadium.

'The Germans', as our European partners are affectionately known, are alarmingly good at beating us. They beat us in the Olympics, in car production, and with their beach towels.

The greatest pain, in recent years, has been inflicted on the football pitch. In 1990 they knocked us out of the World Cup semi-finals on penalties and went on to win. Who can forget Gazza's tears? The nation wept. At the 1996 European Championships, on our home soil, they had the audacity to do it again. Then, in the last match ever to be held at Wembley, one of England's great shrines, they failed to read the script and in the symbolic rain brought down the curtain not only on the famous stadium but also on Kevin Keegan's career as England manager.

The one-man football table tour rocked up in Munich in time for 1 September 2001. England, after losing to the Germans at Wembley, were heading for second place in their

World Cup qualifying group and the potentially lethal play-offs. The importance of a victory in Munich could not be emphasised enough. It is a date that will not be forgotten for a very long time.

It is not just the English that the Germans have been beating. Both the French and the Dutch still harbour painful memories of wounds inflicted on the football field. On 7 July 1974 the Dutch lost the World Cup final to Germany, their neighbours. A television poll twenty years later revealed that every sentient Dutch person recalled precisely where they were and what they were doing. Led by the genius of Cruyff it was Holland's greatest-ever team yet the Germans beat them. It was a genuine sporting tragedy and became a vehicle for unresolved feelings from Nazi Germany's occupation of Holland.

'After World War II football took the place of nationalism,' says Hermann Van der Dunk, a Professor at the University of Utrecht. Wars were not fought any more but played out on the football field. '1974 saw the young, a new generation, confronted again by a Germany who defeated Holland.'

The day before the final the German tabloid newspaper *Bild Zeitung* published a story about a 'naked party' that took place on the eve of Holland's semi-final against Brazil. Allegedly, when the story broke, Cruyff's wife called her husband and kept him up on the phone all night. It is reputed to be the most influential telephone call in the history of football, arguably determining the outcome of two World Cups (it is rumoured that she prevented him from travelling to the 1978 World Cup in Argentina).

In turn, the French, in a poll after the 1982 World Cup, voted the German goalkeeper, Schumacher, the most hated German ever. He came one vote ahead of Hitler. His fame stemmed from a horrific foul on the French striker Battiston in the semi-final. Schumacher appeared to ignore the ball and clattered into Battiston inflicting four broken ribs, five lost teeth, and an immediate trip to hospital, yet, amazingly, not conceding a free kick. The French went 3–1 up in rage but could not maintain their composure. The game finished 3–3 and the Germans remorselessly beat them on penalties.

To compound their agony, the French were again knocked out by Germany in the semi-finals of the 1986 World Cup four years later. David Baddiel, the English comedian, aptly pointed out that, 'having won three European Championships and three World Cups the Germans are more or less the villains of world history'.

Few people are aware that when England first played Germany at football in 1899 the result was 13–0 in our favour. I put this to a spokesperson for the Munich police whom I interviewed the day before the now legendary match in Munich. I had simply knocked on the door of police HQ, stood tall and asked politely for an interview. He laughed, 'No, no I do not think any big results will happen again, we are far too strong.'

'So you don't think the German team will fold on Saturday?' I replied. Again, another laugh; 'Definitely not.' The result was 5–1 to England.

5–1 to England. Not one, not two, three or four, but five goals against the Germans. Germany had only lost one home qualifier in their last sixty and that was way back in 1984. In ninety minutes the England team took us from torturous depths of despair to heavenly heights and, more importantly, reunited us with the dream that England could and would lift the World Cup trophy.

The result was even more satisfying because the table had graced the centre circle of the Olympic stadium on the outskirts of Munich just a couple of days previously. It also appeared on the front page of the *Guardian* on the day of the game, and its caretaker, me, can be made out under the scoreboard in the shots of the stadium that night, the pictures of which rest under gloriously triumphant headlines.

'Nobody, nobody, nobody beats the Germans 5–1, nobody,' explained an official at the Austrian FA while trying his hand at the table some days later. 'They may be our brothers as such but we enjoyed it very much.'

After arriving from Zurich, while having a shave in my new Munich youth hostel, I met a guy from Middlesbrough. To his disbelief, 24 hours later, he found himself playing tablefootball on the pitch of the Olympic stadium.

The 'Olympic stadium' was built for the 1972 Olympic Games. It was also the venue for the 1974 World Cup final when the Dutch self-destructed after scoring the fastest final goal ever (the German goalie was the first German player to touch the ball and his first touch was to pick the ball out of his net). The stadium is an awesome mass of swirling girdered roofing and is sunk into the hillside so that on one side the gates lead straight to the top of the stand.

First port of call when attempting to get onto a pitch with a football table is the stadium-tour ticket office. The lady behind the desk in Munich, who looked like she had never left it, listened intently to our tale and pleas to get onto the pitch then told us she understood nothing and pointed to another building that turned out to be the swimming pool. Maybe it was her way of translating 'go take a running jump'.

Second port of call is the management office, which we finally tracked down half an hour later. The word 'finally' takes on a new, deeper meaning when one is lugging a football table. The lady here was, in the words of Paul, my Middlesbrough sidekick, 'the perfect choice': young, bubbly and with a Union Jack emblazoned across her ample chest. Giggles were all we could hear from her manager's office once I had convinced her that the normal tour would not suffice, that we had to get onto the centre of the pitch, regardless of whether the German TV company currently filming a commercial in the stadium were finished or not. We would wait. We would sit there and play on the table until they were finished. In general we refused to let her say no, and when her manager saw the footage on my camera of Sepp Blatter, the President of FIFA, joining in the table humour, they could not refuse.

The next morning at 9 a.m. we walked unhindered onto the pitch in England shirts carrying Union Jacks and a football table. The lack of security was staggering. A groundsman eventually came over as we started setting up the table. A spitting image of Rudi Voller, the German national coach at the time, he was easily persuaded of our questionable authority by more of Paul's English with a German accent. He was too perplexed to be suspicious. Hooligans do not carry football tables around with them.

We spent an entertaining hour and a half frolicking all over the Germans' pitch and playing on the table in the centre circle. We even ran a lap of honour around the athletics track that surrounded the playing surface, waving our England flags at the bemused Japanese tourists who had been let into the tour areas up in the stands. The only resistance came from a man high up in the floodlight tower who abused us in German. Naturally we obliged and abused him back.

I remember asking Paul if he was excited. He lit up. 'God I'm excited, just think, in 72 hours time Beckham, Scholes and Owen are going to be on this very pitch.' The table beat them to it.

Sadly Paul could not stay in Munich for the match so we shared a few beers that night before his train. On my way home I got lost and, completely accidentally, stumbled across the hotel where England would be staying. In I went.

Two yards later I was stopped. I slurred at the man that I had to play the England players at tablefootball. He looked at me blankly and was about to point to the door when I remembered I had my video camera with me. Once shown pictures of Sepp Blatter challenging me to a game he broke into a field of smiles and called his manager. I was able to leave a letter for the team when they arrived the next day, but as I left I saw the manager already opening the envelope. Still, he had given me hope. England, he said, would win because Germany had only one good player. It was just what I needed to hear before I drifted off to bed and glorious dreams of England victories.

Friday, the day before the match, was almost as entertaining as the match itself. Munich was by then swarming with the English. Beer and sausages were being guzzled in any beer hall that would admit the well-voiced and good-spirited hordes. The Hofbräuhaus, however, closed its doors to the English after Thursday night when they drowned out the oompah band with choruses of the National Anthem, Rule

Britannia and the Dambusters' March. Valiantly, the band played on regardless.

A call to one of the German newspapers had revealed the times of the England press conference and training session. Admittedly I did not wear my England shirt but, armed with a camera and a tripod, I walked straight through the hotel lobby into the conference swirl of press hounds and free sausages. Amazingly, the fact that my video camera was about seventeen times smaller than all others aroused no suspicion.

Beckham was on cracking form attempting to respond to the irresistible questions that presented themselves as he was grilled about his groin injury and the possibility of taking an injection in order to play. 'How does it feel to have the weight of the nation on your groin, David?' He secured additional laughter from the pack by citing his fear of needles as a further reason for not wanting to take an injection. 'What about for your tattoos, though, David?' came the quick reply. 'Oh yeah.' He smiled. Later on he described his treatment as, 'something new, a beam, from Sweden, so it must be good', then sat with his head in his hands laughing and saying, 'God, I can see the headlines already.' Not only was he a star on the pitch, he was not afraid to laugh at himself off it.

Getting into the training session was going to be more difficult. In the Hofbräuhaus on Thursday night more recruits to the mission had been found. There were Andy, Seb, Murray, Chris and Pete, all staggeringly proud, drunk, English, and well up for championing the table's cause. Despite the hangovers, all were ready and waiting in the backpacker lobby first thing the next day, enticed by the childish dream of seeing the England team in the flesh. A short tube ride to the stadium and a quick conversation with security guards revealed that the 'public' training session was no longer public.

'Follow me,' I called to our little army who had been primed to shout at anyone famous until they were on the table. I led them down and round the back of the stadium thinking we might be able to talk our way in through the marathon entrance (where Paul and I had got in two days earlier), or at least get an English press officer out. No chance. But there, waiting outside the same entrance, was Garth Crooks, former Spurs player and now a BBC pundit.

The well-versed followers of the table began their thing: polite, friendly banter, led by Murray with a big 'Gaaarthh'. For the first time on the trip, however, the table was rejected, spurned. One of the darlings of English football coverage, a man you feel is part of your family, did not want to know. 'Garth Crooks don't play table football,' Seb reflected. We had a provisional book title at least. It was eventually dropped because more people associated it with the American country and western singer than our man from the Beeb.

The VIP entrance was nearby and camped outside were the English press in their marauding entirety. We realised they were waiting to be let in for the training session so waited with them but got bored. Murray made the obvious suggestion of killing time on the table. The moment it was set up cameras surrounded us and the media attention extraordinaire began.

Christmas had come early for the cameramen, their boredom broken by the intervention of six guys in England shirts, draped in flags and playing on a football table. CNN, ITV, Channel 5 and BBC News 24 . . . they kept on coming. When the doors to the stadium opened I managed to sneak past the press ID requests thanks to an Australian reporter who claimed I was his cameraman.

The press were only allowed to watch the last twenty minutes of training. Golden Balls (Beckham) looked to be running around fairly free from pain, and there were Macca, Owen, Campbell and Barmby. Magic. Henry Winter from the *Daily Telegraph* took the time to introduce me to Adrian Beavington from the FA (the man who sat next to the players during most of their press conferences) in the hope of sorting me a ticket for the match. He was a nice guy, had lots of requests for tickets, but was amused by the tale and said he would do his best. In the end, unable to bear the wait and the risk, I bought a ticket from a tout on the morning of the game.

Outside the stadium the boys were grinning from ear to ear. Pete had been interviewed by CNN, Seb by somebody else, Murray by one of the radio stations and so the list went on. They had done well making up tales about the table and feeding all sorts of nonsense to the journalists, despite only hooking up with the table tour the previous night.

A photographer from the *Guardian* arranged to meet us later in Marienplatz, the main town square, promising we would be on the front page. The front page of a national broadsheet; what had we started? He was true to his word and even stayed longer than he expected owing to a series of competitive games on the table. To the confusion of everyone back home I was the only one from our group who was not in the photo. My elbow was all that survived the editor's cut. I got emails saying, 'Andy mate, you'll never believe it but there's another guy out there carrying a football table around with him.'

Setting up the table in Marienplatz attracted a lot of attention from circling press (waiting for drunken violence), Japanese tourists and an unbelievably drunk man from Cologne who stood singing songs about his beloved Colognia at the table for a good few minutes before staggering off. Shortly before a live interview with BBC News 24 on a balcony overlooking Marienplatz (in which we forgot to take the opportunity to goad Garth Crooks for blowing us out), we collared two locals in Germany shirts for a game. Channel 5 and ITN camera crews captured the subsequent 5–0 England victory and relished the post-match handshakes between the two nationalities as English fans all around looked skywards and wished for such a score the following day.

Match day finally came. The German security guard at the gate managed to confiscate my deodorant, which had been accidentally left in my bag, yet miss the whopping video camera as I hurried him and made a run for it. When Jancker scored the opening goal for the Germans I honestly thought my luck had run out, but once the score reached

3–1 to England the man behind me lit up a cigar and, as Emile Heskey slammed home the fifth, he was hugged and shaken by his buddy who was singing, 'We're top of the group, we're top of the group.'

I will never forget the band belting out verse after verse of 'The Great Escape' as the English crowd surged out of the stadium like heroes having reached the fields of Elysium, automatic qualification to the world's greatest prize within our grasp. Wembley had been avenged and the table could set out eastwards once more, confident that the dream was still alive.

9. AUSTRIA

Admittedly, Austria became a place between Munich, where the England match had been, and Prague, where Em, my girlfriend, would be. Added to this I was deprived of sleep on the overnight train from Munich by two elderly Hungarian men discussing the merits of young wives with accompanying laughter and entertaining hand gestures, and thus arrived in Vienna viewing it as a place to recharge.

I was pleasantly surprised to find jaw-dropping architecture, a friendly press officer at the Austrian FA and that I was sharing my dorm with an Australian girl who was understudy to Christine in *Phantom of the Opera*. She refused to sing 'Think of Me', but was entertained by the tales of the table.

I managed to get precisely nowhere in an attempt to get the table onto the pitch of the Ernst Happel Stadium, home of the Austrian FA. There was no one about bar a single security guard who spoke no English and did not look as though he ever wanted to learn any. Searching instead for the FA's offices, I stumbled into those of the Austrian Bundesliga and met two ex-professional footballers who readily agreed to play on the table and talk in front of the camera. With long blond hair tucked behind his ears, the shorter of the two was happy to point out (when discussing

England's 5–1 victory over Austria's Germanic brothers) that, 'We don't like the Germans really. You might cheer them against somebody else but at the same time it's nice to see them beaten. They are like a big brother.'

Austrian football was looking to the future, however. By agreement between the clubs, the Austrian second division had instigated a rule that four players under 22 must be on the team sheet for each team in each league match. 'We are a small country. We have to produce quality. Today for tomorrow. There's an Austrian saying: "It's important to see beyond just the nose."'

I eventually found the Austrian FA on the next floor up. The press officer was running around between stadium, training pitch and hotel as Austria were playing Bosnia the following day, but I managed to catch up with him at lunchtime. He claimed he did not have enough time to play on the table but would answer a few quick questions. My first one was, 'How about a game on the table?' He deflected it with good humour.

Austria have qualified seven times for the World Cup and were on course to finish second in their qualifying group this time and make the playoffs. 'For a small country it is an honour just to be able to qualify. With so many foreigners in the Austrian premier league (almost half the premier contingent are from abroad) it is difficult to find quality candidates for the national team. That is why we can never be the best in Europe,' he explained. 'We have never qualified for the European Championships.' True to form, they subsequently failed to qualify for Euro 2004.

10. CZECH REPUBLIC

Arriving in a new city is nearly always daunting. In theory you should bounce off the train in anticipation and charge headlong into another set of sights and sounds, but it is a bit more complicated than that. You normally arrive tired. An overnight train or bus is not conducive to sufficient rest. Fellow passengers are bound to snore or scratch, you are disturbed by border guards at silly hours in the morning once you have finally nodded off and there is the constant concern about the safety of your possessions.

Also, you have probably left behind a good group of people whom you have just got to know and thus feel alone again, tired of going through the find-a-friend saga and bemused by the new language, signs and systems. However, once you have found a hostel, the bags are off your back, you have caught up on sleep and the sun is shining high, the joie de vivre returns and out you charge.

Getting lost in a city is the best way to find your feet. I am quite good at it. Ambling for hours around the back streets in random loops does wonders for orientation later in your stay. It also lets you soak up the true feel of the city away from the bustle of the crowded tourist monuments. The problem is when you get lost before you ditch your pack.

Prague station and the adjoining bus centre baffled me.

Prague was my first taste of Eastern Europe. Until now everything had been exceptionally easy. For the first time I struggled with the various signs and any attempt at the pronunciation of my destination. Judging from the proliferation of Vs, Zs and Ys I was now much closer to Russia. The lack of vowels was troubling. Words such as 'kdy' do not roll easily off an English tongue. Words such as 'pryc' do but presumably have an entirely different meaning. The struggle was not to last long as I was soon helped by friendly locals who turned out to be Scots on holiday. There are a lot of tourists in Prague.

Em was flying out for the weekend but, to her delight, she was not alone in her arrival. It turned out that Murray (of Munich fame) was also Prague-bound in time for England's next qualifier against Albania. Unfortunately, his train hit a herd of cows.

He arrived late but in one piece. 'It was grim,' he confessed, 'poor bastards went everywhere.' With a distinct lack of fences in the Czech Republic it apparently happens quite often. 'The locals will be having one hell of a barbecue,' he added wryly.

'England have a new saviour and his name is Michael Owen,' wrote the tabloids back home. After that magnificent triumph in Munich Sven warned the players they needed to be on their guard in the midst of the euphoria. Owen and Fowler struck two minutes before half-time and full time respectively against Albania to give Sven his sixth win in seven games and put England top of the group. We were level on points with Germany but with a one-goal advantage and one game each to play. If we beat Greece we would qualify automatically for the World Cup finals. All we had to do was beat Greece.

I was a happy bunny in that Czech pub and met Em off her plane at the airport the next day intent on sweeping myself up in her for a weekend and forgetting all about the table mission. Well, that was until somebody told us there was a Slavia Praha match on the following day.

'Maybe they don't have many fans,' quipped my long-suffering girlfriend. Our walk to the stadium had been eerily quiet. Our information was wrong, there was no game. The plan I had hatched with Murray the night before was scuppered. Figuring that security here would be far slacker than in Western Europe and that the stands were unlikely to be full, we reckoned we could probably take the table into the ground and set it up during the match. Sadly, it was not to be, but, with no match on, the pitch was free for an attempted table invasion. It was to give Em a perfect insight into the various tales that had been wafting back from the continent of the table's progress.

It took some hunting to find an office-cum-reception-cum-club-shop manned by a lone Czech. As we approached we spotted someone else. The crowd? Could the match be on after all? No. It was an Englishman, from Leeds. Slavia Praha have played Leeds twice in the UEFA cup so, leaving his wife and kids for an afternoon, he had come to check out the stadium. After exchanging good old English pleasantries in the tradition that a fellow Englishman abroad is to be greeted like a friend from home, we entered the office together.

Before I could tackle the lone Czech about his pitch the Leeds man, having swallowed his curiosity until now, piped up. 'What's, erm, in the bag?' A very reasonable question considering it was a very big and very purple bag. 'A football table' I replied. He smiled, nodded, mouthed 'oh, right' and fell silent. He had already learned that I was on an overland trip backpacking to the World Cup. You could almost hear his mind at work. 'Let me get this straight. You're carrying a football table overland all the way from England to Korea.'

'Yep,' I said with a smile. 'We're knocking on the doors of all the FAs en route and trying to sneak it onto the pitches of all the stadiums we come across.'

'You serious?' His face was a picture. 'Wow, that's great.' He was struggling to comprehend it but something inside him was telling him it was fantastic. 'Good luck mate, that's fantastic, I'll look out for you.'

The lone Czech was not as impressed. 'No' had been the initial reply when I had asked if we could get onto the pitch. His ears had been burning, though, when I was talking to my fellow countryman, and when I opened the bag to show the table he could not help but be captivated. Almost without asking he began locking up the office and took us on a guided tour of the stadium, up into the stands, round the changing rooms and out onto the pitch where he became the most gracious person yet to lose on the table.

His pidgin English was magic. With the stadium behind him we asked if he would say to the camera, 'Welcome to the Czech Republic' in Czech. He was thrilled and delightedly jumped into place. I readied the camera, hit record and signalled thumbs-up. A big smile swept across his face and he said, in English, 'Welcome to Czech Republic, in Czech Republic.' We burst into fits of laughter that only spurred him to do it again, blissfully unaware of his mistake. We were unable to hold a conversation but the table had broken the ice, transcended the language barrier and provided us and this entertaining local, who was not much older than me, with a grand memory to treasure. He led us around with a charm and friendliness that epitomised Prague.

Next to Slavia's home ground lay the remains of a mighty arena. It was about the size of four football stadiums and was the stage for Communist rallies during the days of Soviet occupation. The haunting stands were now overgrown with weeds but the structure stood as a sober reminder of days gone by. On the outside, in massive letters was sprayed a lasting message: 'Hooligans from Poland'.

All too soon Em was gone and I found myself on a train northwards across the border, in the direction of the hooligans.

11. POLAND

'We are Israeli filmmakers, come with us to Amsterdam?' Poland, it seemed, had a few unexpected surprises in store. The table had been lacking attention since the media high of Munich but had attracted new interest in the eastern wilds of Poland.

My knowledge of Poland was limited to its general suffering during the World Wars, its strong Catholic ties and the fact that one of my university housemates, Rob, was of Polish descent. The only time we heard anything about Poland from him was in the build up to each England v Poland game until they inevitably lost, at which point he was English again.

It was another tiring overnight train journey out of Prague and up through the plains to the former royal capital of Krakow. The table and I crossed the Czech/Polish border at 2 a.m. triggering an invasion by a small army of officials and police. It was all quite surreal sitting in the wooded darkness, somewhere in Eastern Europe, as soldiers made their way down the carriage checking documents. It felt like an old war film, with an escaped POW on the run hiding behind his newspaper in the carriage of refugees bound for freedom.

Alongside the horrors of war the country has a rich history. It is full of tales of medieval splendour, castles and knights, which unfortunately I did not have time to explore, but was glad to discover. It is all too easy to live off the stereotypes of a country. You forget that there are millions of people there just as there are in your own country. And with millions of people comes the diversity that makes cultures rich.

When the sun is shining Krakow must be a wonderful place. It greeted me, however, with a cheerless rain, gloomy skies, plunging temperatures and scant football for the table. Whereas Prague had been alive, Krakow was in a dreary slumber.

I was wet, cold, miserable and missing Em, so I decided to surprise her. A brief look in a travel agent's window revealed a cheap return flight the next day from Warsaw to London. Coming from Poland you got Polish prices. It was a tricky choice: three days with Em or a harrowing visit to Auschwitz in the downpour.

The Israeli filmmakers were serious. 'Come with us to Amsterdam,' they said, 'we can make a film about the table on the train.' I had been waiting patiently outside the travel agent's the following morning with my bags when two Israelis joined the queue, consisting solely of me, and we struck up a conversation. The talk culminated in a game of tablefootball in the street and, as the agency opened its doors, they hit me with their dramatic proposal. 'We have to go to Amsterdam to finish a film there. We'd love to follow you but we can't. We were going to fly, but instead we could take the train, it's seventeen hours, we could make a great film.' I hesitated, credit card in hand, flight finally arranged.
    'Really?'
    'Yes, really.' I mulled it over quickly, my mind racing as I looked them over, searching for clues among the madness. Unable to find any I concluded I did not believe them and handed over my card to pay for my flight. I kicked myself almost immediately. It transpired that they *were* proper and respected filmmakers with a large crew and plenty of funding. Bugger, I muttered, as the rest of their team appeared. The lesson was learned. Next time I would take the risk and embrace the adventure.

'We think you have a great project,' they said over a rematch outside the agency. 'Football connects people, it's better than politics.' It was just the motivation I needed. I may not have found myself on a train to Amsterdam, but I had been inspired again to believe in the adventure upon which I had embarked.

Where were you on 11 September 2001? Me, I was on a plane bound for London. I still cannot believe that the pilot told us. We were approaching Heathrow when he relayed the breaking news from America that three planes had been hijacked and two had crashed into the World Trade Center. Messages had been creeping around and mobiles buzzed as people heard the terrifying news from relatives. Everybody was on edge. The pilot must have been on full alert for any suspect-looking persons on our flight. 'Nothing to report, Captain, but there is a lad with a football table in row 24.' We landed safely.

I include this brief sortie home in my tale because, although it broke up the trip, the tragedy of 11 September 2001 puts it into perspective. It was great to see my parents, friends and girlfriend again, albeit briefly, and it was so easy and cheap that I would have been a fool not to. Unfortunately, to his utter delight, Rich, a former housemate, took the opportunity of my return to inflict my first defeat on the table (excluding those handed down by Mike). There was, however, a consolation.

You may have forgotten about my jungle masters from Basel, but they, it seemed, had not forgotten about me. It was 21 days since they started praying so I was due some luck. Matt, my erstwhile partner to be, was readying to fly out to Estonia to join the table's quest and had organised a leaving party in Birmingham that very night. Fitting that the table should be there. The jungle masters had done well.

I only stayed in England for a few days so as not to lose the momentum of the trip, but long enough for the clouds to clear over Poland. Touching down on my return to Warsaw I felt like a seasoned adventurer. The table, however, had yet to see any Polish football action. Before my charge up to Estonia, in time to meet Matt, I had to hit the Polish FA.

I called Tomasz, my sidekick from Rome. He was back home now but under the cosh from work and unable to rejoin the adventure. In Rome, on his birthday, he had painted a rather sorry picture of Polish football that matched the slogan left so visibly in Prague.

'It's hard to say, but there's no football in Poland in my opinion at the moment. I only watch the national team. Football used to be a big thing in the 70s in Poland. Seriously, I mean we had great players, we even made the World Cup finals in 70 something but when all those players retired it was all gone.' Surely it could not be that bad, I asked. 'It is getting better now, but that's the national team, the league is crap.

'It is truly awful. In Poznan, where I live, we had a team that was in the first league called Lecht Poznan. All I remember from their games is just a city destroyed because of football fans. You never found out about the score, you just heard about violence, people fighting and hospitals ...' He paused, took a long, almost mournful, drag on his cigarette, finished his pint, then added, 'But it's getting better now.'

Finding cheap accommodation for the night in the political and economic heart of Poland was surprisingly tricky, so I left my stuff in a locker at the station, where the taxi from the airport had dropped me, and set off via a series of buses to reach an outlying hostel. There, some entrepreneurial Polish lads in my dorm who had won a competition to attend a business conference dragged me into the empty old town and educated me in the delights of Polish vodka.

In the first bar I made my biggest error. A murky looking drink was poured. Summoning up courage I proudly sank it in one mighty gulp. There was no fire, no afterburn; I had taken it like a man. Everybody laughed at me. It was apple juice, poured as a side dish to wash down the vodka and help extinguish any flames as and when the need arose. The barmaid found it very amusing.

'We have a great team, you know.' Wojciech had had a

few vodkas and wanted to talk football. 'We are qualified for the World Cup first time after sixteen years. All the people are happy. I am so happy and I, I can't say more about it. I love our team.'

He seemed a very happy man. Before he staggered off to bed I managed, accidentally, to convince him that David Beckham is Dutch. When said with a Polish accent, it sounds like Bergkamp, and Bergkamp, I rightly insisted, is Dutch. I had misheard him. He wandered off to bed muttering, amazed that he had never realised David Beckham was Dutch.

My final day in Poland was hectic. I was tired and hung over and the incessant rain did not help my spirits. I was due to head for Latvia on the twice-weekly bus that afternoon but knew I had to hit the Polish FA. Without time to go via the locker at the train station and retrieve the table, I set off in the downpour.

The Polish FA, 'Polski Zwiazek Pilki Noznej' (PZPN), was on the edge of the old town, about a forty-minute walk from my hostel. It was shut. Everything was shut. I had to shelter for an hour in a doorway. When opening time finally came I shook off the rain, composed myself and prayed they were not on holiday sharing a beach with their French and Italian counterparts.

I was nervous, which was bizarre considering that I had already thrown myself at the French, Italian and Austrian FAs, FIFA, and talked my way into the stadiums at Caen, Bordeaux, Marseille, Rome, Basel and Prague; but nervous I was as I climbed the stairs to their second-floor offices. This time I did not have the table to hide behind. In my best Polish I asked if anyone spoke English and was thankfully rescued with a welcoming nod. A few more hesitant moments came as I tried to explain what I was doing. As you can imagine, this was especially difficult given that I didn't actually have the table with me.

This was, however, Eastern Europe. They did not get random Englishmen turning up to visit their FA as their colleagues in Spain, Italy and France might do. Therefore, I think my story captured their interest and my dishevelled rain-soaked appearance invoked their sympathy. They were certainly intrigued and once they understood what I was harping on about, were quite keen to join in. After a short wait I was beckoned into the office of Marcin Stefanski, Head of Competitions Department and the Deputy General Secretary of the Polish FA.

I decided to open with a compliment. 'You must be a very happy man now that Poland have qualified for the World Cup.' He nodded, smiling, 'Yes we are very happy because we are in and England are not . . . yet not.' He had a sense of humour. I reminded him that Poland had failed to qualify for the past sixteen years. 'Yes, we almost forgot how to qualify but we are in, and maybe the reason is because we didn't play against England this time.' He had a warm smile and a sharp intelligence in his eye. 'I'm joking, but I think, seriously, we have now a better team than the last sixteen years.'

Encouraged by his enthusiasm I pressed him on what drew him to the game. 'Football is life, the rest is mere details; this is one of the most important things in the world.' He had watched the Germany v England match and enjoyed the surprise result, but explained that the date of the game, 1 September, had an extra significance in Poland. '1 September was a very special day in Poland. It was the date the Germans invaded Poland at the start of the Second World War. I think it is very important for the people who remember these days, but not so important for teenagers. For the teenagers it is important that we qualified for Korea and Japan.'

Polish football has struggled because of the infrastructure it inherited from the communist years. 'In England you have clubs with one hundred years of history and they own their own ground,' explained Stefanski. 'In Poland, for example with Legia Warsaw, you cannot invest any money in the stadium because the army owns the ground. The army does not want to invest and Legia, the company, will not invest money in a ground that does not belong to the company. It is a very difficult situation.

'In Poland, to organise the football game and to arrange

everything, it's a comedy, it's difficult to describe; you have to see it. Everything to do with football in Poland was very funny except the score.' Finally though, the Polish team were creating scorelines to celebrate, not laugh at.

We parted with a friendly handshake and one last question. 'If I had the table-football table with me would you challenge me to a game?'

'Sure,' he replied.

I only wish their World Cup could have been less painful. In their opening game they lost 2–0 to the hosts Korea, then suffered the humiliation of conceding four goals in a thumping by Portugal. The Celtic manager, Martin O'Neill, commented on Pauleta's hat-trick that, 'he'd have had more trouble scoring against his kids in the back garden.' Other comments that they only qualified because they got to play Wales twice were unfair. In their final match, despite being unable to qualify from the group, they remembered how to play football, and dominated the Americans (eventual quarter-finalists) to win 3–1.

My work in Poland was done. Pleased that I had conquered my laziness and been welcomed by another FA I headed for the bus. By the time I had picked up my bag and the table I had twenty minutes to spare. I ran for the tram to the bus station. Once awkwardly aboard the crowded carriage I looked around to stamp my tickets but could only see a wooden block where the usual stamper should have been and could not have reached it anyway. Never mind, I thought, soon enough I would be out of the country so its not as if I would be using them again.

'Off!' I had forgotten about Murphy. If it can go wrong, it will. 'Off!' It was a plain-clothed policeman who had asked for tickets. I had produced both of mine (one for me and one for my pack as is the norm in Poland) but they had not been validated. The stupid bastard had been on the tram when I got on. He must have known, even if he had not seen me try, that there was no chance given what I was carrying, and the crush, for me to be able to get to the validating machine. It did not seem to matter. 'Off!'

He insisted on liberating me of my passport and demanding a fine. As he showed his ID and was joined by a uniformed colleague I realised I was not in much of a position to argue. But I did. I was not impressed and a rage overtook me. He had taken down my passport details, however, and my lack of cash was not a problem to them. They frog-marched me to a cash point having located my money belt and credit card.

Somebody was clearly watching over me as, to my joy, the card did not work. I had been praying for some sort of divine intervention and here it was. The clock was ticking. If I missed this bus to Riga I would have to wait four days for the next one. My parents had arranged a long weekend trip to Tallinn in Estonia to meet me and if I failed to get there they would, rightly, not be amused. It was a straight choice: which was I more afraid of – a Polish jail or a mother's wrath?

There was no choice. I have never launched into anybody in my life quite like I did with those two officers, but my tirade shook them and my appeal to divine justice really hit home. Suddenly they were exceptionally concerned with getting me to my bus station. Maps were out, locals questioned, the quickest route found and then they waited to ensure I got on the right tram. I made the bus to Riga with two minutes to spare.

They may well have the last laugh though. My passport number remained in the officer's notebook. On a future visit to Poland who knows what accumulated delights might await me. I may yet lose the war, but for now I had won the battle and was on my way to Latvia.

12. LITHUANIA

Fell asleep on the bus. Missed it.

13. LATVIA

In one of the towns through which we passed there is a simple monument with two plaques. As you approach it towards Moscow it reads: 'Napoleon Bonaparte marched this way in 1812 with 400,000 men.' On the other side when you face south towards France it reads: 'Napoleon Bonaparte passed this way in 1812 with 9,000 men.' Few if any have headed north and triumphed. But like all those before me I dreamed of success against the odds.

The bus rattled into Riga at the sprightly hour of 4 a.m. No accommodation could be found in Riga at 4 a.m. and there was no onward train service to my preferred destination of Tallinn. Thus, sat on my bench, I had the privilege of watching this indefatigable country come alive.

The first wave were hardened people of the Baltic with wellies, heavy clothes, weathered faces and a resolute step headed for the sea. The second wave were those who had slept-in hurrying to catch the first wave. The third wave consisted of three stunners, dressed to kill, who must have stumbled onto the wrong night bus home from Trafalgar Square. With the fourth wave came the early commuters, the stall owners and shopkeepers. Doors began to open, stock hit shelves, newspapers were in place, Joe Public was finally out of bed, the sound of traffic grew and the sun climbed steadily, weak but life-giving, in the soft northern sky.

The capital of Latvia and former 'Paris of the east', Riga is the Baltic region's major metropolis. It was formerly the home of the feared 'Knights of the Sword' who ruled from Poland to Estonia. Peter the Great succeeded where Ivan the Terrible had failed and conquered Latvia, bringing it within the Russian Empire. It was a subjugation that lasted until 1991.

One invasion that has not troubled the Latvian people came from an unlikely candidate from Wales. The not-so-mighty force of Welsh and world football that is Barry Town FC, led by dreams of European glory, came to Latvia chasing qualification for the Champions League. Skonto Riga, their opponents, had other ideas.

I remember vividly an old Welsh friend of mine animatedly explaining to me the indomitable Welsh spirit. There existed such a passion and belief, she said, that opponents, despite being more talented, more experienced and more successful, could be swept aside as a result of this unique bond. When I got home that night and checked Ceefax, Wales had lost to Holland 7–1.

I told this tale to another Welsh friend some years later. 'No way,' he cried in full Welsh accent. 'I remember that, that was one of the greatest moments of my life. My dad took me to see the game and we scored. We went one-nil up against Holland. Unbelievable. The only problem was that then they went and scored seven.'

In Riga, the Welsh spirit was still in the fight at half-time, but any wayward aspirations were brutally destroyed with two goals in three minutes after the break. A further late double killed the dream before it had even begun. Barry Town were going home.

For the table and me, Latvia was merely a tranquil stop on the road to Estonia. The police Ladas, pretty streets and quiet people would stay in the memory until next time. The table had bigger fish to fry and a new owner to greet north of the border. With a change in management would the success continue or would we be joining Napoleon as another defeated hopeful on the signpost?

14. ESTONIA

Estonia is a small country tucked up above its fellow breakaway states of Latvia and Lithuania. Considering its size and location at the far reaches of Europe it has made a name for itself in politics, history, football and of course, unforgettably, the Eurovision Song Contest.

It was a landmark point of the trip. One would become two again. Matt was finally to join the adventure. I had been getting jittery about the prospect of heading into Russia and possibly down to Iran by myself. I was already in Iron Curtain territory but heading further behind it into its heart was something else. It was good to see him.

Matt hails from a small farm near Sedgeberrow in the vale of Evesham. Despite this his farming knowledge leaves a lot to be desired. Later in the trip I had to explain to him what cowbells were for; and no, Dad, it is not because their horns don't work.

The table now had two owners to guide it to new victories and greater heights as we headed into more extreme foreign pastures. These were places which did not pop up in the holiday adverts of the newspapers but in the 'world news' section after nuclear blasts, riots, demonstrations, severe cold, droughts and cricket; places of extreme religion, extreme poverty, and a very different way of life, but all with the same love of the beautiful game: football. These were places where the rules were different from home; the customs and reasoning varied by centuries of tradition. Yet we found an underlying humanity and kindness that helped wing us on our way to great adventures with many remarkable people.

Matt's first mission, after successfully meeting up with my parents and exploring the delights of Tallinn's medieval heart, was to hit the Estonian FA. He accepted, though his face was quite a picture. It was a mixture of excitement, worry and bemusement at the prospect of turning up un-announced at a national FA with a football table.

Estonia had won the Eurovision Song Contest. Terry Wogan might even have raised an eyebrow. Winning it meant host-ing it and Estonia was proud to welcome the rest of Europe to its pleasant shores.

'I personally don't like music of the Eurovision,' said Indrek Kannik, Vice President of the Estonian Football Federation, laughing 'but for a small country it's a big high-light.' An extravagant nonsense of an event it may be, but it is a European institution and it helped put Estonia back on the map.

We were on the pitch of Estonia's brand spanking-new national stadium interviewing Mr Kannik. He was a charm-ing man, quite young, quite large, quite ginger, smartly dressed, very accommodating and a pleasure to meet.

The Estonian FA was really quite remarkable. Our taxi had flown out of the city and we eventually found ourselves in a very quiet, wooded, country suburb. The ground was clearly visible from the road behind a rusting mesh fence whose gate had given up the ghost many moons ago. A soft track covered in pine needles and broken by tree roots led to the buildings and a football pitch to the left of them sur-rounded by a shale running track. After the city-based FAs of Western Europe – the noise, the clutter, the smog, the attitude and the money – it was idyllic. The home of Estonian football is stuck out in the forest, unsignposted and tucked away in a small facility accessed via the back of what looked like a condemned stand with its own beautifully kept pitch. Trees grew between the buildings as though nature had been in charge there for some considerable time. It was a place unconcerned by the worries of the world, a place where time stands still.

'Hi, errm, we're from English TV,' we stuttered, as the occupants of the long room into which we had just stumbled looked up from their desks. Working on the basis of looking semi-official, with Matt rolling the camera, we hoped that our unusual request would be met with a serious reply. In Western Europe I had concluded it was best to appear as Mickey Mouse as possible and play the humour and/or sympathy card to win affection and access. In Eastern Europe, however, we figured a bit of authority might have more effect.

'Is Trin Adazi here?' I ventured. The lady nearest us got up from her desk, put a file away, said 'no' and answered the phone, adding as an afterthought, 'She works part time and from home.' Phone call over, however, she turned her full attention to us and there were the stirrings of interest from curious workers at the far end of the office. I explained our mission but there remained an air of complete non-comprehension. It was not the sort of place that people just drop into. Let alone two random Englishmen with a football table.

She was friendly enough, however; especially given the limited information we had supplied her with. Another young lady came across to aid translation. With her excellent English we soon established that there was nobody present with sufficient authority whom we could interview or challenge. Both ladies confessed to being secretaries employed solely for their English-speaking skills and having absolutely no knowledge of football. As a consolation the later arrival was stunning. Judging from the camera footage, Matt thought so as well.

The FA consisted of one big long room. Several walls had been knocked through and the room was now divided by filing cabinets topped with trophies and filled with paper. We managed to strike up banter of sorts and, in return, our new acquaintances made a few calls on our behalf. Before we knew it, they had managed to organise a meeting with the Vice President of the FA (who spoke English) at their new stadium on Monday morning. Perhaps, we thought, for the first time our quest had been recognised as a genuine chance of publicity and thus a desire existed to take part.

Matt was on a high. It had been an astounding start to the campaign trail for him. Whereas mine had involved uncomfortably hulking my bags and the table for what seemed like eternity around Portsmouth harbour, he had stepped off his plane and stumbled straight into the bizarre success of being welcomed by the FA of a remote Baltic country. Within a day and a half he had a story for the pub back home that none of his mates would believe. On Monday morning he was due to challenge the Vice President of the Estonian FA to a game of tablefootball on the pitch of the new national showpiece stadium. Not bad. Not bad at all.

Scottish fans know Estonia for the game-that-never-was. In 1996 Scotland travelled to Tallinn to play Estonia in a qualifying match for the 1998 World Cup. At 3 p.m. the Scottish team farcically kicked off the match, in front of an eight-hundred-strong travelling tartan army, without the Estonian team present. The referee blew his whistle three seconds later to call a halt to proceedings, the crowd cheered and Scotland were temporarily awarded a 3–0 victory. If FIFA had been watching Scotland's form in previous matches, they would have awarded them 1–1.

'It was an interesting match,' said Mr Kannik, the Vice President, perched in the stands above the national pitch on Monday morning. 'Scotland demanded agreement from the FIFA delegate that the floodlights were not OK. To us they were fine so the team refused to play at the rearranged earlier time. Italy had played twice under these lights and it had been OK for them. We remember this match in the sense that Scotland had a couple of players injured and booked in their previous match four days before and they were trying to get a victory on paper for this match. Later FIFA took a correct decision, the match was replayed in Monaco and it ended in a goalless draw, which obviously was a very good result from our point of view. It was very sad for both sets of fans though.'

We had met Mr Kannik without a hitch and were led into the stadium via a tunnel opening straight onto the pitch. For a stadium that held only fifteen thousand people it felt substantially bigger owing to the careful design of the stands. He shook hands warmly, shared a joke about the table and asked what we wanted to do. Almost bewildered by such courtesy we hesitated before filming an interview in the stands then challenging him to a game on the table in the centre circle.

The opening game of the new stadium had been against Holland and to the people's delight Estonia had given them a scare. 'We were 2–1 up with seven minutes to go,' said a smiling Mr Kannik, before adding with a sigh, 'unfortunately we lost 4–2.' Agonising. But a sign that progress is being made.

Basketball used to be the biggest sport in Estonia as a result of the Soviet occupation but now football has taken the top spot. 'Football has been getting much better in Estonia during the last six years and development has been quite tremendous', said Mr Kannik. 'I don't want to promise it but I think we will qualify for something in the next decade.' For a country of only 1.5 million it was quite a suggestion nonetheless. 'To qualify for the World Cup, that's our aim.' He gave me a big, knowing smile. 'Well, you have to hope for the best,' he chuckled.

Estonia's biggest match is without doubt against Russia. They had a 'friendly' arranged for March, their first international friendly since they gained independence in August 1991. 'I think it is going to be a very passionate affair,' said Mr Kannik. In 1989, fifty years after the secret Nazi–Soviet Pact that divided Eastern Europe and condemned the Baltics to the Soviet yoke, an estimated two million people formed a 650-kilometre human chain of protest stretching from Vilnius in Lithuania, through Riga and up to Tallinn. To the delight of the people, independence followed soon after, although it was not until 1994 that the last Soviet troops were grudgingly withdrawn from Estonian soil.

Independence is everything to Estonians. 'It has been extremely important to us both politically and economically,' recounted a now grave Mr Kannik. 'The economy of our country during the last ten years has grown tremendously and we really can't compare ourselves any more to the rest of the former Soviet Union. If you are going forward from here to Russia you will see quite a different world.

'In this area of the world, security is of vital importance to us,' he continued. Russia does not have the best record for leaving small states to their own devices. Football is a route into peoples' hearts and minds. It is a phenomenal PR investment. It can change people's entire attitudes to a country. It offers an insight, a means of accessibility, and paves the way for greater trade, investment and general international recognition, which, for a country living under the shadow of a nation like Russia, is very important.

Down on the pitch we had to teach them (Mr Kannik and an FA colleague) how to play tablefootball after they had tried to stand at the ends of the table rather than the sides. With the confusion resolved, they both bent down with gusto. To follow the ball and control your handles requires a fair amount of concentration, which, from the observer's point of view, is most entertaining. Facial expressions accompany the action and it is unheard of for a goal at either end not to be greeted with cries of satisfaction. This day was no exception, although, naturally, we emerged the victors. Mr Kannik had to rush off shortly after, but left with a smile, a handshake and permission for us to remain in the stadium a bit longer to get some shots of the table from up in the stands.

This enabled us to put our new plan into action. We had bought a football. As well as setting the table up on the pitches we would try to actually kick a ball about as well. We could take some penalties; maybe even recreate famous goals. This was why two people are so much better than one. I now had somebody to kick a ball with. The vice president had left. A national football stadium was ours.

We played for quite some time, shooting, crossing and dribbling on the Estonians' hallowed turf. Although on another level from our respective school playgrounds, the running commentary remained the same, 'Sloan to Holyfield who nips past one, rides the challenge, slips it back and what a strike. Sloan wins the World Cup for England, the fans are on the pitch, they think it's all over . . .' It was.

Filled with excitement, but with a wave of trepidation, we found a bus out of Tallinn bound northeast for St Petersburg, deep into the mighty mass of Russia. Mr Kannik's words were ringing in our ears. 'If you are going forward from here to Russia you will see quite a different world.' We had been surprised by Estonia's affluence. Tallinn was filled with classy bars, beautiful women, flash cars, big department stores, multi-screen cinemas, big new fancily designed office blocks, fashion boutiques, Co-Ops filled with fresh produce of every kind and colour on every corner. In ten years of independence they had been able to concentrate on themselves rather than be drained for the greater good of the Soviet nation.

From the moment we hit the Russian border every stereo-type about Russia came true. The Bond films were spot on, with one exception, the women. It looked grim, it looked cold, and I had never seen so many Ladas in my life.

15. RUSSIA

The soldiers wore dark-green trench coats over their dark-green Russian military uniforms as they meticulously searched everything. Even with nothing to fear I found myself unnerved by it. It was a cold day both in look and feel as we crossed the river, which lay beneath old stone forts with cone-topped turrets, a pleasant glimpse of history, the last for some time before we stopped at the border post.

A Lada was being systematically stripped. The people looked tired and miserable. They had nothing yet they were being shaken down as if they had everything. It felt as if we were entering the land of an old, and not particularly well-loved, regime. I held my breath when handing over my passport as the visa was checked, checked and double-checked.

Our arrival in St Petersburg, the 'Venice of the North,' was something of a disillusioned surprise. Our bus had chugged through numerous dreary, bleak towns with run-down houses and old cars before taking an age to weave through the industrial outskirts of the city in the darkness and rapidly falling temperatures. We stepped off the bus into a giant mud pool of a bus station. It was bitterly cold. We must have looked like startled rabbits caught in the glare of headlights. All we could see were Cyrillic signs and wooden newsagent stalls.

It was confirmed that we were in St Petersburg. It was confirmed that we had no idea where. It was confirmed that nobody was about to help us find out. '*Nyet*' means no in Russian. It is a word we became all too familiar with, sometimes before we had even broached a question. The curt, pre-emptive strike of '*nyet*' is a Russian speciality. It even *sounds* menacing and is delivered with a scornful finality. Mr Kannik was right; it was a different world.

A taxi to the city centre, from where we could get our bearings, seemed the only option. Some dodgy-looking locals were ready to pounce standing next to their dodgier-looking Ladas. Our guide book said 'taxi across town: $2.' I rubbed thumb and forefinger together to ask the taxi driver how much and pointed on our map to the centre. 'Ten dollar'. I got stubborn, Matt got cold. After a couple of minutes it became worth ten dollars just to get out of the cold and I had to give in. I could no longer argue with a man who looked like he could stand and bear the intense temperatures until the end of time.

We piled into his barren Lada. He was a big man and could only just about fit into the driver's seat. We rattled off at an alarming pace, slaloming between the traffic, as we were whisked along rivers and over bridges into the heart of St Petersburg, then, worryingly, out the other side into dark unknowns.

We had not counted on an ominous detour at the direction of our driver. We plunged down dark side streets far from the centre, eventually arriving at an eerie youth hostel that wouldn't accept us. Any relief that there was accommodation at the end of our journey and not a watery grave was short-lived as we were held to ransom over our ride back to civilisation. It was gone midnight by the time we escaped. Frustrated and tired, we ended up checking into the outwardly grand 'St Petersburg Hotel' in desperation, and collapsed, somewhat relieved, into a manky room that sufficed until we found our feet and a recognised hostel.

St Petersburg was built by Peter the Great as his 'window on the west' after smashing the Swedes. He celebrated the victory by building his new capital at the site of his triumph. With its many waterways and beautiful palaces you can see why it has been compared with Venice. But here the waterways are massive and, with the freezing temperatures, only a fool would take to a gondola. In January the *average* day and night temperature is minus eight degrees Celsius. It was a positively sweltering four degrees at the time of our passing, but a bitter wind cut straight through my layers of T-shirts. We both made a dash for the long johns in the lingerie section of the nearest department store.

A combination of the bitter cold and the sheer scale of the city meant the table stayed at home. We donned our tourist caps and walked enormous loops around the giant blocks of St Petersburg. The streets are wide, the blocks massive, many of the buildings outwardly run-down, flaking, the pavements cracked, dirty and home to lines of old women selling anything they had in their possession on blankets off the ground, be it nuts, newspapers or simply plastic bags. It was a depressing sight. They looked haggard and beaten.

All was not well in Russia – approximately forty million Russians live below the poverty line. Antiquated concerns and an ongoing, ugly war with Chechnya continue to hold back progress. Only recently did Russia's Supreme Court decide that, contrary to the opinion of four Moscow courts, the Salvation Army was not a subversive paramilitary group dedicated to the violent overthrow of the state. A euphonium would not be my weapon of choice. We chose a football table instead.

St Petersburg was the stage for the first-ever football match between England and Russia. In atrocious conditions the English narrowly won by eleven goals to nil. It was the British colony of traders who introduced organised football to the Russian Empire. By 1901 a championship was in full swing and the impact of football was such that it was later known as 'the opium of the masses' by leftist intellectuals. If the young Tsar Nicholas II had championed football instead of charging into a disastrous war against Japan in an attempt to raise morale and national pride, he just might have survived, or at least delayed, the revolution.

Our route beyond St Petersburg was the subject of much consternation. Pictures, which we had seen on BBC World in Estonia, had cast much doubt on our proposed route through Pakistan. American flags were being burned and the fundamentalists looked to be out in force. Matt raised a more pressing, practical hurdle though. He had not obtained a visa for Pakistan before he left home. Despite initial exclamations at this revelation I had now seen the TV pictures myself and his decision was completely understandable. As events turned out we would never have had time anyway. It was the route through Iran that we were arguing over.

The Islamic Republic of Iran borders Afghanistan and the Americans looked about to start World War III there. Our decision to seek advice at the British Consulate in St Petersburg proved absolutely useless. They simply quoted the Foreign Office website that 'it is not advisable to go to Iran'. No details, no explanations, no 'if you do go, then be careful in x, y and z areas', no, 'don't wave American flags, get drunk in public or sing "you can stick yer Ayatollahs up your arse",' simply 'it is not advisable to go to Iran'. If you were to live by the recommendations of that website then you would miss out on half the world's splendours.

The England cricketers who pulled out of the 2001 tour of India for 'security reasons' missed out on a feast of a trip. Their love for the game was tested and found wanting. They, of all people, should have known how much Indians like cricket. The idea that Indian terrorists would target the England cricket team makes me laugh. They have far more fun beating us on the pitch. It is a sad, irrational fear that everybody not in an England shirt is a potential terrorist. Ironic, therefore, that everybody outside our shores thinks that everyone in an England shirt is one.

There should really be a warning about travelling to England. With IRA and now Al Qaeda bomb attacks in most of our major cities, horrific train crashes, Concorde dropping out of the skies (albeit onto the French), and a high rate of street crime, abroad is your best option. A startling number of my friends have been mugged in England. One in particular got an additional beating because he was so drunk he could not remember his credit card pin. However, this is the same guy who, again having had a drop too many, was convinced that his bank cards had been stolen, so, quickly and intelligently, cancelled them all. How did he cancel them? He took them out of his wallet, turned them over and called the number on the back. Someone once asked Mahatma Gandhi what he thought of Western civilisation. He said he thought it sounded like a very good idea.

Between our first-night joy with taxis, an allergic reaction to some nuts (which, thankfully, did not require a hospital), the fact that every architectural wonder bar the winter palace was under scaffolding in preparation for St Petersburg's tricentennial celebrations, and the mind-numbing cold, we did quite enjoy our wanders around this 'northern Venice'. The real fun, however, was to begin further south. We were on a table mission and it was Moscow not St Petersburg that was home to the Russian FA.

The train line down from St Petersburg was dead straight apart from one long bend that is known as the Tsar's finger and is attributed to the royal digit. According to legend, when Tsar Nicholas I designated the route he drew a straight line with a ruler but accidentally drew around his finger. The engineers were too afraid to point out this mistake so built it into the line. Shortly after we travelled down it, and 150 years after it was built, the Tsar's finger was lopped off, cutting an hour from the journey time.

To our delight Moscow was warmer. The bite had gone. However, the poor bastards suffer an average temperature in January of minus twelve. Can you imagine trying to play football in your shorts at minus twelve? Ninety minutes would seem like three years, six for the spectators. Now I understand why Tsar Nicholas gave up on football and tried to invade Japan.

Our first target with the table was the grand 'Olympiisky Stadium', an enormous circular wall of a thing that we stumbled across near our hostel. Invoking our powers of deduction we concluded that it was used in the Olympics, but walking around its circumference we exchanged increasingly bemused looks as we struggled to find an entrance. There were shops and even a market contained in its vertical sides, but no gates or turnstiles.

Armed with a letter written in Cyrillic by a friendly lady on duty in our 'travellers' hostel' we accosted the guard on duty at the sole entrance we found. He read the letter stone-faced then handed it back unmoved. It explained, in the Russian alphabet, that we were carrying the table overland to the World Cup and trying to sneak it into grand football stadiums en route and a little about our story so far. He contained his excitement well. The typically Russian shrug was executed to precision. '*Nyet*.' He waved us away. We started to stammer a reply but, not even looking at us, he shooed again. We could have argued some more but he spoke no English, we spoke no Russian and he was the one with the gun.

It was a strange moment of defeat. There was nothing we could do. We had asked the only authority we could find and been unequivocally turned away. With the language barrier there was no personal touch that might swing it. It was a simple '*nyet*'. Two days later we found out that it was not a football stadium. It was an indoor events centre about to stage a tennis tournament. No wonder the guard was dismissive. He must have read our letter and thought we were a right pair of plonkers.

Meanwhile, our route-planning in the wake of 11 September had established two options:

A) Head down through Russia and Georgia to Iran, then cross to the UAE and hitch a boat ride to India; or

B) Travel right across Russia then down through Mongolia, China and Tibet to India.

Plan A was administratively the easier as we had already successfully applied for our Iranian visas and arranged with the Iranian Embassy in London to pick them up in Moscow. Plan B would be cold beyond our wildest imagination. The

Russian north, then the Himalayas, both in their brutal midwinter, might be taking fresh air to extremes.

The thought of months upon months of long johns was not appealing. Having failed to linger and buy quality in the lingerie department, our purchases, as befits those generally found in a lingerie department, were failing to cover our needs to the required degree. Then again we could feel the draw of the mountains. It would be a breathtaking journey of a lifetime. But Iran? We had the possibility of trying to gatecrash Iran v Iraq. We could not even begin to comprehend it, Iran v Iraq, a clash with such connotations that we would be foolish to pass it by, especially as we had contact with the Iranian FA. The possibilities were alarmingly exciting.

Keeping our options open, we hunted down the Chinese Embassy to sound out Plan B. The table came along for the ride to help break the ice and explain our innocence in case the Chinese officials objected to the double-entry aspect of our application (we would need to re-enter China from India to get to the World Cup).

We reached the Chinese Embassy at 2.01 p.m. It was shut 2–3 p.m. Muttering questions about who has lunch between 2 and 3 p.m. we sat down on the grassy verge to wait.

Boys being boys, we were on our feet again approximately thirty seconds later. Out came the football, followed shortly by the football table, and within ten minutes the Russian soldiers who were meant to be guarding the Embassy of the People's Republic of China were successfully coaxed into challenging us to a game. The most senior soldier, with a portly waist and chubby smile, also attempted to juggle the football. In the process he tried to head it but forgot about his military hat which toppled onto his nose, blocked his vision and caused him to hump the ball across the road. Regaining his composure he had to stop the traffic and dash out to retrieve it. We were in stitches. When we had arrived these soldiers had been like the guards at Buckingham Palace, rigidly unmovable.

It was as he was making his dash back from the traffic

that a Chinese official's car pulled up at the gate. The man in the passenger seat got out and did not look amused at the sight of his guards playing tablefootball on the embassy frontage. After reprimanding the guards who had snapped back into their rigid positions he spoke to us. 'This is an embassy,' he said. 'Please, for security, no', and he gestured at the table.

On his way back to the car, where his Chinese driver was killing himself with laughter, he conversed with one of the guards. Unable to suppress a smile, he came back over and wished us luck in our voyage to China, 'But please . . . not here.' The international language and love of football had broken through his political concerns. It could not, however, secure us a Chinese visa.

The doors to the embassy eventually opened and it transpired that the visa section was closed until 8 October. There was no other way of us getting Chinese visas. Plan B was officially dead. Iran it was. Fate had decided for us.

But our adventures in Russia were far from over. On the walk homewards we managed to take in Moscow University, five Russian weddings, an Olympic ski jump and the Luzhniki Stadium, the table's next big target.

It took us three days, but we got inside. In the meantime we visited the Kremlin and the Red Square, where, in the past, up to a million soldiers would troop through on parade. We successfully avoided the police that regularly pounce on tourists and demand spurious fines, but made an effort to find a bar showing English football. I watched on gallingly as Spurs lost horribly to Manchester United. The mightiest team in London dismantled the champions 3–0 in the first half, but somehow, to my horror, conceded five goals in the second to lose 5–3. Matt had a field day joining in the celebrations of a barroom full of dedicated Russian Manchester United fans. You don't need to live in Putney to support United.

The Russian FA proved to be the key to the Luzhniki. It was located in the Russian Olympic Committee building near the stadium, an enormous, squat, concrete block, much like many buildings in Moscow. We eventually managed to make ourselves understood at reception by mimicking kicking a football and were led away apprehensively, through a maze of dimly lit corridors and into lifts, under many a suspicious glance. The images from too many films of KGB headquarters were playing tricks with my mind. Matt looked like he was about to have a nervous breakdown when I asked him to keep the camera secretly rolling by his side. To be fair to him he did. It was just unfortunate that he left the lens cap on for much of it.

'The President of the FA does not speak English,' said an English-speaking lady after listening intently to our tale and request. At the end of our maze of cold stares we had reached the 'Football Union of Russia' and been introduced to a particularly cold-shouldered man in colder clothes. The Russian tradition of service with a shrug was in full swing. As in Marseille, Rome and Austria it was a charming lady who rescued us.

She was called Elena Kobak, was average height, with short hair and was, well, Russian-looking. 'OK, anyone who can speak English, like yourself, would be great,' I replied optimistically. 'It's only a few words, bit of a game . . .' She looked taken aback then said, 'Oh no, only the head will do . . . we'll organise a translator.' I nearly fell out of my tree. In the presence of such helpfulness I figured it was worth upping the stakes. 'One other thing, we'd like to try and get the table onto the pitch of the Luzhniki Stadium, can you help us with that? Having got this far, you may as well ask. They can only say *nyet*.

'You'd like to do the interview on the pitch? Sure, we can arrange that,' came the reply, unfazed. She had her colleague telephone Anzhelika Biryukova, the press officer across the road at the stadium. 'She'll meet you at 2 p.m. tomorrow; phone me at 11 a.m. regarding the President.'

It is amazing how perceptions can be changed by a few simple encounters. We went into the building paranoid that we would be strung up for secret filming and rot in the Russian Gulag, but we skipped out of it filled with the joys of spring, albeit in long johns. These were FA workers, people spending twelve hours a day working on football.

They were not about to ask us our name, rank and number. It was a timely wake-up call from our entrenched fears and stereotypes.

A match was taking place that very evening at the Luzhniki between Torpedo Moscow and Rotor. Armed with the then unknown Anzhelika's name we decided to call into the stadium and see what we could blag. It did not take long to get inside and be shown to her office. We were expecting to wrestle with some senior grouch, but she raised her head from her desk to reveal a beautiful young Russian with charm, grace, and a certain inexplicable bashfulness, not to mention knee-high, high-heeled black boots.

Minutes after mentioning Elena Kobak's name we had press passes and sexy green 'TV' bibs. The only blip came when the lady sorting out the bibs asked for our press cards. 'Ah. Well, that's a bit of a long story.' We found ourselves back in the young Anzhelika's office to translate. I told her about the table, about our journey so far, the journey to come and made a good case appealing to their good humour. We were not accredited press, but we could not become accredited press until we had experience such as this. And, hell, we had carried a football table all the way to Russia. It seemed to work. We were in.

I knew nothing about Russian football so had everything to expect. We were thus a bit disillusioned when kick-off came. The 82,000-seater fixture was an absolute sellout of about six hundred fans and five hundred police. I counted four away fans.

The cold was brutal and the echo of the empty stadium made it seem like a practice match. The opposition team sheet provided eight pov's, nov's and kov's. It did not seem like an influx of foreign players was threatening Russian football.

Our camera cut out in sporadic complaint at the cold but the footage of the match, which, due to the shambles of Russian TV rights, we were allowed to film, was revealing. 'I said I had the *chance* to do a cameraman module at university, I didn't actually take it,' said Matt by way of defence as he swore at the camera once more.

Football in Moscow took a bit longer to take hold than in St Petersburg. In 1887 an English mill owner brought a ball over from England, inflated it in front of his mill workers and booted it high up in the air. He watched with amusement when, as it landed with an almighty bang, his Russian workers fled. It soon caught on though, and by the Olympics of 1912 was the top sport in Russia despite the national side losing 16–0 to the Germans.

The problem with the breakdown and disintegration of the USSR is that it destroyed their football team. In its heyday the Soviet team made the final of the European Championships. The Russian team by contrast failed to qualify for France '98 and Euro 2000 (despite beating World Champions and eventual winners France in a qualifying match), but had rediscovered some form and were in the running to reach the World Cup in Korea and Japan.

They eventually succeeded, but only to fall flat on their face like Poland. There were riots on the streets of Moscow. A man was stabbed to death and twenty police were injured. The success of the Russian football team in reaching the World Cup had been a ray of hope that had been all too quickly taken away.

'Foxy lady' (as we renamed Anzhelika) made up for all the *nyet*s. We called the Russian FA at 11 a.m., as instructed, after wrestling with the Russian pay phone system. Miss Kobak had tried her best but was sad to inform us that most of the top officials were not in the country let alone Moscow. 'Maybe next time?' she ventured. I joked half-heartedly to Matt that we could call in on our way back from Japan. Standing in the freezing rain next to the payphone the pained expression on his face summed up the numbness that was beginning to creep through my limbs as the cold, aided by the disappointment, worked its way deeper. However, we still had the 2 p.m. pitch invasion arranged with Anzhelika.

'Nooooo,' she screamed to Matt. 'Andy, noooo,' he shouted as I, table in hand, started to run out onto the pitch. I hesitated, confused, then pressed onward before it became brutally apparent that our poor foxy lady was about to have a heart attack. 'The stadium director has a TV camera pointed at the pitch at all times linked to a monitor in his office,' she exclaimed once I had returned. The boss makes certain no one ventures onto the hallowed turf of Russia's premier football venue. Somehow he managed to miss me running around with a football table.

Foxy lady had been to England once, to Ipswich, when Torpedo Moscow drew them in the UEFA Cup. 'So, did you like Ipswich?' I asked.

'It was dark,' she replied in her well-pronounced but hesitant English.

'Did you see many tractors?' I jested, not being able to resist a reference to Ipswich Town's nickname of the 'tractor boys'.

'Just darkness,' she replied innocently in entertaining fashion.

Beside the pitch, in the depths of the orange-seated cauldron, she giggled and laughed like a little girl as she daintily tried to play on the table. 'We are like little children,' she squealed with delight as the ball scampered back and forth. She was utterly entranced by it.

Afterwards, she offered us a lift in her car to the metro station. It was only our third display of kindness in Russia and rekindled our hope in the Russian people. Admiration for them was also felt as we drove past the open-air Olympic swimming pool that Anzhelika confirmed is used all year round despite the plunging temperatures.

After a bit more cash had exchanged hands we picked up our Iranian visas. The good news was that the weather was warm enough to make me sweat in my long johns. The bad news was that the embassy had started our visas running from 1 October, two days prior to collection, and not the 9th as asked. Despite all our cash, specific requests and reassurances we would lose one week in Iran. Welcome to the world of Asian red tape. It meant we had to get moving.

Having found out that it would take a week to get a visa for Georgia, we opted to head down to Sochi on the edge of the Black Sea, cross by boat to Turkey and get into Iran from there. In a sense, it was a relief to be leaving Moscow, as there had been a mix-up with the registration stamps in our passports. For the past few days we had been carefully dodging the many soldiers and passport checks in the streets and on the metro. It was not really until becoming aware of this that I realised how many Russian workers wore military uniform. They were everywhere, an eerie hangover of times gone by.

It took some time to negotiate the three train stations, forty ticket counters, and innumerable *nyet*s despite having our request written out in Russian, but two tickets eventually materialised in exchange for a large wad of roubles. They were completely in Russian, of course. Matt smiled, patted me on the back and said, 'So we'll be on the chicken-feed train to Siberia then.'

16. GREECE

The match of the century would be taking place on 12 October. In the fanatical cauldron of the Azadi Stadium, hailed by many as the most hostile venue in world football, Iran had a crunch World Cup qualifier against Iraq, the country with whom they fought a bitter war for eight years. We picked up our Iranian visas on 3 October in Moscow. The sprint for Tehran began in earnest.

After 32 hours rattling due south in a big old diesel train with a whopping great red star emblazoned on its nose we reached Sochi. With every passing minute it seemed to get warmer and we eventually stepped off the train to find palm trees, blue skies and some twenty-odd magical degrees of heat. Matt and I shared a cabin of four bunks with two fifty-year-old, potbellied Russians expressly on their way to Sochi 'for the ladies'.

They greeted us on the first morning aboard with fresh coffee, spiked with Armenian whisky. I did not previously drink either; knocking it back in one go I was brought sharply into the world with an abrupt intake of breath and a smack of the lips.

Miles of farmland rushed past the windows and at each remote stop local peasants lined the platform with tantalising home-baked foods and melons. A whole melon cost a mere ten roubles (less than 20p). At the next stop I realised that ten roubles actually entitled you to two melons. Doughy pastries with mashed potato and vegetables, tortilla wraps with melted goat's cheese, fresh tea, coffee, and, of course, vodka were among the other delights that awaited our train's arrival in each and every village.

The conductors helpfully woke us at 4 a.m. to tell us the train would arrive at 7 a.m. Wishing the prospective Casanovas the luck they would need, we headed straight for the ferry only to find that the daily early-morning service across the Black Sea no longer existed. Time was running out so we resolved to break our 'no planes' policy. It would compromise the initial principles of the trip as such, but with a carrot the size of Iran v Iraq we had no qualms. No qualms, that is, until we learned that the plane had just been blown out of the sky by a stray Ukrainian missile. A routine military training exercise had gone badly wrong and the emergency services were scrambled to locate the remains somewhere in the vast expanse of the Black Sea. There were no survivors. We opted to wait for the ferry.

Compared to the grim cold of Moscow, Sochi was paradise. We could feel our toes. It was devoid of sights, history and football, but my mind was, at that time, far more focused on the readings of thermometers. A haven for Russian tourists, it was a pretty place by comparison to the industry of the cities, but a far cry from anywhere truly special. It was the greenery that made it. The only real greenery we had witnessed in Moscow was the optimistic gentleman outside our hostel tower block parked on a stool beside a giant, rusting, metal cage filled with literally hundreds of watermelons. We never saw him sell one.

It took a few hours before the real horror of our situation kicked in. The next ferry was setting sail on Saturday 6 October. We would miss England's decisive World Cup qualifier against Greece. Our chances of the automatic qualifying spot hung on success in this match. I could not miss it; the suspense would kill me. The success of the trip rested on the finale of England lifting the trophy. I could not conceive the thought of receiving the horrifying news of non-qualification from a smirking Turk. In my anguish at the thought of it, and in front of a line of fishermen, I accidentally kicked our football into the harbour. The world seemed almost at an end.

Relief of a sort came when we found out we could delay our run for the ferry long enough to see some of the England game, but we had to resort to watching painfully slow, live updates on the internet courtesy of BBC Sport:

30 minutes: Rio Ferdinand makes a weak clearance and Charisteas shoots low past Martyn from the right corner of the area. England 0–1 Greece.

Our heads fell. We had to leave, but just couldn't.

Half-time: (checking email) 'Hi, I'm a reporter from the *Sun*, I heard about your trip from a mate of mine who works in Aberdeen ...'

Eh?

68 minutes: Eriksson brings on Sheringham and he scores within seconds of his introduction with a header over Nikopolidis from a Beckham free kick.

You beauty!!! Quickly regaining our senses we checked the Germany v Finland score. So long as we had the same or better result than the Germans we would be top of the group. An agonisingly long hunt around BBC and Sky websites revealed ...

Germany 0–0 Finland

Genius. If it finished like that we would be on our way to the World Cup. There would be no slippery playoffs in the trigger-happy Ukraine, no nerve-racking wait; we'd have booked our berth. Relieved, we grabbed our bags ready for the run down the hill to the ferry. 'Just check the England page again,' said Matt unable to resist a final glance. I clicked the button. The Horror.

69 minutes: Greece go ahead within moments of England's equaliser. Nikolaidis beats England's offside trap and holds off Rio Ferdinand before shooting past Martyn from eight yards. England 1–2 Greece.

Words cannot express the shock and desperation. We had to leave. It was a half-hour walk to the ferry without including time for passport control. The ferry was leaving port at 8.30 p.m. The computer monitor read 7.45 p.m. We were way past our check-in time and there were no taxis. England were attacking, but as it stood they were 2–1 down to Greece and the Germany game was still 0–0. The Germans would go top and condemn us to a playoff with the Ukraine. We had to score. We simply had to score.

Painfully lingering until the 80th minute, torn between emotions, our minds aghast at the prospect that we were about to squander the chance of automatic qualification, and even more distraught by the fact that we had to leave before the final whistle, we ran. The last reports I read had England bombarding the Greek goal as we wrenched ourselves away and just ran. We could but pray. Pray, and run.

I did not find out the result until two days later, possibly the longest two days of the year. Our ferry was heinously delayed. We were late to meet it, but it soon became clear it was not going anywhere fast. It was 8 p.m. the following night when we finally set sail, some twenty-four hours late. Twenty-four hours sitting on a Turkish ferry mulling the possibilities. We could have easily watched the end of the match but were now marooned on the wrong side of passport control. As predicted, the suspense was killing me. I was sure we had equalised. I just had to think positively. Matt sensibly sought to counter any disappointment by resigning himself to the playoffs in advance.

To kill time I started writing the names of the England squad and the random personalities we had met so far on the backs of our tablefootball players. I can assure you that fitting 'Sheringham' on the back of a tablefootball player is no mean feat.

At least we had a berth. Our cheap tickets had entitled us to only the 'poor man's berths' i.e. a big dank room with musty seats and a few dirty alcoholics who looked like they had probably not moved for several voyages. So we parked ourselves on the plastic tables and chairs up on the covered deck area waiting in the hope of securing our own cabin, bizarrely promised and duly arranged by the stern ticket collector. Our perch was open to the four winds and the cool breeze from the sea sought to soothe our angst at the delay and provide us with a prime location in which to meet the ship's crew, who, alarmingly, appeared to be drinking heavily.

With the help of 'mad Jim', an overly enthusiastic junior member of the crew, we dragged the Captain down from his bridge to play on the table. Jim was like a kid off his rocker on E-numbers. We had been reprimanded by Russian officials for playing football on the dockside, but once on board Turkish Jim had pounced on us and dragged the football table excitedly out of its bag. He worked behind the spirits bar on the boat and was overjoyed at his discovery. He ran back and forth with an inane grin on his face doing pull ups on the bars of the roof, muttering about his back, fetching us apples and dragging in some of the few other passengers, largely female, to play him on the table. Whenever he scored a goal he demanded a kiss and gleefully ran round the table, turning his cheek and not leaving until he had received a congratulatory peck. Imagine Manuel from *Fawlty Towers*, give him ecstasy and *voilà*, mad Jim.

We were still in port when the storm hit. Waking to find that we still had not sailed, with lorries and cars perpetually being taken on and off the ferry, we watched big, black clouds, shrouding huge lightning crashes, drift slowly down the coast towards us. Finally, at midday, it hit. Darkness fell, rain lashed the boat, the wind ripped through the upper deck destroying the plastic tables and chairs and the sky lit up sporadically with huge forked bolts of lightning.

Having safely stashed the table down below, I returned on deck to film the storm, physically having to hold on tight and shelter behind pillars to avoid the stinging rain, driven horizontally with such force that it bit into my skin. Mother Nature was chucking a mental and you could not help but be exhilarated by the sheer power of it all. The noise of the rain alone was deafening; I had to shout to be heard. The rain turned to hail and huge stones poured aboard the boat. I never imagined that being stranded on a Turkish ferry could be so exciting. Thank God we had not been at sea.

Nobody else seemed the least bit concerned. The boat was on a tilt, it had half a foot of water on its deck, the crew had been up to way gone 4 a.m. drinking with us, a plane had plummeted out of the sky and England's World Cup place was hanging by a thread. Even the two fancy-looking ladies who had come aboard with only their handbags were completely unfazed by our lack of progress and subsequent battering from the elements. Things were clearly done differently here. They appeared to simply accept that when things go wrong they go wrong and that there is no point complaining about it. Matt and I were a tad more worried about our safety, but as our second night on the boat set in the anchor was finally raised and we recommenced the charge for Iran.

We arrived in Turkey in one piece and with the table ready for action. Getting from Sochi to Trabzon had, all in, taken 72 hours. It was now the morning of 8 October. Time had been short before, now it was desperate. A mild-mannered, lightweight local, with a twinkle of strength and knowledge in his eye, who turned out to be a two-time Turkish Army Boxing Champion, befriended us as we passed through customs, beat off the touts and safely saw us aboard a bus bound for Erzerum.

There was still no news on the football. I had run around as soon as we landed trying to ask people using animated hand gestures but without success. We boarded the bus still hoping, still dreaming that somebody, perhaps even Golden Balls himself, had conjured up some magic and saved us in the dying moments of the game.

Iran was closer now, but it would still take two days and two nights of solid bus journeys to reach Tehran. We were knackered but spurred on by the sheer prospect of watching Iran lock horns with Iraq in what could only be a fiery encounter.

Russia had been another world compared to the home comforts of Western Europe, but Turkey was our gateway to Iran and the magical ways of Asia. It held our first taste of true bargaining culture, of predominantly Muslim lifestyle, and the incessant bustle of buyers, sellers, street traders, touts and accompanying explosive tempers, all vying for your Western money. The bus climbed up out of Trabzon over high, twisty, mountain roads, down onto arid plains and through lunaresque landscapes. Stops at Erzerum and Van gave us our first education in shopping around, haggling and not believing a word of most promises concerning local transport.

Eastern Turkey is a far cry from England. It is poor, barren and mountainous, but it held for us a gem, a gem that would have me grinning for days. The man sitting in front of me ten or so hours into our epic bus ride turned the page of his paper to reveal none other than David Beckham sporting a smile the size of Africa. Among the Turkish print next to the picture lay the score: 2–2.

The knowledge that Beckham, in injury time, had rifled home a trademark free kick to put us, England, in the World Cup finals was like a gift from the Gods. A wave of utter joy passed through me. It was going to be our year. Isolated, on a bus filled with unconcerned Turks, deep in Eastern Turkey, two days after the event, it was a strange moment. But it was a triumphant one and we sang nonetheless. We were in seventh heaven. On a wave of ecstasy and with a renewed resolve we crossed the border and plunged into the Islamic Republic of Iran.

17. IRAN v IRAQ

'Welcome to Ireland' read the sign. I read it again. It definitely read, 'Welcome to Ireland'. And it was true, I was in Ireland. What happened to Iran? Last time I looked at a map Ireland was not on the road to Japan. I was meant to be on my way through the Middle East to India. I have heard of many spectacular shortcuts, but a detour via Ireland with the Iranian football team was not one of them. The table tour adventure had just reached a whole new level.

In 1978 Iran reached their first-ever World Cup in which they lost heavily to Peru, drew with Scotland and went out in the group stages. The following year, Ayatollah Khomeini returned home to adoring millions after years in exile to lead the Islamic revolution.

The people lapped up his fiery brand of nationalism and Islamic fundamentalism, everybody loved him; but the adage was true: after the revolution came the revolution. Those Iranians who had wanted to preserve their national identity now found their country dominated by Islam whose roots were Arab. Their duty was not to be good Iranians, but obedient Muslims. Ayatollah Khomeini's clergy-dominated, introspective Islamic Republic was established with brutal efficiency.

The Iraqi President Saddam Hussein sought to take advantage of the turmoil in Iran and seized an oil-rich border region. In doing so he provided the divided country with a common enemy to rally against and the revolution spread by force of arms. The war lasted eight years. America, Russia and the West sided with Iraq against the new Islamic Republic. They (including Britain) sold weapons, allegedly including poison gas, to both sides. Over one million people were killed.

To this historical backdrop we entered Iran. We had been working on the premise that to be able to talk our way into the Iran v Iraq match we would have to be knocking on the door of the Iranian FA two days before kick-off. The match was on 12 October. We hauled into Tehran courtesy of our last overnight bus on the morning of the 10th. We were exhausted, but we had made it.

Tehran was alive with never-ending traffic, mopeds on and off the pavements, hand-drawn carts, people weaving their way through it all, businesses sprawling out of the small, tightly crammed workshops onto the sidewalks and everything, to the eyes of an outsider, mingling into a chaos of activity.

Eyes failing, sun beating down, dust and pollution clouding air and lungs, we were rescued from our tired hunt for cheap lodging by a quiet, friendly man who asked in patchy English, 'Hotel?' He led us off around the corner and parted with a smile and a wave outside the Hotel Tehran. A small doorway under a crowded collection of signs led up a set of stairs to a reception and two floors of basic but clean rooms with en-suite shower and squat toilet. It was time to begin strengthening the thighs. The owner, Habib, greeted us with his droopy eyes, infectious curiosity and affable nature, but no conversation could prevent us from crashing out into a deep slumber. It had been six days of tiresome travel since we left Moscow.

Clutching the letter they had sent me the previous May, we set out for the Football Federation of the Islamic Republic of Iran. The language barrier crushed any conversation with our taxi driver, or comment on the horrific state of his driving, until we mentioned Manchester United. It broke the ice in every cab we took. Suspicious looks vanished and we found ourselves on free detours to see monuments, given presents in the form of bags of nuts and fruit, impressed by even worse displays of outrageous driving; and through sign language and our phrasebooks, we attempted to share knowledge about our families and country. Their generosity was humbling.

The Iranian Football Federation is on the second floor of a simple concrete building on an almost peaceful road just outside Tehran's main ring road. My heart was beating, my palms were sweaty and butterflies haunted my stomach. Yet despite being in a country more hostile than Russia, a country which still has a very active death penalty, huge restrictions on lifestyle and dress, and red tape to almost match that of China, I felt strangely confident.

For a start, they had had the decency to reply to me, the only FA to do so bar the belated Germans. On the few occasions I had tried to contact them from England there had been excited chatter when I mentioned 'Table Football', which was how I was remembered in their office. I was Mr Tablefootball. I was just hoping that they still found my unusual quest amusing.

My hopes and prayers were answered. They welcomed us with open arms. Grins of recognition met us and we were ushered with our big purple bag into the office of the International Department. It was a large room with four desks, a grand conference table and broad windows looking out over a rugged football pitch surrounded by a sports track. On the wall hung a picture of their pride and joy, the mighty Azadi Stadium. We were hastily beckoned to sit down, given tea, and made to feel like old friends.

The boss, Mr Torabian, was called. He remembered my letter and asked what we wanted to do. I aimed high and asked to follow the Iranian team, but rather undermined my position by saying that, basically, if we could get access to the match against Iraq that would be fantastic.

Mr Torabian carried more authority on his shoulders, and

appeared sterner, than the others in the office. To our amazement, he quickly established that were we to follow the team a contract would have to be drawn up and a percentage of any monies made would go to the FA. We would never have dreamed of asking this much yet already it was being presented to us on a plate. At the very least he said he could get us tickets for the big game. Confusion arose from the fact that we were just passing through Iran and not hoping to do a specific film on just them. Sadly therefore, his proposals could neither be met by us nor arranged in time during our short stay.

We must have looked like right cowboys. But the fact that we had made the effort and travelled so far to knock on their door struck a chord with the Iranians. Mr Torabian gave us another cup of tea, asked to hear all about the trip and then requested passport photos. 'We might be able to get you accredited.' He said he would also introduce us to his son who would show us around and help get the table onto the pitch of the Azadi Stadium. This latter gesture really bowled us over. We had only just met the man, but were already being introduced to his family. It pains me to say it, but I cannot always imagine such a reception in England.

Another FA employee, Mr Doroudgar, walked into the room. 'Wow, is that a football table? I am a great champion; let's have a game. Bring it to my office when you are finished here.' He was a big, strong guy with short, dark, wavy hair and sported the almost obligatory, classic Iranian moustache. Given his enthusiasm I thought it wise not to refuse.

Our hopes of accreditation, of a chance to get backstage at Iran v Iraq, were dealt a blow by the appearance of the Head of Security. The bearded Mr Husseini asked the routine questions of which company we worked for and the location of our press cards. 'Well . . .' I began my increasingly polished explanation of our exploits that finished gently with the fact that we had no accreditation. It caused quite a commotion.

Unfortunately we had not counted on the heavy requirements and restrictions placed on foreign journalists. Everybody had to be thoroughly vetted and approved by the ominously titled 'Ministry of Guidance'. Mr Husseini was just doing his job. He could see no way of us getting past the Ministry at this late hour without press cards or the backing of a recognised company. Even with them it would have been difficult.

We had been in the office for about half an hour and it seemed that Mr Wazeri and Mr Karimpour, the two members of the International Department who had first greeted us, had taken a shine to our trip. They jovially hassled the rather severe frown of Mr Husseini and coaxed him into making some more calls. His initial suspicions of us seemed to abate and eventually he hatched a plan and picked up the phone one last time. Still unaccustomed to hearing Farsi we were unable to ascertain from the highs and lows what the outcome was. He finished and looked up.

'Bring your photos to the Physical Education Organisation at 8.30 a.m. tomorrow morning. Meet me there.' Smiles reigned supreme. Business seemingly at an end, the big man, Mr Doroudgar, walked back in, slapped his hands together, rubbed them gleefully and demanded his game with a big smile of excitement and another declaration that he was champion of the world. Business was about to begin.

'One nil to England,' I was able to cry before he walloped me off the table. I would like to say I let him win but my unbeaten *away* record (I haven't forgotten you, Rich, how could you possibly let me?) was spirited into extinction by a ferocious competitiveness. He attacked the table with such force that by the end of the game he was bleeding.

It finished 10–4 and two of my four strikes were own goals scored by him. An enormous grin crossed his face as he won. He was a big-hearted, competitive man and gave me a warm handshake. 'Have nice time, you very welcome,' he said as he briskly marched out of the office back to his work. Within a few seconds he had returned to show off his wound. Raising his bleeding finger to the camera he said, 'This is blood, we give blood to be champion.' Grinning, and proud, he left us once more. Losing to a man prepared to bleed, at the Football Federation of the Islamic Republic of Iran, was not a bad way for the record to fall.

Back at Hotel Tehran we excitedly related our tales. Football in Iran has a massive following and our hosts were no exception; they were all ears about our visit to the headquarters of their heroes. We eventually escaped to bed but were later awoken by a knock on our door. Amin, Habib's sidekick, was on the other side. 'Err, Manchester United,' he said excitedly and pointed downstairs in the direction of the small reception office that had a TV in the corner. He did not leave us an option; he stood there until we had thrown on tops and hustled out. We were in Iran; we were watching Manchester United on TV. Iran has nearly four hours of European football on TV every night.

Once settled in the office Matt managed to bemuse one of our new-found friends completely. He was trying to say that Andy Cole is crap, something many England supporters have been trying to say for years. To convey his meaning he said, 'Iran', grinned and did a big thumbs-up sign, then said, 'Andy Cole', and turned his thumb down. To our horror we were later told by a journalist that thumbs-up in Iran basically means f*** off. To complicate Matt's situation Andy Cole went and scored.

Meanwhile, Habib had proudly called up our details onto his computer screen for the benefit of our video camera. Name, Age, Date of Birth, Country ... Occupation. This last criterion was blank. He paused, smiled, fumbled a dictionary and said, 'free'.

At midnight the real football started. We had spent the last two nights on buses, the two nights before that on a boat and were desperately in need of sleep, but the streets of Tehran were clear and our hosts were raring to go. By day the road outside the hotel was a four-lane nightmare, by night a field of dreams. Small, homemade goals were put in place and the game began. Playing football as we were, in our England shirts, late at night on the streets of downtown Tehran, you might have thought for a moment that the world was in perfect harmony, that the conflict only a thousand kilometres to the East in Afghanistan was a million miles from there, and for that moment, you would have been right.

The following morning Habib insisted on hailing a taxi

for us. The P.E. Organisation was only a ten-minute walk but the pollution in Tehran is simply shocking. Ironically, as a result, everybody adds to it by taking the car instead of walking. In summer, people with heart conditions are advised to stay indoors.

'This is definitely it,' I said, looking again at the map, the address and weighing up the advice of the last passer-by we had asked. The security guard still shook his head and refused to let us in. He had already sent us away twice. But I was now convinced that this was the right building. We attempted to reason once more through a number of appalling drawings, sign language and general begging. It was no good; he was not going to change his mind. But, equally, we were not about to let his stubbornness undo our goals. Matt provided an excellent decoy, leading the guard's overweight, irritating bulk into the security hut by the gate on the pretence of showing him one of our earlier drawings while I scurried past into the building to try and find Mr Husseini.

My search proved fruitless until I met a man named Ghahreman, which literally means 'champion'. Half an hour of telephone calls and three cups of tea later, Ghahreman and his colleague had established that I was in the right place and that Mr Husseini was late but on his way.

Matt was waved upstairs from a lofty window and conversation with our temporary hosts began in earnest via numerous and dubious sketches, most of which involved using Manchester as a point of bearing. Quite unperturbed by the interruption of their work to entertain foreign guests, Ghahreman and his colleague ensured that black tea after black tea rolled through the doors as we attempted to understand, and answer, their questions in what must have been a comical exchange.

Mr Husseini arrived quiet, straight-faced and smartly dressed, just as we had found him the previous day. He relieved us of our passport photos and gestured to wait while he attempted to contact the one lady who could grant us passes at such a late hour.

As he departed, another Iranian man appeared, sat

himself down and started conversing in Farsi with our two entertainers. He was also suited (though without a tie as is the Iranian custom) and made me feel very underdressed in my shabby brown cords and heavily creased short-sleeved summer shirt, especially considering the favours we were asking. Eventually he turned to us and introduced himself in perfect English. His name was Shahab. Born in Iran, he grew up in England, his parents having moved there before the revolution. He was working in Tehran for the BBC, but had been commissioned to write an article for the English football magazine *4-4-2* on the Iran v Iraq match. Like us he was without a pass and desperately seeking a last-minute solution. As we waited, he acted as translator between us and the 'champion'.

Mr Ghahreman was a shining example of the Iranian love for football. During the 1986 World Cup his town near the Caspian Sea was unable to receive World Cup TV footage. Unperturbed he found a friend with a boat and sailed out into the middle of the Caspian in the hope of picking up Soviet pictures. They were successful. For each game they would set sail or, due to the distances, even spend days at a time out on the boat. Have a look at a map; it was quite an effort.

As he finished retelling this tale for Shahab to translate, he reached into a drawer and took out some pills that he carefully swallowed. He joked through Shahab that although they have a custom in Iran of offering everything, he wasn't offering us these (under 'Ta'rof' everything should be offered and refused three times). These were keeping him alive after losing his kidney. Sensing a story, Shahab pressed him on the incident.

Sure enough, he had sacrificed it in the name of football. Fifteen years before, his local side were on a roll and, so sure was he of a famous victory in the second leg of the cup semi-final against Persepolis (the Manchester United of Iranian football), that he made the 400-kilometre journey over the Alborz Mountains to Tehran. The car was full with people so all he took was the strip he was in. The trip was long and cold and he got very ill, but carried on to the stadium instead of going to hospital. By the time he received medical treatment he had lost a kidney and now had to endure a life of swallowing pills. Would he have it differently? He sat back in his chair and considered the question for a split second before a smile drifted across his face. 'His team won,' translated Shahab.

The deadline for accreditation had passed. The game was the next day. Shahab explained: 'There is no chance of getting a pass at this late hour. The clock stopped last night. We are now working purely on goodwill, and only by goodwill can we get one. But that's how things are often done in this country.' The fact that Mr Husseini was even trying on our behalf meant that we were in a very privileged position. I felt humbled by such good treatment.

After four hours of waiting and listening to a series of heated telephone conversations between Mr Husseini and various officials, we left. Shahab was looking glum. 'There is one lady who can pull this off for us and he can't get hold of her. He said he'll keep trying and will call us the moment he finds out, even if it is one o'clock in the morning. Even the BBC are struggling to get passes. For now, all we can do is wait, but I'm sorry guys, it's so late in the day that our chances are virtually nil.' We were walking down the stairs and out into the sunshine. As we parted I slapped my hand on his shoulder and said, 'Don't worry, magic happens, trust me.'

If David Beckham could bend in a 94th minute winner against Greece to send us to the World Cup then Mr Husseini would manage to magic up some passes. After the bizarre successes of the trip across Europe I felt it in my bones that if we believed hard enough then anything could happen. At 4 p.m. we got the call. An excited Amin knocked on our door to relay the news. Magic happens.

The clock on the wall ticked by agonisingly slowly as we waited in the lobby of the Hotel Azadi, one of Tehran's top hotels. My eyes drifted back and forth across the room until, to my horror, they focused on our table number: thirteen. No sign of Mr Husseini and we were sat at table number thirteen.

An hour behind schedule, he finally ended our nervous

wait. In the most dramatic breakthrough of the table adventure so far, he gifted us two Asian Qualifiers 2002 Photographer passes, our mug shots laminated in place underneath the badge of the Iranian FA. This quiet man had gone out of his way to help us achieve a dream. The passes would give us a free rein of the pitch during the match. We would be behind the goal for the most politically charged game of our lives. He also introduced us to Jeffery.

Jeffery was a legend. He was 21 and employed by the FA as a liaison officer to look after visitors. Today his charges were the FIFA referees from Korea. Initially we had no idea who he was and assumed that he must be Mr Torabian's son. He chatted animatedly for a few minutes, ordered us some tea, told us about the timetable for the game and his plans for us to eat with him and the referees at the Hotel Azadi that night. My head was starting to spin.

Three courses later and we were on first name terms with the referee. I nearly even had to inject the fourth official, who needed an immunisation injection in the buttock. He was over six-foot tall and a black belt at Taekwondo, but too squeamish to handle a needle. In the end the task fell to the Iranian Director of Refereeing, the sharpest decision of his career.

The waiters flurried away the plates and Jeffery led us out after having made sure his entrusted guests were happy and knew what time he was coming to collect them the next day. A blacked-out, chauffeur-driven FA van pulled up and in we climbed. 'To the Esteghal Hotel,' said Jeffery. 'We are going to have interviews with the players.'

Jeffery had a confident, friendly and completely unfazed manner that made us happy to follow whatever he suggested. Hell, it was only the night before a vital World Cup Qualifying match against a bitter rival who took the lives of half a million of Iran's forefathers. Of course the Iranian heroes, the Beckhams, Owens and Sheringhams of Iran would be up for chatting to random Westerners at gone ten o'clock. We didn't have the table with us, but we had a new approach: Jeffery.

To my amazement all the players were there. Jeffery handed us an Asian Qualifiers magazine that profiled Iran's danger men and there they were milling around us, slightly less sweaty than their photos and surrounded by family, friends and well-wishers in the hotel lounge. 'Whom would you like to meet?' said Jeffery, a glint in his eye.

The past 24 hours caught up with me like a slap in the face. I was completely overawed. I felt dizzy and my brain tried to shut down. I couldn't take it all in. I was in the Islamic Republic of Iran. Iran! I was in the Iranian players' hotel. It was the night before their match against Iraq. It was an impossible situation. I should have been back home, dribbling with hay fever, playing football on boggy marshes, and slaving away at some underpaid boredom. Imagine Scarlett Johansson turning up on your doorstep saying 'Hey babe', handing you the keys to your birthday present Ferrari and telling you Spurs had won the Premiership. My brain had simply overloaded.

Matt had to hand me the camera and, to his horror, do the talking himself. Fair play to him, he shouldered the burden well, albeit without a choice, for I was barely able to speak with nerves. Our first Iranian superstar approached. Pulling myself together, I steadied the camera on Matt and the man we thought was Hamed Kavienpour, Iran's young midfield maestro who had been in talks with Newcastle United.

He looked a lot bigger than in the photo, but Matt courageously leaped in regardless. Sure enough, it was not our man; it was his agent. Embarrassed, Matt attempted to disguise the fact that we really had no idea who he was and, as the real Kavienpour was called over, started again.

The conversation was nervous, the questions were awful, but Matt was doing far better than my cowardly run for the camera. Then he asked, 'Next week you [Iran] are playing Bahrain, you must think you have a good chance against Bahrain as it is a lesser opponent than Iraq.'

'He actually thinks Bahrain are a far better team,' replied the agent.

'Really?' gulped Matt.

'Oh yes,' came the reply. Our faces must have been a picture. We had been rumbled.

A last-ditch effort to rescue the situation was needed: 'Was Bobby Robson [the former Newcastle manager] the nicest person you've ever met?' Before the translator could begin, the 'tough-tackling' Hamed smiled, nodded, and his set, focused eyes wavered for a moment with recognition and fondness that indicated he had indeed met Sir Bobby. Sadly, because of his choice to stay in Iran for the international qualifiers, his window of opportunity with Newcastle disappeared. We did learn from his agent, however, that Saudi Arabia had allegedly offered Bahrain a million dollars a man if they beat Iran in their potentially decisive final match.

As we wished him good luck and turned away, Jeffery introduced us to Mr Sharifi. 'OK Andy, this guy, Mr Sharifi, is responsible for TV and media in the stadium.' He had his arm around the shoulders of a short, stout, grey-bearded man. 'Also, if you want to go to changing rooms you can arrange with him. Also, I am in the stadium, you can find me, we go to teams' changing rooms.' As we tried to pick our jaws off the floor, Mr Sharifi shook our hands and hurried off. He was a busy man.

Jeffery worked the room like he owned it. He would wander off, shake hands with somebody, exchange compliments, make them laugh, introduce us, then chat warmly during a lengthy farewell handshake. He even led us upstairs around the corridors knocking on hotel room doors looking for the manager, Miroslav Blazevic, the fiery Croatian who took his native country to third place in the 1998 World Cup. Thankfully we didn't find him. I don't think my poor heart could have taken it.

The highlight was talking to Iran's great hope, the mercurial Ali Karimi. Described in our magazine as an 'attacking talent with a phenomenal ability to waltz past even the most experienced defenders'. Unfortunately he could also struggle to hit a barn door. He was friendlier in manner than Kavienpour, looked us in the eye, and in general was more open to our questions, translated by Jeffery. He eyed us with what almost amounted to amusement. We certainly did not appear very professional considering our age, the size of our camera and our wide-eyed 'my God, we're in Iran' look. But then that was the point; we weren't professionals. We were just two normal guys taking a rather long road to the World Cup.

'The game tomorrow, you must be a little bit excited?' I had overcome my nerves and was warming to the occasion. Matt had slipped back behind the camera. It was a better combination as he was good at pitching in when I ran dry and I was better at general meeting and greeting and more prepared to mingle with 'the natives' in order to break the ice and spark opportunities.

'If we win tomorrow people will come to the streets', replied Karimi. 'Celebration should be reserved until after the Bahrain game but if we win tomorrow for sure people will come to the streets. It'll be big ceremony.' His eyes glowed at the prospect. Finishing with a flourish, I asked if he would score a goal for us the next day. 'It's the score over-all that's more important,' he replied, bashfully diplomatic. 'He'll score for sure,' said Jeffery nudging him in the ribs. They both beamed.

Jeffery waved for the van. Whether it was the way we left the building accompanied by FA officials, the fact that we stood out being two young white guys, or simply because of our means of transport, some of the fans lingering outside mistook us for someone important. As Matt continued to film, I signed autographs, shook hands and told them I was from Tottenham Hotspur. Recognition of the name only really took hold as I climbed into the van's backseats. They clapped and cheered, 'Tottenham, Tottenham, Tottenham'. I grinned with delight as the door was closed on me and we were whisked away, driven back across Iran to our slightly more humble lodgings. Spinning round to Matt I checked, 'Did you get it?!'

'Bollocks, shit, bloody, stupid camera,' was all I got by way of reply. I know it's hard, but you'll just have to believe me. They were chanting for Spurs.

Friday 12 October finally arrived. After all the travel, the hype, the expectation, the unknowns, the fears, the successes, and our raw, simple hope, this was it. Back in England I had joked over many pints about this very day. 'Can you imagine? Iran v Iraq, bloody hell!' The hour had come.

The city was buzzing. Flags and smiles adorned faces and lampposts in an outbreak of nationalistic fervour. To the Iranians, such matches were a chance to take pride in being Iranian. Under the Islamic Republic they are told that nationality should not be championed, Islam is all that should occupy their thoughts and actions. While they are all devoutly Muslim, one can never strip a man of his national pride. The people, once part of the mighty Persian Empire, take pride in their homeland and their spirit is strong.

115,000 Iranians were making their way to the new Mecca of the day, the Azadi Stadium. With an excuse to use their car horns more than normal, they obliged with the glee of a nation poised to qualify for their third World Cup. The name 'Azadi' means 'Freedom' and the people were once again about to taste the joys of the finals as they had done in France in 1998. Blazevic's praise and hope for this current Iranian team was manna from heaven for the people of Iran. Fingering an English dictionary, a local had pointed out to us what the World Cup meant to him. 'Everything.'

Football was giving them a chance to find a place for themselves again in the world. At the World Cup in France 1998, even more significant than the glorified political point made by beating the 'Great Satan' (the USA), Iran had placed itself on the world stage for all the right reasons and rubbed shoulders with not just the hosts, France, but the thirty other nations as well. It was an opportunity that both the nation and the national team grasped with both hands.

The Azadi Stadium gains its might from its people. Its curving, open, two-tiered concrete bowl, high at the sides, lower at the ends and cut down into the ground, seats a sardined hundred thousand official ticket-holders on basic concrete steps. Up to fifteen thousand extra 'standing' tickets are illegally sold at the turnstiles. By kick-off, all steps, exits and walls would disappear from view under a rippling sea of support and expectation. The Alborz mountain range towered behind the stadium providing a magnificent backdrop to this dusty suburb of Tehran as the sun beat down. With three and a half hours still to go until kick-off, nearly fifty thousand fans were already in place.

Matt looked terrified. I had admittedly been too afraid to wear my England shirt, just in case. We were the only white people, two freckled strays among a surge of fanaticism. I felt vulnerable. England had never been high on Iran's popularity list, but after the Americans' decision to bomb their brothers in Afghanistan, Tony Blair's support had made us and him 'legitimate targets' in the words of one hard-line Islamic cleric at a Friday Mass. Yet, as we walked down the vast avenue approach to the stadium, we were greeted not with abuse but with warmth and cries of friendly banter. One guy was even wearing an old England shirt. There is a clear distinction between the governments of opposing countries and the people who live under them. This was football, not politics, and Iranians love their football.

The thunderous roar of the Azadi is something truly special. It sounds like a plague of locusts; thousands of horns and hooters creating a swarming buzz of noise. The passion, desire, excitement and sheer, unadulterated fanaticism deafened me into trepidation. Matt turned on the camera. 'Welcome to the Azadi Stadium, Tehran, Iran. We're here with a hundred and fifteen thousand screaming Iranians. If they win, we are going to have the night of our lives; if they lose . . . my God, if they lose we could be in a whole heap of trouble.'

There is a reason why the Azadi is labelled by away teams as one of the most terrifying sports arenas in the world. Women are not allowed to attend and the favourite chant, echoed from a hundred thousand vocal males, which reverberates through your mind, body and soul, is: 'What will Iran do to you? Iran will put holes in you.'

Iran and Iraq fought bitterly for the duration of the 80s. On this occasion the battle would last just ninety minutes. NOW THE WAR BEGINS IN EARNEST was a relatively tame headline from one of Iran's eight polemic sporting daily newspapers. As an act of 'reconciliation', Iranian war wounded were paraded in front of the Iraqi team before kick-off and showered with flowers by the home side.

Iraq had no chance of qualification. All army officers, they were playing for pride. Alone, in front of a stadium packed solely with a partisan Iranian crowd (no Iraqi fans being allowed) they were also playing for their lives. The Iraqi Football Federation was, at that time, run by the notorious son of Saddam Hussein, Uday. When they lost to Iran in Baghdad eight players were sacked. In the past certain players had disappeared or been publicly beaten.

The teams emerged to a tumultuous roar. As they lined up for the anthems, the referee, Mr Kim Young Joo, gave me a wink. The Iranian Director of Refereeing was at my side. He was grinning like a madman. 'How many people will watch this match on TV?' I asked.

'All of them . . . all women, all man, watch.' There was delight on his face, his eyes creased by joyous smiles. 'If Iran win,' he said, raising his fist to the crowd, 'then . . .' But the crowd literally drowned him out. I was two feet away but could not hear a thing. Whatever he had shouted ended with '. . . party, party, party', and a warm, confident handshake of shared anticipation.

Before the national anthems came a stirring, eerie recital from the Holy Koran. The crowd repeated every line in sombre throat as we took our places behind the Iraqi goal. Iran were in white, Iraq were in black. It could not have been more clear cut. The battle was about to begin.

Iran hurled themselves at the Iraqis and after only ten minutes they scored. The crowd erupted, the players wheeled away in celebration, but Mr Kim Young Joo remained where he was, his whistle in his mouth and his arm in the air. Offside. It remained 0–0.

The Iranians proceeded to set up camp well inside the Iraqi half but could not deliver the final ball, despite some nice passing moves. Our man Karimi was working his magic; he skinned three Iraqi defenders on the edge of the area and laid the ball off to former Charlton player Bhagheri who agonisingly buffooned it wide from six yards. The Iraqis were overrun but holding on.

The breakthrough finally came after 27 minutes when Iran's German-based number two, Mahdivikia, slotted home from the edge of the area. The crowd went berserk. This was what they had come to see. Caught up in the euphoria, we cheered and shouted and jumped about, joining in the celebrations. It was a great moment. Iran 1 Iraq 0.

At half-time the Iranian substitutes stayed on the bench. Shahab, who had also succeeded in getting a pass, joined us behind the goal and translated as we tried to persuade the subs to show us some tricks. One of the youngest came close to actually saying yes, but eventually got too shy for the camera. As we walked past the Iranian bench to take our positions for the second half he acknowledged his abstinence and gave a cheeky salute for the camera.

Iran sat back. It was horrifying to see them self-destruct in such an obvious manner. They let the Iraqis come at them and the inevitable happened: the Iraqis equalised. I completely missed it. The crowd were stunned. The thousands of horns continued but the roar behind them was gone. At 1–1 Iran would lose their automatic berth. They had to score.

The tension in the stadium built with every passing minute. The pure, white shirts of the home side streamed forward but every move lacked the killer punch. We had been in the country but two days yet we were cheering for them as if we had spent a lifetime in their arms. The frustration grew and the crowd agonised as the clock ticked ever closer to the ninety-minute mark. The tackles became more heated, the Iraqis stayed down longer and a desperation set into Iran's play spurred on by the fighting spirit that Blazevic had driven into them. They knew the game was theirs for the taking.

With twenty minutes to go Mr Sharifi walked past, checking the line of media. He tapped us on the shoulder, shook hands, smiled his shuffling smile and gestured not to worry; Iran would score in a few minutes.

Two minutes later Mahdivikia made a break down the right towards us. Matt had been explaining to the camera that Iran must score. He nodded at me, calm as you like, and gestured for me to swing the camera back around to the pitch. Mahdivikia surged into the Iraqi area and squared the ball confidently across the box, beyond the reaches of the out-coming keeper. Our man Karimi was there. It was an absolute sitter. There was no way he could miss it.

Connecting with the ball, he drove it home. It crashed sweetly into the back of the net; the crowd roared their delight, Karimi wheeled away arms in the air and the celebrations began.

The entire place went absolutely mental. We leaped, we hugged, we danced, we sang. It was magnificent to see the dreams of so many come that one vital step closer to realisation. And the noise, the noise was simply deafening.

We had attracted the attention of the other photographers and cameramen behind the goal during the match with our verbal contributions and animated excitement. As Karimi stroked in the winner they ran over to share a multitude of euphoric hugs while the main Iranian TV camera turned away from the celebrating players to film the two white guys cheering for Iran. It was a phenomenally charged moment of emotion. The experience of 115,000 Iranians breaking into instantaneous ecstasy in a match with such history and such passion, both from the Iraqi–Iranian sense and from the awe-ridden gaze of a foreigner, was breathtaking.

The dying minutes were almost unbearable. When the final whistle came a further roar erupted. This time it was a roar of relief as the Iraqis, to their credit, had tested the Iranian defence and aged most of the audience in the closing stages. We charged onto the pitch to greet the players. It was simply amazing.

Then the fighting began. The desolated Iraqi players had trudged off to their subterranean changing room, down a flight of stairs behind the goal. On their way they were pelted with water bottles, eggs, tomatoes and general waste from the jeering crowd. The humiliation of it all was just too much and they retaliated. All they did was throw back a few water bottles, but this was all the justification the fans and security needed to give them a hiding, and we shortly found ourselves caught up in a thirty- or forty-man brawl. Punches flew, arguments raged, and the Iraqis attempted to flee.

The rush of press to the scene complicated everything. The staircase down to the changing rooms and relative safety became blocked with bodies, cameras were ripped off shoulders and the remaining fans in the stands were chased away by a security charge. Just before they cut the floodlights I saw a beast of an Iranian security guard land a sneaky punch through a crowd of people. It connected with the back of an Iraqi player's head. There was a sickening thump and the player crashed down the stairs, adding to the frenzied pile.

We remained on the fringes of it all and kept our camera rolling throughout. I had never seen anything like it. Everybody charged into the mêlée to witness it, but when the floodlights were cut we quickly backed away, afraid for our safety. Suddenly we were feeling very English and conscious of our unique position among the throng. Journalists who had ventured too close were coming back sporting bruises. It was time to retreat.

With the floodlights out the stadium was an impressive sight. The pitch was almost in complete darkness, but the stands were lit up by hundreds of small bonfires of programmes, newspapers and Islamic flyers, like so many candles lighting up the sky. Dusting ourselves off and regaining our composure, we descended into the heart of the main stand and the managers' press conference. The Iraqi manager was late due to the scuffles involving his team and by the time he finally arrived the temperature had risen significantly.

Unsure how wise it would be for us to leave the stadium and join the rampaging throngs we sought out Mr Husseini to say thank you. He was a changed man. His job done, he had relaxed completely and, after the right result, was beaming smiles in all directions. He spoke only a very few words of English but his words touched me deeply. 'Thiiiis, my friend,' he managed, making everybody laugh with his struggle to remember and pronounce the words. 'Welcome tooo Iran . . . err . . . I hope . . . err . . . I hope to go to . . .' Still keeping his eyes on me he started laughing at his attempts and held out his hand towards Shahab, beckoning him in to translate.

'He says you're really welcome to Tehran, he hopes you'll come here again . . . he says film him!' Matt, who had the camera pointed at Shahab as he translated, swung it back round to Mr Husseini who was enjoying his little moment. I did a thumbs-up as if to say 'there you go, you're back on camera' which only caused more hilarity among our growing crowd of officials as Shahab quickly grabbed my hand and reminded me of its consequences. Fortunately they all saw the funny side of our confusion.

'The President will speak to you now,' said an official who had just tapped me on the shoulder. I stuttered a 'beg your pardon?' in response. 'The President? Really? Me?' A blurred minute later I was being introduced by Shahab and welcomed once more to Iran, but this time by the President of the Iranian Football Federation. It seemed that the tale of two Englishmen behind the scenes at his FA had spread and he wished to learn more and welcome us officially. It was a fantastic end to a dramatic evening. He knew we were not properly accredited media, that we were on an adventure of our own, but recognised our desire to spread the good word of what we saw and the good nature of our trip. He was glad we had enjoyed such close-up, first-hand experience of Iranian football. I thanked him profusely, and when he said he hoped I would visit Iran again, I replied that I would pray to see him first in Korea and Japan. 'I hope so,' he replied, 'I hope so.'

18. IRAN v THE REST OF THE WORLD

We had thought it best not to take the table with us to the Iraq game, feeling too scared that we might be pushing the limits of our cheekiness. Instead we called round to the FA the following day to thank them and ask official permission to take the table onto the grass of the Azadi. Mr Husseini said nothing was possible for that day but he would see what he could do and call us on Sunday morning.

Iran is the home of kebabs and loose women. Loosely clothed women, that is. The message was quite clear. Mingle too much and you will be swinging from a tree. The Islamic regime demanded that outside of one's own home women must cover up completely in loose, dark-coloured robes and headscarves. It is quite a daunting sight for a visitor unused to such restrictions.

The kebabs on the other hand are fully exposed everywhere, loud and proud in their glory. They are the national dish. Unlike the fatty mix of 'non-specific meat content' we grease our faces on after last orders in England, these kebabs are well cooked, well presented and served with rice and vegetables. It was one such kebab – ordered from Habib's brother's place just down the road and delivered on a tray with a soft drink to our room, all for just over a dollar – that became a staple diet during our stay at the Hotel Tehran. We rested and waited for the phone call from the FA.

It was bad news. Due to his exceptionally small amount of English all Mr Husseini was able to say to me on the phone when he called the next morning was 'sorry, sorry . . . bye.' But then Jeffery called. 'I'll pick you up at 10.30; the FA couldn't arrange anything? OK, well, we'll go to the stadium anyway.' Legend. At the entrance to the huge Azadi sports complex the FA badge on the car was checked, but the stadium itself seemed to have no security. We walked straight out onto the pitch with the table. A quick chat with an old groundsman was all it took. Jeffery and a friend of his, Faraz, spoke to him. The pitch had just been watered, so if we could just wait twenty minutes for it to dry then sure, no problem. He trundled off.

The table stood in the centre circle of Iran's showpiece stadium under the watchful gaze of President Khatami and Ayatollah Khomeini whose portraits were placed at the highest point of the stand. It was hard to picture the drama that had unfolded there the Friday before. The empty, sun-drenched stands kept their stories to themselves. We played for a few minutes before a burly man started walking out across the grass towards us. 'OK, let's go,' said Jeffery after a nervous glance at the new addition striding our way. They say first impressions can be deceptive but this one was spot on.

Content with the table's latest conquest we jumped in the car and almost turned down the offer of driving to the Iranian team's training camp. We were tired and shy about imposing ourselves. As we started to drive away, however, I came to my senses. It was a golden opportunity. When would we ever be in this position again? This was what we had been hoping for all along, we could not let a few nerves and tiredness stop us. It was staggering that we had let ourselves almost pass it up. The human trait of idleness is quite something, even after doing so much it can still creep up. We were not about to let it triumph.

In we drove and lingered in the car while Jeffery went off

to investigate. He came back with a grin on his face. 'The football team are no longer here but the futsal (six-a-side indoor football) team are. They're Asian Champions, fancy meeting them?'

Our final afternoon in the capital city of Iran was thus spent playing football with some of Asia's most technically talented footballers. I can safely say that they made a complete mockery of us. Within minutes we were gasping, bright red and useless. Even more humbling was the fact that most of them were playing in flip-flops.

The table went down a storm. The entire squad gathered around cheering, joking, trying to distract whoever was playing and championing every goal. It was another remarkable chapter in the table's colourful last few months. As we left we drove past a sign for the 'Beach Volley Federation'; maybe next time.

It had been six magical days in the city that the Lonely Planet suggests you get in and out of as quickly as possible. There may be little taste of the Orient left in this sprawling mass at the foot of the Alborz Mountains but it is still the heart of the country. Simply riding the streets in a shared taxi, seeing the countless giant murals of soldiers and Ayatollahs, experiencing the crazy traffic and watching the covered women wearing their black hejab was an education in itself.

Carting the table across Iran was equally magical. Wherever we set it up swarms of kids and adults gathered around enchanted. Unfortunately it quite often meant more tea, but the moments we shared were worth it.

Tea is a big problem for the tourist in Iran. Possibly even one of the greatest dangers. Iranians love tea. Great, no problem, I like tea too. But combine their love of tea with their unfathomed hospitality and suddenly you are spending your stay desperately seeking toilets. I have never drunk so much tea in my life. Unlike India, or France to a certain extent, you cannot just find a tree, or pee in the street. With the strict codes on covering up I hate to think what eye-watering punishment might be dished out.

We bussed our way East through plains and mountains. With the table forever present we took in the magnificent bridges and mosques at Esfahan, the ruins of ancient empires at Shiraz and the remarkably restored ancient mud citadel at Bam. Not only were we treated to these many, beautiful and historic sights, the table adventure was in full swing.

One particular occasion sticks in my mind. Outside Shiraz, at the ruins of Persepolis and on top of the hill overlooking the remains of past glories, we set up the table. An old guide who perched himself up there as the guardian of a tomb that was cut into the hillside, introduced himself in his best Farsi. He sidled over to the table and poked it. Clearly he had never seen one before and had no conception of how to play. It was fascinating to see something we took for granted become so foreign. Once explained though, it was hard to get him off it.

Esfahan is the jewel of Iran, boasting some of the finest mosques and architecture in the Islamic world. In a stroke of good fortune our hostel was next door to a football stadium, which doubled as the HQ of the regional FA and provided us with a sneak preview of the next generation of Iranian footballers. The hostel owner knew the President, Mr Satek, and arranged for us to meet him the day after our arrival.

With a new companion in tow, a Dutchman called Vince, the first Westerner we had seen for some time, we accepted a subsequent invitation to watch the closing match of a round-robin style, regional Under-20s tournament. We were met warmly, ushered into a small stand and informed that, if the two teams playing in front of us drew, then they would both travel to the national final in Tehran. It was Esfahan 0 Yazd 0, and uninspiring. Yet in the ninetieth minute something extraordinary happened.

It took an hour and a half of uneventful football to produce the goal but what a goal it was. Esfahan's little number ten picked up the ball on the right flank, just inside the Yazd half. Rolling it forward he shaped to lob a long ball into the box. He hit it with some clout, the ball rocketed skywards and, to the horror of the keeper, flew in slow motion over his head, dropping spectacularly into the far top left corner of the goal.

It was a wonder strike from out of the blue, the sort of shot that the former Arsenal and England goalkeeper, David Seaman, has nightmares about. Had I been able to see into the future I may well not have cheered so much at the goal-keeper's misfortune. Certain events in Japan were to change my opinion on such 'lucky strikes'. His team-mates mobbed him and the Yazd goalkeeper fell distraught to the floor and into a disconsolate malaise.

Iran's final World Cup qualifier was against Bahrain, in Bahrain. If they won it they were in the World Cup. Bahrain is not much bigger than the Isle of Wight; Iran has a popula-tion of 65 million. Yet the Iranian people were worried and conspiracy theories were flying around.

We learned that after the Iraq match four hundred peo-ple had been arrested for little more than enthusiastic cele-bration. The government did not like such displays of emotion. They were not the actions of a good Muslim. They believed people should be more reserved, more Islamic. There was thus a strong belief and a growing anger that the national team might be ordered to lose against Bahrain.

It is ironic in a way that the government should try to stem the support for football. They had used the team's away trip to Iraq as a propaganda tour, state TV showing nothing but pictures of the team visiting Muslim shrines, and could surely have used World Cup fever as a tool to engender support for their ideals as Franco did in Spain. I am not about to argue with them, though.

We watched the Bahrain match in Shiraz, appropriately known as the 'House of Learning' in days gone by. Gherkins, although a pet hate of mine, proved the key to our invitation to watch it in a local TV shop. My insistence on their removal from my sandwich provided for an entertain-ing exchange with the owner of a sandwich shop opposite our £2.50-a-night hotel. The owner proved to be best mates with the local television specialist.

In a locked-up mall we sat down in front of ten TVs with ten Iranians. Iran had never lost to Bahrain before. As Saudi Arabia staked their claim for the top spot in the group with an emphatic 4–1 win over Thailand, Iran faltered. After only seven minutes Bahrain took the lead and by half-time Iran were trailing 2–0. The captain, Ali Daei, was not impressed and savagely bundled a Bahrain player to the floor in frustration.

Our new-found friends in Shiraz were not quite as perturbed. They put on some music, forgot about the football and had a little party, the other closed-up shops in the mall turning out occupants of their own to form a veritable crowd of clapping dancers. It was all a little bit bizarre. Perhaps they knew Iran would lose, perhaps they were resigned to the inevitable. But come the second half the music stopped and everybody scuttled back to their respective screens. Hope still remained and the shouts during the closing minutes revealed their distress. Yet lose they did.

The match finished 3–1 to Bahrain with three red cards. Ali Daei had given Iran a glimmer of hope by bringing the score to 2–1 in the 81st minute but Bahrain put it beyond doubt shortly after. Iran had lost to the equivalent of the Isle of Wight. Conspiracy theories still buzzing in my mind, I could almost have sworn that the Iranian keeper dived the wrong way for the final goal. It was irrelevant. Bahrain's players had scooped their pot of Saudi money and Iran were condemned to the playoffs. Our friends again turned off the TV and resorted once more to their own entertainment. It was at least something they knew they could put their faith in. They wheeled off into the night attempting to fit four of them on a moped.

After our chain of successes, this was a shock defeat. Fate had been good to us and the chance of meeting up again with our Iranian friends in Japan seemed like a glorious piece of destiny and an unrivalled chance to get behind the scenes of the World Cup. Evidently it was not meant to be. Iran now faced a playoff against the UAE. Where were we heading? You got it, the UAE. We would see our friends again, sooner than we thought.

While looking around Shiraz a middle-aged man named Rahimdeghani had quietly approached us and asked if we could help him with his English. He had a few tattered pages of an ancient, yet treasured, English exercise book tucked under his arm and a list of all the words he had learned. He followed us all day asking questions and guiding us about. The next day he waited at a point he knew we'd pass so as to innocently say hello once more. It was touching. He even came with us to the bus station when we left. It was sad to leave him as we had seemingly made his day and he looked like he didn't want to go home. But as we were waiting to leave he was able to translate the latest fantastic news: FIFA had overruled Bahrain's victory and declared Iran the winners. Iran *were* going to the World Cup. Saudi's money had been in vain.

Or were they? More questions revealed that the following morning FIFA were going to make an announcement about a complaint lodged by Iran that some of Bahrain's players had been ineligible. In reality it was an unlikely attempt to cover their poor performance and repair the heartbreak of the Iranian nation. Iran were *not* going directly to the World Cup.

Bam is a small, relaxed town only 300 kilometres from the Afghan border, famous for its two-thousand-year-old mud city. Unlike most ancient sites, the Arg-e-Bam left nothing to the imagination. With painstaking reconstruction the whole city and its raised citadel had been completed. When a former Iranian President visited it he was so taken that he urged every Iranian to make the journey at least once in their lives. It was the perfect place to make one of the most unexpected and successful contacts of the entire adventure.

Tragically, Bam as we know it is no more. A vicious earthquake struck without warning in 2003 killing some thirty thousand of the local population and razing the historic citadel. I recall watching the aftermath on the news, clutching my face, my jaw wide open in horror; I didn't even think there were thirty thousand people in Bam. The thought still makes me quiver. Plans are afoot to rebuild, but despite an appeal from HRH the Prince of Wales during a visit shortly after the tragedy, its majesty will not be seen again for some time.

Our contact's name was Daniela Da Rugna. She was Swiss, from Zurich, and had grown up in Basel of all places. We met her at our hostel in Bam enjoying time not having to cover up and then saw her again at the Arg-e-Bam clad in the mandatory coverings. This time we had the table on display, dramatically poised on the roof of the citadel. She was amazed and listened with awe to our stories about the Iraq match and the trip in general.

As I talked about our greatest goal of all being somehow to get into the World Cup final she broke into laughter. 'My cousin works for FIFA,' she said. 'He's quite high up, he's organising the World Cup. He was probably there the day you met Mr Blatter. He got my dad tickets for the final in '98.' I was stunned. 'I could email him if you like and get him to help you. He'd love the sound of your trip.'

These were the depths of Eastern Iran. We were perched up in a two-thousand-year-old mud citadel. On one level it was a staggeringly fortunate meeting, on another level it was something else. What is meant to be is meant to be indeed, and from that moment on I have kept my eyes wide open to any and all possibilities and never stopped believing in the impossible.

Akbar, the owner of the hostel in which we bunked down, was able to fill us in on the events surrounding the football. Iran's appeal had been turned down. They would face play-offs against the UAE and then Ireland. After the loss to Bahrain thousands of fans had taken to the streets of Tehran in demonstration and clashed with police. They had heard the rumours that the Mullahs had ordered the team to lose. Some fans even claimed the players had been told that, if they dared to win, their flight home would be shot down. The loss also provided an excuse to react in protest against the regime under the thin veil of football. The next night, following the failed outcome of Iran's appeal, even more people had taken to the streets. It was not pretty. Some eight hundred more Iranians were arrested.

Despite the unrest, when Akbar told us that the first leg of the playoff against the UAE was to be staged in Iran, my spirits rose. Matt reached out and turned on the camera. 'I've just been rudely awakened by Andy. He's looking very happy. I've got a horrible feeling we're about to go on a charge back to Tehran. Let's do it.'

It was 3 p.m. We were in Bam 1,200 kilometres from Tehran with 24 hours until kick-off. Mr Karimpour had confirmed that our passes from the Iraq match would be valid and I couldn't resist the opportunity of a return to the Hotel Tehran and the mighty Azadi. By 3.30 p.m. we were packed and in the first taxi we could hail, thundering along the 200 kilometres to the nearest airport at Kerman. It cost us ten dollars, but nearly cost us our lives. The driver's overtaking manoeuvres were death defying. He wasn't hurrying for our sake; he was just overtaking Iranian style.

Despite finding that the promised flight did not exist, surviving a brush with the police after an overzealous bout of haggling with another greedy taxi driver and a bizarre encounter with the Iranian grass-skiing team, we eventually made it to Tehran in time.

There was no return to normality, though. Our taxi driver from Tehran airport managed to use the slipway off the motorway as a route onto it, took a short cut diagonally up and across four solid lanes of one-way traffic and delivered us to the Football Federation in record time.

Just hours later, entering the Azadi Stadium once more, we stumbled into none other than the Irish manager at the time, Mick McCarthy, surrounded by television cameras. His translator was unmistakable: Jeffery. Breaking off mid-sentence he waved and shouted at us, causing McCarthy to look over with a puzzled expression. McCarthy, in Iran to scout Ireland's potential opponents, was in the midst of commenting on the intriguing events in Bahrain. 'I thought Iran would win. I think they are the best team and I thought they would qualify. But strange things happen.' The latter was said with a wry smile.

Iran strolled out with a look of confidence. They won the match 1–0, but the score line did not do justice to the drama for it could easily have been 10–4. Karimi was on fire, dribbling through the UAE's defence with ease, but unable to hit the mark. Barn door syndrome was back to haunt him. As the match entered its final minutes, one of the cameramen behind the goal produced a small carpet, walked back a few yards into the space between the track and the pitch, and knelt down to pray. It was a remarkable sight. Despite Iran's sheer number of chances the UAE were battling and still very much in the game until the final whistle blew.

Familiar faces had greeted us at the ground. There was Mr Sharifi buzzing around, the photographer who plied us with sweets, the Saudi camera crew, Mr Torabian, Mr Husseini and even the same referee. After the final whistle we spoke to Cristina D'Alessio, the general manager of West Asia for the Asian Football Confederation. At a guess it was she who had granted our passes for the Iraq match. She was Italian, lived in Lebanon and spoke perfect English. She was also in exceptional circumstances, being the only lady allowed into the stadium, which, as a result of the defeat against Bahrain, was only three-quarters full.

To my unjustified surprise she was extremely friendly. One of her henchmen had been talking to us and we had revealed to him the story of our trip. He looked a bit surprised when we told him we weren't accredited media and, after watching him relate this to Cristina, who looked very much in charge, we thought we had better introduce ourselves. One of her colleagues had laid into Matt at the Iraq game for having managed to sneak in outside of the official channels. Whoever he was, he was not amused that his authority had been usurped and had a poor way of expressing it. He failed to endear himself to Matt, who naturally took affront to being spoken to in such a manner, called the guy a wanker, and walked off.

Cristina was the perfect person to consult about our chances of getting into the return leg in Abu Dhabi. Most helpful, she said we would have no problem, despite our lack of paper accreditation, but that if we came unstuck we could contact her colleague who was in charge of the match.

The managers' post-match press conference was an entertaining affair. The Iranian press were heatedly laying into Blazevic, incensed by the fact they had not won by more than a single goal, and by his tactics in Bahrain. His translator was working overtime mimicking the emotions of the reporters and the fiery replies of his employer.

The UAE's coach, Tini Ruijs, was Dutch and spoke good English like the rest of his countrymen. Able to tap him on the shoulder in the mêlée afterwards, I asked, 'With Holland knocked out of the World Cup by Ireland, are they selling UAE shirts instead?' He laughed for the first time in the past hour. 'There will come a lot of Dutch at the second leg against Iran. In football the ball is round; it can go either way. We are only one goal behind. If we score at home it is 1–1 and then we will see which way the ball will roll. I hope to meet Ireland so they can see the Dutch colours again.'

Gallingly, we missed Mick McCarthy after the match and at his hotel the next morning by a matter of minutes. Promises to leave early the night before had turned, come morning, into cries for a lie-in. We ended up getting neither. It was pathetic to have come so far yet miss someone by minutes. The end result was effort without reward, which irritated us all. There was a consolation prize, though, as we tried not to abuse each other in the respectable confines of the Esteghal Hotel lobby: Jeffery appeared.

With him was the referee, Mr Kim Young Joo. Matt set up the table while I tapped Kim on the shoulder. He was in his late fifties, a small, sprightly Korean with a ready smile and friendly eyes. He loved it. The Iranian Director of Refereeing told us they did not have time and that they had to get to the airport, but he was actually the first to jump on the table with glee once it was up and ready. They all ended up laughing, shouting and gesticulating while playing on the magic table. Mr Kim in particular put in a freestyle performance with legs and arms flailing all over the place. There was no neutrality in his performance. High fives greeted every goal.

We were in the middle of the lobby of a five-star hotel on a beautiful Persian rug. Our audience consisted of a number of white-robed Sheiks. We were probably playing in front of royalty. Eventually Jeffery had to prise them away to ensure they caught their plane, dragging them off to the airport while promising to try and talk to McCarthy about a table adventure in Dubai.

Before we left we had a quick word in the ear of the hotel manager who had thoroughly enjoyed the excited antics with the table. 'If Iran beat the UAE and play Ireland, will the Irish team be staying here?' we asked.

'Yes, McCarthy come here and team come here,' he replied.

'Would we be able to bring along the table, set it up in the lobby and have your help in trying to meet the Irish players?' He didn't answer. He flashed a smile. It was a smile of utter delight at the prospect.

Before we crossed the Gulf to Abu Dhabi, the FA was in need of one last visit. I wanted to get their thoughts on the qualifiers, say thank you and film another game on the table. Our taxi driver was a very well educated man who spoke good English. Like all Iranian males he loved to talk football, but when we came round to the Bahrain game he was very cagey. 'You are young intelligent guys,' he said when we asked him about the rumours that the match was thrown and, more importantly, *why* it would have been thrown.

'You don't need to ask me that question,' he said. 'Maybe I know, but I not tell you. I get myself killed.' It was a staggering revelation. 'You English are clever, you can work it out,' he added, his eyes rising to meet mine in the rear view mirror. I spun round to Matt who was filming the conversation. He was glaring at the camera with a look of hate as though it had just bitten him. Somehow it had managed to cut out at the exact moment of the priceless footage. 'Never mind,' I said, smiling weakly. I apologised later for other, more choice comments.

It snapped us back into reality. We had been careful and respectful during our stay, but were conscious of being drawn across the line into politics, a politics the ins and outs of which we knew little about. It was best that we put our thoughts on the Bahrain game to bed and concentrated on the future, at least until we had left Iran.

Dr Hassan Ghafari, the Deputy General Secretary of the Iranian Football Federation, was what you would call a very nice man. 'I don't think the goal posts can help them two matches in a row,' he joked, happy with the first-leg match against the UAE. Of the playoffs in general he remarked, 'It is very exciting but also nerve-breaking. Now is do or die. Everything is possible in football. That is the beauty of it. A third division team can win the Cup; everyone can have hope, even Tottenham fans.' He looked at me and laughed heavily. 'Iran *could* beat Ireland.'

He rounded off our interview poignantly: 'Football, and sport in general, is special. It unites people. It forms friendships. If it weren't for football I wouldn't be meeting you now and I doubt you would be here in Iran. It brings countries together. That is one main goal of any sport, especially football.' We had one last question:

'Are you any good at tablefootball?'

'No,' he replied, laughing, 'but I'll challenge you to a game.'

Perhaps it was the football angle from which we had approached Iran, and the warmth of our successes, that lent us to view the country fondly. But in comparison to the Russian shrugs, the Spanish laziness, and the brash, loud Americans of Paris, the hospitality, sights and staggeringly good treatment we had encountered in this Persian wonderland had been a revelation. The country had an intimidating side to it, with its strict codes and military presence, but with respect and understanding these simply added to the experience of our stay. I had cheered and prayed for them to beat Bahrain and qualify directly for the World Cup, but providence had lined up an earlier meeting than in Japan. We were on our way to the UAE.

19. UNITED ARAB EMIRATES

Iran won comfortably, 3–0. True to the words of Cristina D'Alessio, the football authorities in the UAE proved to be as accommodating as the Iranians across the gulf and press passes for the match were issued without hesitation to the fine representatives of 'Because its Football Productions'.

'You've blagged it,' cried Amir on seeing our passes, as we stood behind the Iranian goal at half-time. We were not the only ones. Amir, a producer for the BBC, and his camera-man were in the UAE filming a documentary about the aftermath of 11 September called 'Letter to America'. They had flashed their BBC cards to earn a free ticket to the match, the same cards that we later flashed to gain free entry to see the touring Shaolin monks a week later in Dubai.

What struck me most about the UAE were the women. I had only been in Iran for three weeks yet the first lady we passed dazzled me with her hair and figure. The effect stunned me because it was something that I had previously taken for granted. The character and the beauty contained in those two simple elements were quite something. To deprive the women in Iran of this, to cloak and shroud their beauty transformed them into a uniformed group, stripping them of their distinctiveness, and made this lady in front of me spectacular.

Almost as spectacular was Ali Daei's first-half free kick. Down to ten men within eight minutes of play, Iran needed a touch of class to break the resolve of their opponents. It was duly supplied by their talismanic captain to put them 1–0 up. Officially the highest international goalscorer in the history of international football with over one hundred goals in just over 130 appearances, Ali Daei didn't even play football before he was twenty. This particular curling right-foot shot proved he was close to mastering the art.

Iran's class had been plain to see during the training sessions the evening before. The UAE had displayed admirable industry, but the Iranians oozed confidence, despite the oppressive heat. We, however, were less accustomed to the sweltering temperature and it seemed to be taking its toll. Post-training we managed to speak with one of the UAE players. Trying our luck once more, we asked him if he would score a goal for us. His head rolled back as he roared with laughter and answered, 'but of course'. It was only the next day, as the teams emerged from the tunnel into the floodlit night, that we realised he was in fact the goalie.

Equally suffering in the humidity were hordes of Irish journalists. No doubt they had been delighted at the chance of a few days in the sun 'researching' first-hand Ireland's potential opponents. One in particular, Emmet Malone, informed us on our chances of nobbling Mick McCarthy, who was also in the UAE, continuing his scouting mission. 'The problem,' he said, 'is that he's playing golf like a f***ing lunatic. You can try approaching him tonight. He's attending a meet and greet thing at the Crown Plaza Hotel. You know, meet the local Irish community, shake a few hands, a bit like the Queen. All he can do is tell you to f*** off.' We did. He did, but in the nicest possible way and with the caveat that if we caught up with him at the stadium the next day he would oblige. Needless to say we missed him once more.

A red card early in the second half sealed the fate of the UAE. As the third goal went in Amir declared it was going to become a rout. Needless to say no more goals were scored. 'Marshallah, marshallah' (God has willed it) sang the five-hundred-strong Iranian crowd, drowning out the twenty thousand white-robed Arabs. It was official: Iran would face Ireland.

The night before, Mr Sharifi had approached us as we watched the Iranians being put through their paces. After the usual smiles, handshakes and kisses he pointed at the team and said, 'So, you come Irland? You come Irland with us?' We nearly choked, taken aback, and explained that, first, it was far from on the way to Japan and, second, that the Irish FA would never be as accommodating as the Iranian and Emirates' had been in granting us press passes. He issued a few gruff sentences and hurried on his way. Ten minutes later he was back. 'You come with us,' he said. Before we knew it we were handing over passport photos and, dumbstruck, were included in the Iranian contingent bound for the Republic of Ireland.

Twenty-four hours later, with the expected result against the UAE etched in history, the Iranian press were singing to a new tune. The ringleader of the previous critical attack on Blazevic rose to his feet and, with the full attention of everyone in the room, addressed the Iranian manager: 'Last time against Bahrain when we lost I asked you what you had to say to our great nation of Iran and you said that you were sorry. Now I would like to congratulate you and all the players of our great nation and ask you again your thoughts.'

The stage was set. Blazevic composed himself. 'Before everything I want to congratulate my colleague [the UAE's manager, Tini Ruijs] and the Emirates team for their good sportsmanship. The changes made with the players available to him showed the work of a great trainer. But maybe now it is time for me to talk of a phenomenal team that has the name of Iran. This winning of our team is a gift for the great nation of Iran because they are deserving much more satisfaction than this. I congratulate my players because they have realised everything that we have talked of and this win is going to be our springboard into the game against Ireland. My dear Iranians I thank you' (applause). The Iranian contingent roared approval as Blazevic walked with a royal swagger out of the room.

All the UAE's manager could do was stand and watch. I felt sorry for him standing there, alone, his dreams in tatters as Blazevic milked the moment. Iran may have been the better side, but the diminutive UAE had asked some questions and had had their chances. Regardless, Ruijs happily added his signature to the table as we added our commiserations.

In my search for Sharifi, at the Hilton Hotel that evening, a security guard waved me outside into a private dining area, amid palm trees and silver service. Sharifi, who was surrounded by the team, the officials and Blazevic, gave me a big wave, ushered me over and pointed to a seat. I was in my England shirt and grinning in disbelief. A detour to Ireland was about to become reality. Marshallah indeed.

20. IRELAND

The border-crossing into Iran had led me to Ireland. It was a comic touch from somebody upstairs, for when we first arrived at the Iranian border we had been escorted into a special room, welcomed politely, and asked questions about Ireland. 'We're not Irish,' I said. 'We're English.'

'No,' said the guard, pointing at our passports. 'Where is English, there no English.' Sure enough he was right. They read 'Great Britain and Northern Ireland.' So be it. We were Irish. Welcome home.

The Iranians had a treat in store for them on landing: snow. It was November and it was freezing. Having ridden with the smell of death on a Bangladeshi Airlines flight home, I was ready for the fresh, cooler air of our fair Isles but not the biting wall of cold that confronted me. Admittedly shorts and sandals didn't help the situation or my memory of it. The route home was uneventful bar the pilot's choice of airspace. We seemed to fly directly over Iraq and then Israel. Fortunately there was no detour near the Ukraine.

Matt had decided not to come. Maybe he was happy with his decision to head instead for the beaches of Goa; maybe he was sick of me. Whatever it was I found it hard to comprehend, but his absence paved the way for another to accompany me to Ireland. I had spoken with Sharifi, explaining that Matt was not going and whether it would be possible to get a pass for his replacement, my girlfriend. He told me yes, so long as I brought two photos to the team hotel two days before the match. I flew home, knocked on Em's door, packed her a bag and, without her knowing where we were going, whisked her off on the overnight ferry to meet the Iranian football team in Dublin. Who says romance is dead?

'We didn't shit ourselves in advance' roared Blazevic to the Irish press as the Iranian team settled in. Come match day it looked like they had. The keeper wasted more time than was humanly possible, the defence and midfield looked terrified of losing possession and the attack, well, they disappeared into the midfield among the negative tactics. It did not bode well for the colourful Croatian manager who had vowed to kill himself if the Iranians failed to qualify.

The night before the big match the Iranians' captain and star striker did not leave the lobby until close to midnight. Why? He was playing tablefootball. It had inadvertently taken four matches and three countries, but finally Ali Daei graced the magic table; and after his endorsement his team-mates were quick to follow, especially our man Ali Karimi. A fine way for him to celebrate his birthday.

The Burlington hotel lobby was alive that Friday night. There is quite a large Iranian community in Ireland and this was a chance for them to get back in touch with a homeland most hadn't visited since the revolution in 1979. Whole families appeared, the kids dressed in face paint and balloons, the parents armed with flags and hooters. There were no (or very few) headscarves, some of the Irish-based Iranians were enjoying a drink, and laughter filled the lobby as bemused, holidaying American golfers returned to the hotel from eighteen holes of wind and rain.

In the middle of it all I spotted the English comedian Nick Hancock. I had been hanging around the lobby most of the day chasing visas and Mr Sharifi, and had missed countless golden opportunities to whip out the table through sheer lack of confidence and inept shyness. It was inexplicable considering the story of the table so far, but I had just been unable to move.

Finally plucking up the courage to act, I tapped Nick on the shoulder. His wife is Iranian, and when Iran qualified for the World Cup in France 1998 he and a friend decided to make a documentary charting their progress in the tournament. At first he was a bit offish, said he was with the wife and kids and about to head home, as he continued to stand drinking in the same spot with a couple of mates for the rest of the night. His mates, however, thought the table was absolutely brilliant. While Nick fine-tuned his portly figure with another bottle of the local brew, they insisted I set it up and set to with gusto.

Nick eventually warmed up as he realised that my travels had brought encounters with some of the same people he had wrestled with at the Iranian FA. Everybody loves to relive their adventures and he was no exception, recalling his initial meeting with the Football Federation when he first went to pitch his film to them.

Unbeknown to many, Nick Hancock once appeared in an episode of Mr Bean. He played a thief who steals Mr Bean's camera in a park and is later caught, but only after having a park bin pulled over his head and being jabbed in the ribs by Mr Bean in the ensuing chase. In the police line-up Mr Bean can't identify him, so asks if he can put a bin over each of the suspects' heads and poke them with a pen. He recognises his man from the noise.

Mr Torabian at the Iranian FA had not been warming to Nick's film proposal. But, as the negotiations appeared to be stumbling, he stopped, looked straight at Nick and asked, 'Were you in Mr Bean?'

Mr Bean is huge in Iran. Consequently, the meeting took a funny turn. 'Can you be you and I'll be Mr Bean?' asked Mr Torabian. 'You put this bin over your head and I'll poke you with my pen . . .?' Nick broke into laughter at the memory of it all. 'Well, I couldn't exactly say no, could I,' he said. They got the deal.

As the night progressed, Em put on an Iranian team shirt I had bought in Tehran and, armed with a black marker pen, approached the players. Ali Karimi's eyes nearly popped out of his head. To see a beautiful lady in figure hugging clothes was probably a delight but the blonde hair was really something. You just don't get blonde hair in Iran, and the previously aloof captain, Ali Daei, was adding his inky flourish just moments after Karimi, dropping his defences and afterwards venturing onto the table. It was quite an evening.

There was still the minor problem of tickets to the game and visas for the return leg. I began to think I had fallen foul of Ta'rof, the Iranian tradition of offering and refusing everything three times. Everything had been offered but nothing had materialised. I tried desperately to recall any refusals. It didn't aid my plight or the sinking feeling gnawing at my stomach. My memory reverberated with the number of times I had repeated the phrase 'this is too good to be true' as, increasingly nervously, I chased Mr Sharifi during the two days before the match.

10 a.m. came on match day and passes were still yet to replace the promises. My attentions, however, were distracted by a crew from the TV show 'Football Mondial'. The producer had approached me in the lobby the night before, a disbelieving look on his face, and asked about the table. 'I read about you in the paper,' he said. 'I remember thinking wow; they're carrying that thing all the way to the World Cup! We were looking for a story around Iran and this game and I thought, this is perfect, it would be a great story for us, I wonder where their next stop is. You were in Abu Dhabi at the time so when I walked in here and saw the table I thought, no, no way, is this the same story? It can't be!'

I set the table up for their cameras and in turn they microphoned me up for an interview about the trip so far. The programme went out to 145 countries and undoubtedly aided our success later in the journey. As I finished, the Iranian players started to come down from their rooms, readying for the bus to the stadium. A few quick waves later and I was challenging Kavienpour then Minavand on the table, in front of a crowd of onlookers. Defeated by the English they were eventually forced to play among themselves in the chase for a victory. It brought drama and loud cries of both jubilation and frustration to the lobby, breaking any remaining tension before the big game.

At about 2 p.m. Mr Sharifi told me to go to the press centre at 4 p.m. to pick up my pass for the match. When I pressed him about Em's pass he laughed and said she didn't have one, she should be at home watching it on TV. The two cultures had collided.

I was stunned and Em was visibly rocked. It shocked us both for her to be looked down on in such a manner. I had seen and learned a lot, but this was a first-hand experience of the way women are treated in Iran.

My emotions, however, were mixed. This was the way he had been brought up. I was mad at his despicable treatment of my better half yet understood that I should have expected it at some stage and somehow pre-empted it. I am still divided about it. Why hadn't he said something earlier? Common courtesy could have avoided such a painful confrontation for all concerned.

Mr Sharifi was always on the move, shaking hands and organising. Aside from this incident he had been very good to Matt and me and was probably trying to hold together too many favours in too little time. Fortunately, he eventually reassured me that Em did have a ticket and, although there were no press passes waiting for us when we got to the ground, Mr Sharifi had lined up two complimentary tickets.

Without drama there is little glory, and hurrying into the fuelled-up roar of Lansdowne Road after the stresses and strains of the afternoon was a special moment. It was impossible not to be swept away by the atmosphere and our frustrations were blown away by the fevered desire on that cold November night.

While the newspapers were dramatising the return leg in deepest darkest Tehran, Lansdowne Road that evening was certainly not a place for the faint-hearted. It was passionate, loud and with a tinge of hostility not usually associated with the easy-going Irish. They had failed to qualify for the past two World Cups and the pain ran deep. This was due to be third time lucky. They ran out comfortable winners and journeyed to Iran with a clean sheet and two goals in the bank.

It was the end of our Iranian affair. I was unable to get a return visa to Iran for the second leg. By the time the back-door routes had fallen through there were not enough days to process a standard visa, despite a trip to the embassy in London and phone calls to Jeffery, the Iranian FA and even the Iranian Ambassador to Norway with whom I had shared a drink in Dublin.

Instead I watched with sadness as Iran's World Cup dream died, a Bristol pub my venue for the decisive second leg. They created chances, they hit the woodwork, but they were up against the luck of the Irish. A goal in the dying minutes gave ninety seconds of hope but it had come ninety minutes too late. It was Ireland, not Iran, who were on their way to Korea and Japan.

I was on English soil long enough to witness the draw for the World Cup. In the words of the England manager Sven-Goran Eriksson, 'It couldn't have been worse.' It was to prove a double blow. Not only were England to be based in money-guzzling Japan, but we also found ourselves in exalted company, the group of death to be precise. Argentina knocked us out of the World Cup in both 1986 and 1998; we hadn't beaten Sweden since 1968; and Nigeria were the strongest team in Africa. With Argentina tipped to win the group, our route to the World Cup podium had the potential run of France, Brazil, Argentina (again) and Italy. If we were to win, then we would have to win in style.

21. INDIA: THE CRICKETING SOUTH

You can smell it before you land. The must, the magic, creeping in through the vents of the plane to enchant, lament and deceive. We were about to plunge into a billion-strong world steeped in cultural mysticism, an ever-changing landscape of beauty and squalor, cities roaring into the e-age future amid crumbling infrastructures and staggering poverty, rural life unchanged for thousands of years and a people nuts about cricket.

'Actually, more people in India play football than cricket,' stated our man from the Indian Football Association. 'All thirty-eight States in India play football, only twelve play cricket.' He was very proud of this fact.

'Who do you think will win the World Cup?' I asked.

'Australia,' he replied, without hesitation. I tried to remind him that Australia had not qualified, but he was resolute; Australia would win the World Cup. He may have been working for the Indian Football Association, but he was talking cricket.

India boasts some of the world's greatest natural defences. Soaring mountain ranges, waterless deserts, mighty rivers and, of course, the understanding of cricket. Yet, of 21 attempted invasions of India over the centuries, eighteen have been successful. Could we add our names to the likes of

Alexander the Great, Darius the Persian, and Babur the Turk? The table had begun its approach run.

My plan was simple: find Matt, hit the Indian FA, nobble the touring English cricket team, see the Taj Mahal, track down His Holiness the Dalai Lama, then head for Everest.

I landed in Mumbai (Bombay) with the table and Will, a friend from home who had bravely volunteered to help at a school in Calcutta for six months. He had been to India before. As we touched down he turned to me and grinned. 'You are going to love this.'

Bombay was to be my first taste of a country that no amount of fancy superlatives can truly describe. The airport was a dirty chaos and we fought for nearly two hours to get out into the early morning Bombay crowd where, waiting for us, were the mosquitoes – almost as many in number and annoyance as the taxi drivers scrambling for our bags. My senses were assaulted. The noise, the dust, the crumbling air of past glories and a booming population swirled around me. The biggest impact by far was made minutes later as I caught my first horrifying sights of true poverty.

It is India's stark contrasts that both attract and repel foreign visitors. Some are on the first plane out, others never leave. As we were to find out, it is only by embracing everything that India has to offer, both the good and the bad, that you can even begin to understand it.

What in Europe are problems to solve, in Asia become limitations to accept. Certain events must simply be acknowledged and can only be worked around. To the Western tourist, India can appear full of such immobility, such as regularly being assured, categorically, that the hotel you are seeking no longer exists, or attempting to post a parcel without having had it checked (before it can be checked it must be wrapped, but once wrapped, it cannot be checked).

Our first task was to find Matt. Mumbai boasts majestic colonial buildings, crowds of colourful street-life, Asia's largest slums, and the home of Bollywood, but Matt would not be there. Turning down bit parts in one of the umpteen Hindi films churned out each year, we could not resist a childish peek at the 'Wankhede' Stadium before jumping on a train south to Margao and the beaches of Goa. If Matt were anywhere he would be on a beach.

There are a lot of beaches in Goa. Our chances of running into Matt were slim. But on the train south I had my first taste of Indian magic. I was sitting opposite a white-robed Indian man, a spitting image of one of the bad guys from *Indiana Jones and the Temple of Doom*. He was smiling at me in a direct and unnerving fashion. Finally he leaned forward, clasped my hands, and in a quiet but controlled voice said, 'I can see you have a lot of dreams.' He sat back again looking smug, as though he had solved a great problem, or lifted a mighty burden off my shoulders, then proceeded to explain.

'Keep smiling,' he said after a lengthy talk about energy, auras, tantric healing and visualisation, 'because when you smile people come to you. Things happen.' Content that he had taught me enough, he was silent for the rest of the journey, but a twinkle remained in his watchful eye.

The first beach we hit, we found him. Basking in the setting sun, lobster tan glowing, Matt looked at peace. Unbeknown to him it was only seconds before he was to be dragged back into the hectic world of adventures with a football table. I tapped him on the shoulder and gave him the fright of his life.

Nestled into the Nehru Stadium just outside the small, sunny town of Margao in Goa, the Indian FA was something of an anticlimax. Since it potentially covered a talent pot of over a billion people I had expected a little more than two unoccupied, paint-peeling rooms many miles from the major cities of the country. We eventually managed to nab a short chubby man in his thirties who was locking up the room next door. His name was Anil Kamat. He worked for the Goa Football Association and informed us that the staff of the All India FA were currently up in Delhi on business. Training inside the stadium itself were not the elite of Indian football youth, but rather the participants of an Under-12s sports day.

In Bombay we had seen banners loudly preaching, 'Ban

cricket for the sake of India sports.' Mr Kamat explained: 'The government is totally looking after cricket, not other sports. Other sports need more money otherwise it is not possible as there are no compulsory sports at school. We are the second largest populated country in the world but about sports we are right down there because of this government policy.'

'What do you think the score would be between England and India?' I asked while packing away the table after doing the necessaries. He paused thoughtfully, then replied, 'I think it is very difficult for England to beat India, in India,' and sat back smugly. He was talking cricket again. The 'Ban Cricket' campaign could take some time.

Buses and trains, delays and cancellations, crowds and sweat, bumps and rally driving, a night sleeping on a bus station floor and the table's closest shave with death yet took us to the small, hilly town of Madikeri. We were met by riots.

According to a sign at the station it was 'Vigilance Awareness Week'. Judging by the age of the sign, it had been 'Vigilance Awareness Week' for some time. The week we arrived appeared to be more in tune with vigilantism. Several cases of sacrilegious vandalism between Hindus and Muslims had sparked retributive attacks leaving numerous dead. As we stepped off the bus three trucks of armed police sped past us into town.

The Kodagu district in which Madikeri lies is hailed as India's Switzerland (minus snow, chalets, yodelling, fondue and about a thousand metres in height). The region did have rolling hills and clean air, and provided a much-needed break from the pollution of the lowlands, but it is difficult to compare Swiss and Indian habits and lifestyles.

Kodagu was to be our training ground for something wilder, a dream that captures every inch of the imagination: Everest. Until now the table had always been carried over one shoulder in the bag made by Mike's mum. For hiking this was not possible due to the intense pain that set in after only a mile or so. Buying some rope, we lashed the table to the back of my rucksack. Our guide watched on, bemused, before leading us off into the hills. We knew it before, but now it was brutally confirmed: carrying a football table up to Everest would require a tad more fitness. The highest peak in the Kodagu district was 1,750 metres. To get to Everest we would have to climb to over 5,000 metres in altitude and notch up some 10,000 metres of actual ascent on the long walk in; and it would be midwinter.

As I delicately lifted my pack back onto my aching torso for the second day, Vijay, our guide, informed us that we might have to run from elephants. At that moment I would have been entirely content to let them trample the table, and me with it. Apparently, should you choose to flee, climbing the nearest tree will not save you from an angry elephant. If it can't knock the tree down, it will wait. A local man had recently fallen foul of this tactic and died. After waiting two and a half days, dehydrated and exhausted, he had fallen out of his tree and under the feet of the elephant he had troubled. Remember, elephants never forget.

Neither do policemen. Threatening a policeman is never a good idea, especially in a foreign country. Before leaving for the table training-trek, Matt nearly landed us in a lot of trouble. Unable to get to sleep because of Hindi music screeching from the TV next door, he had taken affairs into his own hands and, after they ignored a polite initial plea for silence, he charged round and loudly abused them.

The next morning, we walked out of town to a waterfall. On the way back, slowly plodding up a long hill in the heat, Matt stopped in his tracks. Ahead, on the brow of the hill, hands on hips, fighter pilot shades reflecting the glaring sun and uniform neatly arranged, stood a policeman, staring down at us. 'That's one of the guys I shouted at last night,' whispered Matt, not nearly as boldly as his declarations twelve hours earlier. 'Shit,' he added.

We were in a country lane, two miles away from the nearest houses. There were no witnesses. We were well and truly at his mercy. The policeman drew himself up to his full height as we approached. He appeared alone and unarmed, but just as my spirits rose with this discovery, a police jeep rattled over the hill and halted alongside him. He was not alone and he was not unarmed.

'Conquer thyself, conquer the world' had been the motto for Vigilance Awareness Week. If my shoulders survived the next three days of trekking with the table on my back I would certainly be ready for anything, but my more immediate existence was now in question. There seemed a frightening possibility that we might be conquered by someone else before we had a chance to conquer ourselves.

The policeman's head wobbled from side to side as he sized us up. Then he hit us: 'Would you like a lift?' It was the last thing I had expected and we both stood in stunned silence. It was almost an anti-climax, as if we had wanted a beating. A lift doesn't make nearly as good a story. Hopefully, bowel-shaking fear will suffice.

Once more our prejudices had been unjustified. 'You like the English then?' I asked. 'Oh yes,' replied the driver of the jeep. 'There is English in us all. This is India.'

Having subsequently proceeded thoroughly to conquer my shoulders, I was looking forward to sitting back in the sun, beer in hand for a few days, learning a bit about the mystical game of cricket. Our first few weeks in India had been spent eating with our hands, pissing virtually in the street and, outside the cities, washing in streams. We marvelled at the basic lifestyles, the colourful sari dress of the women and the religious ceremonies and beliefs that pervade all aspects of Indian life. Bangalore was a stark contrast. Bright, flashing neon signs, Nike, Adidas, Levi's, Western brand name stores, KFC, bars, nightclubs and girls shunning their saris and attired in Western garb.

I have never been a big fan of cricket. It always seems to rain mid-test and inevitably ends in a draw. At school, the idea of the local giant hurling rocks at me before I was confined to a mind-numbing number of hours standing in the outfield just didn't strike a chord. However, I approached the third test of the England cricket tour of India with an open mind. I was ready to sit back with my beer and give it another try. Sachin Tendulkar, India's talismanic batsman, was present and both sides were promising victory. It rained. They drew.

After the events of 11 September 2001 and the subsequent bombing of Afghanistan it was feared that the England team might be targets for further attacks. Fortunately the tour went ahead but with startling levels of security. The team will thus be thrilled to learn that we managed to walk, talk and wait our way past two metal detectors, four sets of Indian security and befriend the two guards at the back door to the team's changing room, all while carrying a huge purple bag and a rucksack full of electrical equipment.

It was not the team we were seeking to nobble, however, so we decided not to give them a scare. It was Ian Botham and David Gower we were after. Both former cricket legends for England, they have since distinguished themselves further: Botham for much charity work and various revelations involving Miss Barbados, and Gower for his dry wit on the TV show *They Think It's All Over* alongside Gary Lineker and Nick Hancock. It did not take very much to get past the security and up into the press centre where they worked.

While we were at it we also got two days of free grandstand seating in the members-only clubhouse. According to the robed gentleman next to me on the first day, I was sitting in front of an Indian princess. The same white-garmented guru also attempted to cure my sore throat by cosmic healing. When I revealed that I was a bit under the weather he gave me a shock by reaching out and grabbing my neck. After thirty seconds or so he slowly removed his hand and shook it, as though shaking off water or dirt. Sadly, I then had to lie for the next hour about how much better I felt.

'Quite frankly, lads, I couldn't give a monkey's about football.' Gower wasn't as friendly as we had hoped. It seemed like we had caught him at a bad time. This was not the reaction I had expected. Having just finished a live TV interview on the pitch in front of the clubhouse, he was walking back into it when I tried to nobble him. Taken aback, he seemed bemused by my tale about a football table, so threw something back at me about monkeys and walked off.

It was quite a sorry moment. Such a curt, uninterested

rebuff left no room for a cheery comeback or fighting talk, just an 'Oh well, guess that's that then', and back to guessing when the rain might stop for the Indians to resume their potential rout.

Indians are nuts about cricket. The vast majority are also exceptionally poor. While the visiting English, and comparatively wealthy Indians, forked out 100 rupees (about £1.26) for plastic garden chairs and plenty of space in the '100 rupee stand', the masses piled into the screaming, partisan cauldron that was the '50 rupee stand'. For day two of the test I decided to take the plunge.

Sitting on the concrete steps, the only white face in the rapidly filling stand, I attracted a lot of attention, not least because of my England shirt. When India came out to bat, every 'four' brought a torrent of wild abuse in my direction. Sachin Tendulkar, their hero, made a mockery of the English bowling and the packed stadium was overjoyed. With Tendulkar stroking away balls to the boundary, the impoverished throngs beamed from ear to ear.

No smile was bigger than that of Peter. I had seen him on the street when we first arrived in Bangalore. A very young, short, skinny lad with brow-length brown hair, he had approached me and begged that I give him money for a doctor's prescription. You experience a never-ending stream of beggars in India and have to harden your heart. I walked on by. I gave money to disabled beggars and the helpless old ladies on the train station platforms, but for him, I walked on by.

I felt bad. There are many scams to get tourists to part with their money, but more often than not there are real pleas for help. It is very easy to carry on walking, thinking about your own travel budget and forgetting basic humanity – these people have no home, little food, no possessions and no future. You cannot help everybody and it is a tough call whether by giving handouts you encourage begging which undermines and distracts people from attempting to earn a living through genuine work initiatives; but no handout is too small.

The second time I saw him I just did not have the heart to

say no. Excited, he thanked me profusely and led the way off down the main street. It took a long time to reach the stall from which he ordered the medicine and to which I handed over the money. Doubts had been running through my mind, but they were dispelled by his story.

Peter lived on the streets, an orphan. He had run away from his orphanage when he could take the beatings no longer. They had been so severe he now had trouble passing urine. 'You know what urine is?' he said, looking up at me with big, wide eyes, eyes filled with pure innocence.

Peter told his tale as though he was the luckiest boy on earth. Barefoot and dirty, he jabbered away at my side as we walked, asking questions about England and the English, ever inquisitive, eager to learn and dream. As the chemist went through the doctor's tatty prescription (he had been begging for ten days), I braced myself for the tally. Three hundred rupees, not even four pounds; four pounds to enable a young boy to pass urine pain-free. Nothing.

As we walked back into the main area of shops, he kept thanking me. 'Today is like Christmas; I shall always remember this, thank you. Will you come say hello tomorrow?' He was a little boy alone on the streets. I had offered an arm of friendship and couldn't just walk away, so I decided to really make his day; it was the least I could do. I would soon leave to carry on a tour around the world, while he would be left alone to battle and beg for his next meal.

His eyes exploded with light as I handed him the ticket. 'I think you should have this,' I said. He stopped dead in his tracks, took the ticket and held it as if it was the most precious thing in the world. He was in disbelief. You could see the questions rushing through his brain, too fast to speak. He had never been to a cricket match before. 'You'd better hurry,' I said, 'lunch will have finished and they'll be coming out again. Guess who's batting?'

'Who?' he asked, eyes bulging with excitement.

'Sachin.' The little intake of stunned breath made my year. He readied to go, nervous with joy, but then checked, looked around and found me unmoved. 'What about you? I'm not going if you're not going.' It almost brought a tear to my eye.

Ian Botham was standing behind me all along. Matt, who was facing him, with the camera rolling, never told me, never batted an eyelid. The man we had been expressly trying to catch up with had been practising his golf swing anonymously behind me, and Matt forgot to mention it.

After watching Sachin Tendulkar almost notch up a century (to little Peter's unbridled delight), the rain ended any potential excitement on the pitch and probably saved us a mauling from the locals, so we had got back on the table trail and in search of the big man, Botham. Breaching security was by now a doddle as they recognised us, and we had been seen chatting with the Secretary of the Bangalore Cricket Club, thereby securing tacit approval. Obviously we hadn't known who he was at the time, but we carried it off and managed not to get thrown out in the process.

It was then that the silver fox reappeared. Bowling around the corner of the press centre, Gower was slightly startled to see us again. We were in supposedly more secure areas. He broke into a relaxed smile and said, 'Sorry about before, lads, you caught me at a bad time.' He had a pleasant manner and found time to talk about squat toilets, fine wine, 'jug ears' Lineker and Nick Hancock, 'The greatest sportsman I know. He knows more about my career than I do.'

Sky TV had given its presenters the choice of joining the tour after all the hoo-ha about security, but there was never any doubt in Gower's mind. 'India's great. It's not the first time I've been here, but it's a fascinating country, the hospitality is great and since I first came everything's improved dramatically. You still have to pay an awful lot for a not very good bottle of wine, but there you go.'

Regarding himself as a 'lapsed' football fan, he refused to take up the table challenge – 'it's a matter of principle' – but did reckon that Botham would be more than happy to say hello. 'He'd probably break it he's so competitive. He was down here a minute ago, I'll go give him a nudge.' I turned to Matt. 'Down here a minute ago?' Matt laughed and told me about the golf swings. Much as I wanted to murder him, to his credit, he had secured some entertaining footage of 'beefy' and my complete ignorance of his presence.

After celebrating my birthday, rather randomly in the company of a Nepalese fighter pilot it, was time to move on. The jungle was calling. We were off in the footsteps of Baloo, Kaa and Mowgli. There was little chance of finding my masters, but there might be a tiger or two. We were still under a duty, though, to hit the England team hotel before we left.

Expecting heavy security, we were amazed to be able to stroll right in and up to the captain himself, Nasser Hussein. In truth we had a few beers at the bar first before Matt valiantly plucked up the confidence to approach Nasser as he finished his supper. Another guy called Matt, who we'd met at the stadium, then approached one of the bowlers, but both were dismissed with a depressed air. England had lost the series. On holiday, in their five-star hotel, the players were a bit down. We joined in with the Mexican lobby band's version of 'Moon River' instead.

22. INDIA: THE TIBETAN NORTH

Mowgli found freedom and friendship in Rudyard
Kipling's *Jungle Book*. In Kanha National Park, where
the book was set, I got nothing but food poisoning. So did
my younger brother, Malcolm. It was New Year's Eve.
Welcome to India.

Malc had joined the trip by flying into the hole that is
Chennai after putting on hold his bid to become a rock star.
Forced back into the real world, he had lined up a job at a
bank. With six months freedom remaining, and having successfully applied for World Cup tickets like myself, he joined
the table tour to Japan. Law of the sod dictated that my little brother would beat me in our first game on the table. He
obliged with glee.

Matt declared that he would not leave the Kanha
National Park until he had seen a tiger. While Malc and I
dashed back and forth from our lean-to greenhouse to the
field behind (there were no toilets), he got up early and
braved the freezing cold to roam the park in a jeep, and then
again at dusk, for two days: four trips, no sightings and
much discomfort. We were now on India's central plateau
and the nightly temperatures hit freezing. There had also
been a freak cyclone somewhere out to sea that had given
India some of its worst weather for years. Upon recovery,

Malc and I went out once. Much to the bemusement of the park authorities we took the table with us and, to Matt's unpublishable response, we saw four majestic tigers.

The tigers were an interlude on our long trek up into the far north of India in search of His Holiness the Dalai Lama. Taking in the Taj Mahal, Delhi, many trains and buses, more late-night Hindi film music, early morning mosques and Indian emergency medical care, it was quite a week.

It had started auspiciously. In Chennai, Malc and I met a forty-year-old Australian called Morris in one of the local snack bars. A father of three, and qualified as a doctor, he had spent twenty years of his life searching for a problem. Sporting a neatly trimmed beard, solid build and relaxed manner, he explained that he had found an ancient script in a boxload of inherited papers. Many journeys to many places over many painstaking years had revealed that the script was a prophecy. Discovered buried alongside its master's servant, the script held the solution to a problem that would arise some seven hundred years after it was written.

Morris finally thought he had found the problem to which his document held the key: the dispute between China and the Tibetan government in exile as to who was the real reincarnation of the Buddhist Karmapa of the North. Morris was now in India seeking an audience with the Dalai Lama, and his work had just been accepted by His Holiness for examination.

In turn we told him about our aim to try and seek an audience with the table. Laughing, he told us it would be 'nigh on impossible'. While still encouraging us to give it a try, he brought us down to earth as he explained the reality of getting close to the Buddhist equivalent of the Pope. 'It's his private secretary to whom you have to get a letter,' he said. 'He is the one man who could arrange something for you, but as you can expect, he is inundated by everybody.'

Tucking into our morning masala dosas and ignoring the usual glass of lethal tap water, we resolved to head to the home of His Holiness, up in McLeod Ganj, in a bid to reach him before he departed for a festival in Bodhgaya. It would be our only real hope. Morris's knowledge and advice had instilled a sense of realism and awe into us that, far from curtailing our dreams, had simply fanned the flames.

As his travels and research had brought him into close contact with Buddhism, Morris had become spiritually practised. I was therefore very surprised when this calm-talking man lost his temper as the Indian on the till made error after error in supplying him with his change. But that is what India can do to you; it gets to everyone, eventually. Everybody is human, no matter how spiritually content they are.

The Taj Mahal is a true wonder of the world. The building lived up to every expectation and we were lucky to see it. After all the security talk following 11 September, and a subsequent terrorist attack on the Indian Parliament, plans had been laid to camouflage the Taj. Yes, you read correctly. Only in India could someone even possibly suggest something as crazy as constructing a giant camouflage net to hide the massive, white, marble building from a cunning aerial bomber. Fortunately this plan to make an eyesore of one of the world's greatest wonders was scrapped.

Regrettably, the increased security fears put paid to any chance of taking the table into the Taj complex. We tried at each of the gates in turn, creating a crowd of mystified Indian onlookers as we hammed up our gesticulations at the unfortunate guards on duty. Eventually, we resorted to setting the table up in front of the southern gate. It caused a stampede of interest, completely blocking the street and driving the soldiers to distraction. The crowd were oblivious to the barking orders and, used to being beaten by impatient police sticks on a regular basis, were quite happy to stand their ground. Malc's cheeky attempt to bribe the policemen, however, did not exactly help the situation.

The solution in the end was to take the table down to the river behind the Taj. The view from there is arguably better than the classic, head on, catalogue shot inside the main complex. The sun sets behind the Taj and its orange reflection flickers in the river waters that wander past its northern confines. A boatman will pole you across the filthy expanse of water for a very negotiable fee. We had company in the form of a host of playful kids on the far bank who were distracted from their cheerful, cheeky begging attempts by the table, as was a newspaper reporter for the *Hindustan Times*.

The reporter was there to do a story and take pictures on security measures at the country's finest monument, but ended up running a piece on three English lads with a football table. A billion further unsuspecting people were exposed to our tale, via this magnificent monument to love.

Suffering from a nut allergy and travelling in Asia are not the best of combinations. A significant number of Asian dishes are laced with potentially lethal substances for allergy sufferers, and those meals that aren't may well be prepared with utensils that are. I resorted to employing my companions as tasters for every dish I was unsure of and then stuck rigidly to two or three that I knew were nut-free. Much as it was a shame to be denied the opportunity to explore the culinary delights of each region, it was marginally preferable to death or painful suffering.

It was on the one occasion when adventure got the better of me, my taste buds clamoured for more and I tried something new, that I was struck down. Allergic reactions are funny things. First I get a strange but distinct taste in the back of my throat. No teeth brushing, water swilling or vomiting can rid me of it. It is at this point that I know I am in trouble. I am meant to carry on my person, at all times, adrenalin injections, but these are invariably left in the hotel room, so a sprint to return to them swiftly ensues. The people I am eating with are normally calmly asked for the room key, address, or money for the swiftest form of local transport, then are left looking in bewilderment as my chair shoots back and I hurtle out of the room and off down the street, careering through the traffic in true Hollywood fashion. The adrenalin injection calms everything down. My throat relaxes and any rash disappears. But sometimes the reaction comes back at me, and that is when I need a hospital.

The hospital in Jabalpur was interesting to say the least.

My face and hands were swelling up at quite a rate and a rash had spread over my chest and back. Malc and Matt had piled me into a rickshaw and shouted at the unfazed driver to hurry. I was concentrating on my nads. I get a very, very itchy nether region. With a swollen face, struggling to breathe and desperately trying not to itch down below, I was hurried, by my concerned companions, into a dark, dirty corridor. While lacking any of the recognisable features of a hospital, it was one up on the first place the rickshaw driver had taken us – which was derelict.

Through the dim light of the bare bulbs hanging precariously from the high ceiling of the corridor, a local, shrouded in an oversized, badly knitted jumper, with a scarf wrapped around his head for warmth, signalled that a doctor could be found in a room on the right. To my relief the doctor spoke English but, unperturbed by my deathly appearance, beckoned me to wait. Scared by the extent of my reaction I attempted to explain that time was not on my side and that I was in dire need of adrenalin. He responded by putting a finger to his lips and pointing again to a seat. After what seemed to me like days of feverish suffering he waved me over and beckoned me to lie down on a padded bench.

The British adventurer George Hayward once said 'I shall wander the wilds of central Asia possessed of an insane desire to try the effects of cold steel across my throat.' In 1870 it happened. He was treacherously murdered in Dardistan by a local chieftain. My adventures caused me to feel the effects of cold steel only twice. Using needles that I had brought with me from home, the doctor inflicted two of the most painful injections I have ever had. My left buttock was sore for days.

Health problems should never be viewed as a barrier to travel, but common sense is needed. Although standards vary enormously across the globe, nearly all modern medicines are available across India and Asia for those with the money to pay for them – which is where your holiday insurance does what it says on the tin. Even more can be bought without a prescription over the counter. I had three serious reactions during my trip and survived them all thanks to a little bit of foresight and the care, concern and knowledge of my travel companions, Mike, Malc and Matt.

Surviving Delhi was something different. A hellish train journey deposited us there for a day before we swiftly escaped, catching a fourteen-hour bus up to Dharamshala in India's mountainous north.

Transport in general, in India, is one of the highlights. A highlight in the sense of a tale to tell, be it exasperating, amusing or simply different. On the trains, the incessant cry of 'Chai, Chai' (tea, tea), served in terracotta cups to be carelessly tossed out of the window once drained, along with the rest of any rubbish; the beggar kids crawling on hands and feet, using their solitary rag to sweep around your sandals in the hope of a rupee; your ability to hang out of the doors, your life in your hands, to admire the country-side; and the sheer length of some of the journeys shared with entire families, are a million miles from the sterile journeys of home.

With the buses it is often your responsibility to secure your own bags up on the roof of the bombed-out hulks that carry you. In rural areas necessity excludes comfort, establishing a policy that if two people get off a packed bus then four can get on. In Kodagu I counted 150 on a single bus. Schoolchildren formed human extensions to the seating arrangements, clinging to classmates who were already hanging out of the rear door as the bus set off again, forcing those inside to breath in that extra inch and haul them in.

Beside the common horrors of retching, belching, spitting, phlegming and snoring locals during our many hours and nights exploring the railroads of the nation, we suffered the usual trick of seat stealing. It was this that really got my goat, especially when it was literally a goat that got my seat. Through insistence, flustering and a basic reliance on our obvious inability to read Hindi, the offending locals per-suaded us that our seat was not in fact our seat. Once we had politely moved, apologised, then subsequently realised that it was in fact our seat and there were no others free for fourteen hours, there was no chance of getting it back.

Trying to manoeuvre around a cramped train carriage with three big rucksacks, a football table and camera bags as a host of people, boxes, sacks and animals are attempting to get on and off, or barge past, is difficult, disruptive and heated. Our final tactic was to refuse to move until the particular joker could produce a matching ticket with the correct seat number on it. It drove them mad, but sure enough they eventually acknowledged our right to the seats in question.

Amid one such mêlée, I confess to losing my temper when a local, who seemed about to reason quietly with me over the petulant actions of his friend, said ever so politely, 'Aren't people in England meant to have manners?' I lost it, completely. Even if we had wanted to, we were unable to move and they refused to show us their tickets, so we had no intention. Why on earth they didn't produce the tickets until the conductor came along I have no idea but, to my horror, on that particular occasion, they were right. We had identical seat numbers on an identically timetabled, but different, train. Only in India.

The spiritual leader of Tibet, His Holiness the 14th Dalai Lama, Tenzin Gyatso, lives in exile in India. In May 1949 the Communist Government of China signed a treaty declaring sovereignty over Tibet and shortly afterwards the army marched into the country to impose Chinese rule. It was the start of a brutal subordination that has left some 1.2 million Tibetans dead and destroyed 90 per cent of Tibet's monasteries and temples.

Against his wishes the Dalai Lama was advised to lead his people into exile in 1959. He escaped the Chinese by making a perilous crossing of the Himalayas on foot into India. Since that date some three hundred thousand Tibetans have made the same journey, ill equipped, through brutally cold conditions. Many more have died trying. India granted the exiled Tibetan government political asylum and now they continue their fight for freedom from the beautiful slopes of McLeod Ganj, under the watchful gaze of the snowy peaks and ridges that divide them from their homeland.

It is another world when compared with the fume-filled streets of Delhi. Perched up on the hillside among a host of fir trees, McLeod Ganj looks out over the plains of Himachal Pradesh, high enough to avoid the oppressive Indian heat and nursed instead by the fresh mountain air. It is a beautiful, peaceful place and the area was the perfect training ground for our fast-approaching Everest adventure. We also dared to hope that it might yield us the immense privilege of an audience with His Holiness.

Buddhism is not centred on a God, but is a system of philosophy and a code of morality. Essentially, it provides guidance on how to live a pure and compassionate life, and a lot of the teachings on how to manage anger and overcome worries are largely common sense. My favourite example of the logic imparted by His Holiness is this:

If you can solve a problem then there is no point worrying about it. If there is no solution to a problem then there is no point worrying about it either.

When you are angry, he says, look at yourself in the mirror. Do you like what you see? Neither do the people around you, so how do you expect them to react? We cannot overcome all our enemies, but by overcoming our own hatred we effectively overcome all our enemies. If everybody took two seconds to think like this, imagine how much happier our lives would become.

The prospect of meeting this remarkable man, a master of his emotions to the extent that he has the power to forgive those who have tortured and raped his homeland, and a man who travels the world campaigning for peace, freedom and inner contemplation, was possibly the greatest opportunity of my life. I was sure that his infectious smile would be further widened by our tale. Football unites people and throughout our journey we had sparked many great moments of excitement and laughter that had broken down barriers of language, race and class. To have the blessing of His Holiness would be quite something.

I wrote a letter to his secretary and submitted it at the

security gate to his house. Audiences, we had learned, were only by advance booking (of at least four months) and a special committee existed to sift through the thousands of requests. We would have to be extremely lucky. The fact that we had delivered our letter in person, having travelled so far, could only count in our favour.

Our wait was broken by an email from FIFA that lit up the inbox of my email account. Daniela, the Swiss girl from Iran, had come through for us. It was from the 'Head of World Cup Events'. Her cousin had received the letter and video clips I had sent and been quite taken by it, to the extent that he passed it on to FIFA's Director of Communications, the man who dealt with press passes and who, he said, would contact us within a fortnight. We were a massive step closer to our dream.

Feeling lucky, we hurried through torrential rain down to the Dalai Lama's hilltop lodgings to find out the latest progress report on our letter. We had the table and the camera and to our nervous delight were beckoned into the security hut, awarded security passes and led inside the gates that we had previously been told were impassable. We walked past security barracks, a basketball court and into a peaceful little garden with a modest-looking, raised bungalow on the left and the remaining three sides lined with homely, single-storey offices.

A far cry from the pomp and circumstance of the Vatican, this was the humble abode of one of the world's holiest and most revered individuals. Winner of the Nobel Peace prize in 1989, it was from here that His Holiness conducted his day-to-day campaign for the freedom of his people, while practising and teaching his Buddhist beliefs. We had been invited inside with a football table.

His secretary, personal friend and general right-hand man, Tenzin Geyche Tethong, was a kind-looking fellow. Short by Western standards but solidly built, like most Tibetans, he must have been about fifty, with grey hair and big glasses. He had a warm face, the trademark high, broad, fleshy cheekbones of Tibetans that are so welcoming, and was wearing a relaxed shirt with a V-neck jumper, cotton trousers and black shoes. He was, naturally, rather bemused as I tried to explain our story. For a man who deals daily with thousands of requests by religious practitioners, Tibetan refugees, leading world media, and many, many followers, our reasons must have stood out from the crowd.

'We'd like to challenge His Holiness to a game,' I ventured. I felt ridiculous, but you just never know until you ask. Having explained our hopes of adding the blessing of His Holiness to our trip, he replied that he was sure it would have made His Holiness smile, but that, unfortunately, he was a very busy man.

He was not at home. He was also unwell. His physician had ordered him to rest. After teachings in Bodhgaya he would be returning to McLeod Ganj, but would go into a strict retreat for several months, before commencing a tour of Europe. Our window of opportunity just wasn't wide enough. We had already dramatically altered our plans and time was against us. Perhaps in the next life we will have the honour.

Mr Tenzin Geyche Tethong was also a very busy man, but as we talked his initial bemusement evaporated. He agreed to answer a few questions and give us a game. Watching his curiosity develop over that half an hour was quite an insight. By the time we left he was thoroughly enjoying himself and chuckling away. He felt like an old friend; but he was an old friend whose country had been taken from him.

'I honestly think Tibet will be free again,' he said. 'The situation in Tibet is very bad and things are in fact getting worse, but what His Holiness says seems to make a lot of sense ... he feels that because of the tremendous changes that are taking place [in China], changes for the better, that sooner or later it is inevitable China will become more free, more democratic and when that happens, the situation in Tibet will definitely improve. If you look at it from that angle, when China becomes more democratic, I think yes there is possibility for Tibet to be free.

'Even as a Tibetan,' he continued, 'I am really amazed with the strong spirit of the Tibetan people, especially when I hear about many of the young Tibetans who know very well what the consequences will be if the Chinese arrest them. They still go and demonstrate and do something that the Chinese are annoyed about. Unfortunately, even now, these people are being imprisoned, tortured, for such acts as waving the Tibetan national flag, or saying Tibet is independent, or saying the Chinese get out of Tibet. I'm amazed.' He broke off and his eyes trailed downwards, away from my own and the camera, in mournful remembrance.

The prospect of seeing China at the World Cup, lapping attention and applause on the world stage, made him sad. 'Of course, in some ways I might feel sad that Tibetans don't have the same opportunity. Tibetans just love sport and I am sure that in the future, I don't know if they'd be world-class, but in the future there will definitely be a football team. Since the occupation of Tibet, Tibetans not having many of the things other free countries enjoy, always makes us feel sad, like a world football tournament where Tibetans are not represented. We've lost our freedom, we've lost our country.' Despite this deep hurt he held no desire to see the Chinese team lose and wished them well, but at the mention of a Tibetan side his heart appeared to swell.

'His Holiness says that because sometimes things are difficult, it makes us stronger and more determined. It makes us more determined to carry on our struggle for justice.'

It was an engagingly powerful half an hour. As he talked, his eyes glistened with both sadness and hope. He focused on my face as he spoke, giving his words the emotiveness they needed to convey the horrors that were, and still are, being perpetrated in Tibet. That he can continue to talk about compassion and forgiveness is a tribute to both himself and his people.

McLeod Ganj was emptying. Every day the square was filled with hundreds of orange-robed monks stowing bags on roofs and piling onto buses heading for Bodhgaya. We were to follow the monks some of the way, but our destination, unhappily, was not Bodhgaya. England were playing a one-day match against India in Calcutta; we had been distracted by cricket. I wanted to get Botham on the table.

We broke our journey to Calcutta with a stay in Varanasi, one of the holiest places in India. After twelve hours on a bus from McLeod Ganj, then fifteen hours on a train from Delhi, tired, and feeling harassed by rickshaw wallahs, I succeeded in supplementing my failing humour by slipping up in cow shit on the banks of the Ganges. Sixty thousand people a day bathe in the sacred Ganges off the concrete ghats of Varanasi; I was not about to join them. Along the same stretch of river thirty sewers discharge their largely untreated effluent. Apparently, water safe for bathing should have less than 500 faecal coliform bacteria per 100 millilitres of water. Samples at Varanasi have shown 1.5 million. The locals use it to clean their teeth.

The water of the mother Ganges is said to wash away all sins, making the city an auspicious place in which to die. Every day hundreds of people are burned on the city's ghats, their ashes sprinkled into the holy river. If you cannot afford the required amount of wood for the official pyres, then bodies are often cast in direct. We hired one of the many tiny boats for a row up the river; both bodies and, to my surprise, dolphins slid under our oars.

The table was set up on one of the many non-burning ghats. As the setting sun cast the city in a magical light the sadhus (holy men) gathered round in awe. The various colours of their body paints mirrored the variations in the sunset as it glistened on the water, basked on the bold faces of the tall river-front buildings, and vanished into the deep alleyways between them. Varanasi is a city that challenges many of our most refined Western ideals, but enchants with a vibrant mysticism that will remain with the visitor for many years to come and which embraced the table in its own unique, auspicious way.

'This is not your train,' said the conductor of our 7.26 p.m. train to Calcutta. There were, it turned out, in true Indian fashion, two 7.26 p.m. trains to Calcutta. 'It is only ten minutes behind. Please get off here and wait.' We obliged at the next stop, Gaya.

At 1.30 a.m., five hours later, our train finally arrived. The doors were locked. The passengers sitting within view ignored our pleas to open them. It blew my mind. As they turned their heads away, rage swept through me. India had finally got to me. I lost it, completely. We had waited for hours, kicking our heels in the dank, dusty darkness. Our chances of making the cricket had been hit for six. I was not alone. One glance through the red mist at the tired, drawn and angered faces of my companions showed that they too had been pushed too far. It must have been quite a sight. We attacked that train. Shouting, kicking and swearing, we waved our fists at the skies, at the carriage, at the passengers and at any tout or rickshaw wallah who came within a fifty-metre radius.

We should have learned by now that the big man upstairs generally has something better in store for us. We were after all, lucky bastards. Gaya, it turned out, was but a bone-jarring, forty-minute rickshaw ride away from Bodhgaya, the most important Buddhist pilgrimage destination in the world, and where the Buddhist Kalashakra festival was about to begin. Our cricketing ambitions had been stumped, but we were subsequently treated to two days journeying into the beautiful, palm-ridden Bodhgaya, to marvel at the thousands upon thousands of Buddhist monks and the legendary Bodhi tree, under which Buddha attained enlightenment.

On a slightly smaller scale of success, I received news from home that the *Guardian* newspaper had featured me as their 'Graduate of the Week'. They must be avid readers of the *Hindustan Times*.

Among many other sacrifices, Tibetan monks must abstain from football. On becoming a monk they take many oaths, which include a renunciation of sport and competition. Yet football is a great love and many stories exist of monks sneaking out of their monasteries to watch games. In McLeod Ganj we saw an infamous Tibetan film called *The Cup*. It tells the tale of a young monk called Orygen who snuck out of his monastery in the mountains to the local village to watch the 1998 World Cup, and of his tribulations in convincing the Abbot to allow the monks to hire a TV to watch the final.

The end credits reveal that it was a true story, that Orygen still dreams of founding the first Tibetan national team and that many monks were excitedly awaiting the next World Cup.

At Bodhgaya, to our disbelief, we met a monk who not only knew Orygen, but was virtually related to him. Picking a particularly busy street, we had decided to test out the monk-pulling power of the table. I climbed up a tree with the camera and Malc opened up our big, purple bag. We nearly started a riot. Within seconds Malc had disappeared from view in a stampede of shaved heads and orange robes. Physically jostling for position as the games got under way, cheers and boos attracted impossible levels of interest from the milling throngs. They absolutely loved it. The police absolutely did not.

Ghinley Gorji had travelled down to Bodhgaya from a remote, mountainous monastery of four pupils and a single teacher in Bhutan, three days on horseback from the Chinese border. Ghinley loved football. After the police had gone, he led us through a short maze of alleyways to a quiet courtyard where we could set up the table again and continue playing.

Ghinley knew Orygen from Bhutan where the young monk lived. He told us that *The Cup* was very true to life. To see games he (Ghinley) had to sneak out to the nearest village just like in the film. Rising to the occasion, this extraordinarily friendly young monk had an even better tale for us. His cousin was the national goalkeeper of Bhutan. The trip was getting more ridiculous by the day. The odds were too great for it to be anything other than magic. Getting on the wrong identical train, then getting locked out of the right one, then, out of two hundred thousand monks, stumbling into Ghinley, who had such football connections. I've said it once and I'll say it again, magic happens. What we didn't know was that there was a further, odds-shattering twist still to come, later on in our journey.

Before departing Ghinley's glowing company we asked him, 'How good is the Bhutanese national team?' He laughed hard before finally choosing the word, 'improving', and beaming one of his unforgettable smiles.

23. NEPAL

We had seen a whole mountain range, little by little, the lesser to the greater until, incredibly higher in the sky than imagination had ventured to dream, the top of Everest itself appeared.

George Mallory

Nepal. The roof of the world. Home to Mount Everest, the highest point on earth. 'Surely the Gods live here,' said Rudyard Kipling's Kim. Our aim was to take the table to the Gods, to carry it for three lung-busting weeks to the roof of the world and the foot of the world's greatest mountain.

With every mile north of the Indian border the landscape grew greener and cleaner. Our bus joined the path of a vast riverbed, snaking between ever-growing hills, lush with forest or etched by paddy field terraces, resplendent in their many shades of green. As the riverbed narrowed into a dramatic gorge, the road started to climb. It twisted and turned its way into the heart of Nepal and finally, as the mighty, snow-laden peaks rose from behind the lines of hills, delivered us over the horizon into the mysterious and chaotic valley of Kathmandu.

Six months earlier a tragedy of love had plunged the unstable governance of Nepal into further disorder. The

Crown Prince Dipendra had argued with his parents over his choice of bride. His love was deemed unsuitable and marriage had been forbidden. In a rage of despair he massacred the King, Queen and numerous other members of the royal family before turning his gun on himself. The news rocked Nepal. His uncle was, for the second time, hastily crowned King of Nepal, fulfilling an astronomer's prophecy that he would be enthroned twice (he had been a child king in the 50s when the true monarch had temporarily fled to India as a result of civil unrest).

The deeply religious nation was shocked by the massacre. Public outpouring of grief for the royal family, and disbelief at such an act, aroused a renewed discontent focused on the replacement King and the Prime Minister. Troubled by Maoist insurgency, the King had called a state of emergency.

Kathmandu was under a strict curfew and police checks littered our route from the border. Although we were made continually aware of the situation, and suffered first-hand experience of Maoist attacks, tourists are usually safe. Recognising foreigners as Nepal's main source of income, the rebels were smart enough not to cut off the hand that feeds them. Trekkers had been stopped at gunpoint and relieved of their belongings but were issued with receipts for everything taken and were not harmed in any way. I was able to fill my postcards home with tales of shootouts, bank robberies, bombings and minefields although I was never in any immediate personal danger.

'You don't assault Everest,' said climbing legend Ed Viesters, 'you sneak up on it and then get the hell outta there.' Former Tengboche monk Phurba Sorba explained the Buddhist view: 'A goal can never be reached through force or by aspiration and ambition alone. But if the nature of the motivation is pure, stemming from a compassionate desire to help others, the goal will almost always be reached.'

Our goals were simple and our intentions pure. We wished to take the table to the roof of the world, respectfully to embrace the might of the mountains and to introduce the table to the Sherpas of the Everest region. The omens were good as another series of exciting developments and outrageous meetings swept our way.

Cristina D'Alessio, whom we had met in the Azadi Stadium in Tehran, had passed on our tale to her colleague at the Asian Football Confederation, Steve Flynn. He had sent an email saying hello and that the AFC's football TV show based in Singapore, which went out across Asia, would like to do a feature on us. The ball was well and truly rolling. After the incessant worry about the success of the trip and the daily concerns that it would all fall flat, that I would reach the World Cup to a chorus of *nyet*s, events and opportunities were now simply unfolding in front of us. I was beginning to believe in the unbelievable and the unbelievable was beginning to seek us out.

Cue the entry of Per Henrikson. Since the age of 21, Per had been travelling the world touting his services as a professional goalkeeper. Over the years he had played in Ireland, England, Pakistan and Bangladesh before coaching national sides in the Philippines, Sri Lanka and Costa Rica. At the age of 32, while recovering from a shoulder operation, he caught sight of the table in our bare-walled, three-bed room at the Hotel Annapurna and introduced himself. He was looking for a job as a goalkeeping coach to the national team of, wait for it, Bhutan.

The unlikeliness of the connections had us all clutching our sides with laughter and disbelief for the rest of the day. We hatched plans to travel to Bhutan after our trek to meet our friend Ghinley, his cousin and the rest of the national team of Bhutan. 'Bhutan is one of the remotest kingdoms of the world,' said Per. 'The government wants to keep it that way so they impose rules saying that without an invitation you can only go as a tour group and have to spend 100 dollars a day. Televisions are banned. It's a hard-core, remote place. You guys have just made my day.'

Unfortunately, due to a lack of time and money we never made it to Bhutan. Per, however, did make the journey to the mountain kingdom, and in March of that year exceeded his goal, becoming head coach of the Bhutanese national team.

Our other plan of hitting the Nepalese FA also fell by the

wayside. Our contact, the President, had lost his wife to cancer just three days before. Out of respect we decided not to
call.

Nepal was never going to have been about the football
anyhow. A lot of the country is so mountainous that football
simply is not even conceivable. Nepal, for us, was to be
about something equally as emotional, something that can
seize and dispense with the entire spectrum of your emotions
at its whim, in the same style as football: Mount Everest.

Throughout the journey so far our minds had been casting
ahead to this moment, for Everest is a mountain that captures the imagination like no other. Its history alone grants
an awe that draws people towards its treacherous slopes.
Mallory and Irving, Hillary and Tenzing are names that
inspire and bewitch with their tales. Success and tragedy,
Everest has them all. I cannot even begin to dream of the
feeling of standing atop its mighty peak, standing literally on
top of the world. To date, over 180 people have lost their
lives trying. Of great sadness is the fact that a third of those
who have died were Sherpas. One high-altitude porter has
been well quoted in summing up the dangers of an attempt
on Everest: 'Tomorrow or the next life, you never know
which will come first.'

We followed the path taken by Mallory and Irving. In
their day the airport at Lukla was not even dreamed of. The
road from Kathmandu stopped at Jiri, from where it took
seven days trekking to pass Lukla and reach the Sherpa capital of Namche Bazaar. Deep in the mountains and perched
1,000 metres above the Dodh Kosi river at an altitude of
3,400 metres, Namche is the final staging post. It is a last
chance to replace faulty gear and stock up on Mars bars.

The main trekking season starts in March. We had heard
horror stories of trails packed with panting tour parties,
slipping and sliding in the freshly thawed mud of spring,
but, as it was February, we were delighted to have the entire
national park virtually to ourselves. In January of the previous year some 250 people had been in the park, in February,
650, in March . . . seven thousand.

Walking in sync with us each day, at varying paces and

start times from their different lodgings, were five Aussies, two Frenchmen, and a couple of English lads. The latters' gap year drinking habits were curtailed by the fact that the Maoists had stolen all the rum, but the Aussies suffered far greater hardship later in the trek, eventually being forced to call for an air rescue by Russian helicopter to take them to Kathmandu.

As a direct result of the booming trekking trade, there are plenty of lodges dotted every few hours or so along the trail. We were their only guests, so the beds were free; we paid our keep by eating. The lodges consisted of simple stone or wood constructions with plywood twin rooms barely big enough for two beds, or rooms with one long bunk sleeping 8–10. To keep out the cold we would huddle, every evening, around a dung-fuelled stove with the wife of the lodge. Our few phrases of Nepalese were richly rewarded beyond their efforts. 'Ramro' (good) and 'mero khushi' (me happy), accompanied by a belly rubbing gesture, became trademark comments, always quick to bring giggles of laughter from our overly generous cook and host.

To see how they lived was humbling. High up in the mountains, exposed to extreme cold with only badly fitted wooden planks, stone walls and blankets to fight it. They had very few possessions and worked hard during the day on the terraced paddies, cutting wood, building lodges or working as porters. Yet they are some of the most privileged people in the world because they are happy. Happy to live every day in the lap of the gods, blessed with the fresh, clean, exhilarating air of the Himalayas, free from the trials of city rat races, Western decadences and the vices that come with them.

The porters were a sensation. To pass a man in threadbare rubber plimsolls carrying 40 kilograms in a wicker basket, via a strap across his forehead, quickly puts paid to any quiet mutterings of discomfort. The table, in its voluminous purple sheath, lashed to my pack, made me look like the back of a bus and attracted much interest from the Sherpas. As my load weighed a mere 20 kilograms I felt like a fraud; my shoulders over the first few days reminded me that it was all relative.

'Life in the mountains draws out the character of those that journey there,' says Pheriche Aid Post doctor Jim Litch in a book on Everest. 'Maybe this is the reason why we climb, to see ourselves at the core, not packaged and contained as we are when living within the constraints of technology and consumerism.' I was worried Matt might see a bit too much. It was only down to eight degrees Celsius on our first couple of nights, yet he was wrapped in a six (yes six) season sleeping bag with his thermals and woolly hat on. We were due nightly plunges to minus fifteen when the water bottles next to our beds would freeze solid and our sleeping bags would be crusty with ice. The banter began, but to his credit Matt was to wrestle with his very core and come out fighting.

Badly fitting boots were of a far greater concern in the first few days. I had picked up a decent pair of second-hand boots in Kathmandu. It meant blisters breaking them in, but I had had no intention of carrying a pair all the way from home. They had fitted perfectly in the shop, but only hours into the trail my heel was catching and by day two I was nearly crippled.

Having hauled myself step by step up and over the snow-covered Lamjura pass at 3,500 metres on day three, the pain overcame me, and at the start of day four I collapsed in a heap on the trail. Tears running down my face, and swearing profusely, I threw off my boots and shook my fist at the sky. Enough was enough and desperate measures were called for.

Once I had finished a second round of abuse, this time unjustifiably directed at Matt and Malc, I put on the spare pair of rainbow-coloured woolly socks in my bag, then wrapped them up with duct tape to make rudimentary footwear, and blazed off in a heavenly, pain-free, surge of relief. The only problem came on the next descent. The path was muddy in places and my shiny duct tape, weighed down by a football table, was never going to grip. The table and I managed to stay vertical for an impressive ten metres or so before careering across the path and into a series of thorny plants, much to the amusement of those following behind me.

For the remaining four days, until we reached Namche, I walked like the locals in camo plimsolls, purchased for £2.50 from a tiny village on the trail. They were excellent for inducing cold feet and sprained ankles in the snow, but perfect medicine for my badly bruised heels. The locals were very amused to see a Westerner shunning his boots (which dangled from my pack) and sharing in their meagre choice of footwear, especially a Westerner with a load almost as big as their own.

Each night on the trail we challenged the owners of the lodge we stayed in to a game on the table in what proved to be a phenomenal ice-breaker. On day five we reached Bhupsa, our destination for the day, at 2 p.m. We had been setting off earlier and earlier in the mornings as, by midday, clouds would start to gather and move slowly up the valleys, obscuring the breathtaking views and energy-giving sunlight. There was also the small matter of about ten degrees temperature difference.

We set up the table outside our chosen lodge and immediately attracted a bunch of locals. Eventually leaving them to it, we retreated to the warmth of the stove and then our sleeping bags; they continued playing until gone 9 p.m. when the savage cold finally defeated them. Undeterred, however, they simply took it indoors and when we arose the next morning they were still playing.

As we made to leave they begged me to sell them the table. 'We buy, we buy,' they clammered. Pausing, I decided it would at least be fun to get an indication of its worth. 'How much?' I asked. The Sherpa's eyes lit up; he looked the table up and down, smiled and said, 'Two hundred Mars bars.'

We had carried it a long way; we had had more than our fair share of adventures, triumphs, failures and happy memories. It couldn't last; I understood that now. Our legs were sore and our bodies tired of our ceaseless table quest. Perhaps it was time to call it a day. It would certainly be a fittingly amusing way to end it all. Two hundred Mars Bars. It was a done deal.

24. EVEREST

Of course we didn't take the Mars Bars. I dreamed about them for many nights but our pot of gold was still to come. There was no way I could part with the table now. Not for a thousand Mars Bars. My watchful jungle masters would never have forgiven me. The 2002 FIFA World Cup was just over the horizon of Everest. As we walked steadily onward towards our Himalayan goal, I fantasised about what lay ahead in the Far East destinations of Korea and Japan. Could it really be our year? So many coincidences, so many ridiculous triumphs, a whirlwind of luck so bizarre, and so strong, that surely it was destined to go our way; it was written in the stars.

Unwritten and certainly not predictable, diarrhoea was an accepted daily topic of conversation. It had been so for some time. I had never realised the sheer variety of stool the human body is capable of producing. Although our stomachs had largely adjusted to the gastric delights of the sub-continent, the sheer quantity of bugs and bacteria in everything we ate and drank kept things flowing. The toilets of our lodges were huts outside, at the end of the Yak paddock, built over deep holes, or hanging over streams. Due to the cold, piles of frozen faeces had formed, like stalagmites reaching up to the ominously stained and rotten wooden hole in the floor.

Lodge selection, especially higher up in the snow, was often based on how far the toilet was from the lodge. Cold temperatures and altitude are not friends of bladder retention, causing numerous pit-stops during already sleepless nights. It soon got so cold outside that we learned to use our bottles inside.

While we acclimatised in Namche with the table, the Maoists struck. Two days running they bombed the airport at Lukla then robbed the bank in Namche and shot a policeman. Although the runway was still intact, the pilots, naturally, were refusing to fly. Anyone planning to fly out now faced a seven-day walk to Jiri, then an eight-hour bus trip to Kathmandu. Then came the news that trekkers had been turned back and robbed on the trail to Jiri.

A short walk up from the town was an army base. A strict curfew of 6 p.m. was in force because of the Maoist activity and we were warned by our lodge owner not to venture outside for any reason, even to nip next door. The soldiers would shoot on sight and ask questions later. This particularly perturbed the two English lads, Sean and Andy; their toilet was outside.

Matt braved it. He had to. It was potentially his last chance to get tickets. You may recall that I had got him a set of World Cup tickets through the FIFA website. To my utter astonishment the plonker let them slip away. When the acceptance letter came he decided he could not afford to send the banker's draft and, instead of calling me, or offering them to a friend, or finding some way to keep them, he simply let them go, like gold dust slipping between his fingers.

As we got ever closer to the World Cup Matt naturally began to kick himself. The tickets' actual cost dwindled as he realised their true value. FIFA had one final stage of ticket allocation, first-come-first-served via the internet at 3 p.m. GMT, a cruel blow time-wise for those six hours ahead in Nepal under a 6 p.m. curfew.

Remarkably, there was an email facility in Namche, but via a satellite phone that cost a small fortune. Urging Matt to imagine how much he might be prepared to pay a tout for a ticket we managed to convince him that it was well worth it and struck a deal with the owner of the satellite phone.

Matt snuck round after dark. Three hours later he returned £30 lighter and in a foul mood. He had got onto the FIFA website and right the way through to the credit card details page, when the satellite phone crashed. Not the most patient of people, he was rather upset, as you can well imagine. Looking on the bright side, at least he did not get shot.

When I suggested, the next morning, that he try again, the glare nearly killed me; but try he did and within twenty minutes he was back and beaming. It had worked like a dream. Tickets on the website had been classed as 'available'. He had selected them, put down his details and now just had to wait.

Before I lead the reader up the trail, Namche's position has to be described. Imagine an amphitheatre, nestled halfway up a mountain, facing out across a valley. The valley floor is at 1,500 metres; the mountain opposite rises to over 6,000 metres. Namche is at 3,400 metres. You could fit Ben Nevis beneath and above it.

'There is nothing wrong with getting altitude sickness, there is everything wrong with dying from it.' This motto is plastered in all the guidebooks and in the lodges along the trail. 'AMS' affects everyone differently and is a serious consideration from 2,500 metres upwards. Every year, despite the warnings, people die from it. We therefore took our time and only after three nights of acclimatising in Namche, and proud wearers of clean boxer shorts and socks, did we set off in the sunshine through the snow. Proud, because they were one of only two pairs. Carrying the table, camera equipment and cold weather gear, we had to keep everything else to a minimum so each took only one change of clothes. The first was worn on the seven days from Jiri to Namche, the second for the rest of the trip. It would not have been a good time to stumble across your dream girl. As we wove our way round the side of Khumbila, which rises above Namche and is home to the god and protector of the

Khumbu region, Khumbu'i Yulha, gunshots and cries echoed loudly around the valley. The army base was in full alert training.

Four days later we reached Gokyo in near-blizzard conditions. On the way we had had an afternoon to spare at Dole so had set up the table and built two snowmen either side of it, dressed in hats and glasses. When the owner of the lodge returned, driving in his herd of yaks for the night, he stopped dead in his tracks. He had never seen a football table before, let alone one being played by two snowmen and at first glance it gave him quite a shock.

In Gokyo we shared our lodge with a team of Germans who were acclimatising for an attempt on Island Peak. To our astonishment, several months later in Laos, we bumped into an Irishman we had met in Namche who had also stumbled across these Germans. It was with great sadness that we learned from him of the their ill-fated summit day. One of them celebrated his 50th birthday when he reached the top of the peak. Tragically, it was his last. Shortly after reaching the top, he fell to his death.

En route to Gokyo we spent a night in a lodge at Machhermo. A small collection of huts and yaks nestled between two spurs, Machhermo was home to Mr Chhuldin Dorje Sherpa, his wife and three sons. There was a certificate on the wall of his brand new lodge (we were his first lodgers) that read, 'Summited Everest in Autumn Season 1989'.

Dorje worked for Adventure Consultants and for the past seven years had been a high-altitude climbing porter supplying camp four on Everest's south col, affectionately known as 'the death zone'. In short, he had an obscene amount of mountaineering experience. It also meant that he was working on Everest during the well-chronicled tragedy on 10 May 1996 when a storm caught two climbing parties too high, too late in the day and claimed the lives of eight people.

An IMAX crew, who were on the mountain filming an attempt of their own, came to the rescue of the survivors. At the same time they were able to document the terrible events as they unfolded. One of the leaders, Rob Hall, was stranded on the south summit. He was severely frozen, with little chance of survival, and too high for a rescue attempt in the fearsome weather. His crew at base camp managed to radio him through to his pregnant wife in New Zealand to share a heartbreaking few words. Coupled with the inspiring account of the miraculous recovery of Beck Weathers, who was left for dead in the snow, it is a tale that will bring tears to your eyes. Whether witnessed in the subsequent film, *Everest*, through Jon Krakauer's book *Into Thin Air*, or the late Anatoli Boukreev's response to Krakauer's version of events *The Climb*, it is a sobering account of the dangers of the mountain.

To our honour, Dorje agreed, over a game of tablefootball, to guide us across the Cho-la pass with the table. At first, due to the time of year, he had been very hesitant, claiming it was too dangerous and unpredictable. However, after an evening's competition on the table he could see we were keen and could not resist accepting. He beamed and shook our hands. Then a thought occurred, clearly registered on his face. 'Must ask wife!' Wife wasn't too happy but eventually let her man go. He agreed to meet us in Gokyo three days hence on the strict condition that there was no more snow.

Thankfully the next two days were stunning. We all over-came initial waves of altitude sickness and were able to walk along the massive Ngozumpa glacier to Scoundrel's view-point, so named because it grants stunning views of Everest's north face with minimum effort. Looking up the glacier we mistook Ngozumpa-tse to be the viewpoint and were quickly given an insight into the weakness of men: ambition. Ngozumpa-tse looked like a wee bump from a distance as Cho Oyu rises to over 8,000 metres behind it. The closer we got the bigger it became though and its summit seemed almost unreachable. We pushed on past our agreed turn around time, heads burning, stopping every ten steps to gasp and gulp in what air we could. The summit was irresistible, and worth it.

I felt like I was on top of the world. The glacier, Nepal's largest, flowed out in front of us between vast mountains. We were so high it looked surreal, as though we could see the curvature of the earth, as though we could reach out and touch heaven among the beautiful peaks all around us. It was quite a moment. I have since returned to the region to climb Cho Oyu itself. Reaching the summit was all of the above and more, an experience of magnificence and wonder beyond words.

I can now better understand the captivation of Everest. 'The summit of Everest can deliver you from the prison of ambition,' said the British climber Peter Boardman. I can well believe his words following our day of clear, isolated beauty. During our trek, however, we talked with many Sherpas. They told us they could not understand Western desires to climb such mountains. Several, including Dorje, worked on Everest. 'With every step I think about my family,' he said. 'I fear for my safety, I fear for their security, and I wish to be with them.' Yet when I asked him what it felt like to be stood on top of the world, he stopped and smiled. A look of calmness and wonder crossed his face. 'You forget about your family,' he said.

'Without guide, very difficult. With guide, not terrible.' The Gokyo lodge owner was not inspiring confidence in us about going over Cho-la. He was also smashed on vodka. When Dorje walked into the lodge the owner's reaction had been quite something. It seemed we were very privileged to have him as our guide. The owner hung off his every word and sang his praises non-stop.

Earlier in the evening, while we had been talking about our determination to climb over Cho-la, he had, with a sudden seriousness, looked into my eyes and said, intently, in his broken English, 'You good. I think you success. The heavens smile.' Malc was to be less fortunate. In the midst of ten hours hard walking the next day, at 5,500 metres and in rapidly deteriorating conditions his trousers tore substantially at the crutch. The draught must have been something else.

Matt had made the sensible decision of walking the two days round Cho-la, rather than over it, as he was not in good physical shape, suffering from coughs, stomach cramps and the shits. The table, however, was destined for the heights. Dorje told us some sobering stories, pointing out places on the route where climbers had died from avalanches, rockfalls or exposure. But we had timed our crossing to perfection, managing to capture the small window of sufficient snow to cover the dangerous ice sections and forgo the need for crampons, but not enough snow to start avalanches or render the route impassable.

At the top of the pass, in the biting wind, we set up the table, and Dorje, with the touch of a magician, pulled three cans of beer out of his bag. Climbing down the glacier on the other side of the pass, Malc captured a world-first on video as, losing my footing and falling face first on my belly, I slid off down the glacier with a football table on my back.

I survived the fall, and with hindsight, we were able to laugh about it, as we hurried, exhausted, into the lodge at Dugla just as the storm hit. Malc awoke to a mystical blanket of fresh snow outside. I had been up for some hours. Sleeping next to the window, I had been woken from my heavy slumber by two inches of not so mystical white powder. The force of the blizzard had driven it in through the tiny cracks in the window frame and onto my sleeping bag. My bladder had also been plaguing me. It was not a problem until the third call of nature, for the satisfaction of which there was no option but to don my gear and brave the raging storm outside; I had filled my piss bottle.

Matt appeared two days later in even worse physical condition from having to break trail through the fresh snow. Together we covered the last couple of days up the valley to the foot of the mountain that had been in our thoughts and minds for so long. It was everything I had expected, and more.

En route we passed a dramatic line of stone chortens commemorating climbers and Sherpas who had lost their lives on Everest. One of them was for an English lad, Michael Matthews, who had reached the summit but never made it down alive, disappearing forever during his descent. He was only 22 years old. For us, even Everest Base Camp was unreachable. The heavy snows had turned back Sherpas sent to begin preparations for the wave of expeditions that would descend on the area come 1 March. Our sights had not been set on the camp, however, but on the view. It was Everest we had come to admire and the best place to view it up close is the comparatively tiny peak of Kalar Pattar.

Hearing the national anthem float across the clear Himalayan skies was a truly euphoric moment. With our England shirts stretched over our bulky down jackets, we stood beside the table in the snow and faced Mount Everest. It was a moment of triumph. Against the odds, the table had made it in one piece to the roof of the world. As the music played, we became enveloped by a joyous sensation of victory. Laughing, dancing and singing in the virgin snow under faultless skies, 5,500 metres above it all, and in awe of the mighty mountain that had drawn us to its passionate embrace, we shared in an extraordinary moment of wonder and delight. Our brains were starved of oxygen and we were revelling in its liberating effects.

Standing opposite Everest, I had an overwhelming desire to climb. It was calling. I could have sat there for days just staring at it, alone in my thoughts. I felt like I had come a very long way to be there, both physically and mentally, and I did not want to leave. So I didn't. I climbed the peak again after the others had started the walk back to Namche, and watched the sun set over Everest. For over two hours I gazed on, transfixed, as the shadows swept slowly across the glacier and up its treacherous face until only the black triangular peak remained, basking in the day's final golden rays, the last to see the night. It was Valentine's Day and I was smitten.

After a month in the mountains we were dirty, tired and in need of a few luxuries. Matt had been suffering from what turned out to be giardia and, since the start of the walk, had picked up a ticklish cough from the dry air. Unable to get his breathing in time with his stride, his knees complaining at the work rate, and with his stomach doing the unmentionable, it had taken a Herculean effort for him to get to Everest. He had been pushed to the limit, and beyond, of his temper and tolerance, but had found sanctity in the peace of the mountains and decided to stay.

As my brother and I boarded a plane at Lukla for the resumed service back to Kathmandu, he set off alone to settle his mind on the long walk out. After the tantrums getting him up the valleys and out of his sleeping bag, I have to say I didn't think he would go through with it. Fair play mate, you surprised us all.

Back in Kathmandu, as Malc and I readied the table for a flight to Singapore and the home straight, Matt set off for the Annapurna circuit. He had fallen for the mountains but was to learn much more about their potentially fatal embrace before we met again in Bangkok a month later.

Mother Nature must surely reside in Nepal. It is a country to which I have already returned, its beauty, scale and power an irresistible draw. For now though, my brother and I were hanging up our boots and putting the emotional encounters out of our minds. We were off to the crystal waters and sandy beaches of South East Asia's paradise islands. Leaving Mother Nature behind, we were taking the table to her eighteen-year-old daughter.

25. SINGAPORE

The film crew were waiting and before we knew it the tale of the table was broadcast, not just to Iran and India, but across the entire world. Using some of our tapes from Nepal, Iran and India, World Sports Group cut a ten-minute story about our trip that headlined on Sky Sports, Star Sports (Rupert Murdoch's Asian equivalent of Sky Sports) and ESPN, i.e. to the whole world. An embarrassing number of people had now seen me slip up in shit on the edge of the Ganges, throw a tantrum and march off in taped-up rainbow socks in the Himalayas and reach Everest in my England shirt with a football table and our national anthem. One of Malc's friends even fell off his running machine with surprise when he saw us on TV in a London gym.

The Singaporean locals and visiting golfing professionals, by contrast, were stoic in resisting the lures of the table. Nick Faldo was in town, but somehow he went all the way to the final playoff of the Singapore Golf Open leaving no time for the potential encounter we had lined up courtesy of his beautifully spoken agent, whose telephone number we had obtained at the offices of World Sports Group, the makers of the TV show *Football Asia*.

After the rice, hard wooden beds and basic living of Nepal, Singapore seemed like a Western wonderland and the hospitality of Gavin, the producer of *Football Asia*, was flawless. The original plan had been to travel from Kathmandu to Calcutta and get a boat to Singapore. But with June looming on the horizon we treated ourselves to a flight out of Kathmandu and got our first taste of life Singapore style – after much cheeky begging by us on the off-chance, Singapore Airlines upgraded us to business class and sat us on the left side of the plane giving perfect views of Everest imperiously reaching up above the clouds as we left Nepal.

It wasn't long, though, before the sterility of Singapore started to get to us. After the buzz of India and the natural beauty of Nepal, Singapore was too much too soon. It was too easy, too regimented. There is a famous joke in Singapore that university lecturers are now teaching their students the three ways to think freely. We hadn't come all this way to eat McDonald's and wait at traffic lights. A saviour in the form of an old university housemate whom I had thought was working in Australia sparked us on our way.

The email went something like this:

G'day matey,
We're on Ko Pha-Ngan. It's beautiful. The full moon party is in two days time. You know you want to. It's going to be legendary.
Orpen

It would have been rude not to.

26. MALAYSIA

An overnight train from Singapore connected with another overnight train to Thailand. In the six-hour wait between them, we hit the AFC (Asian Football Confederation). The President was away but a number of other employees welcomed us in, gave an interview and accepted the table challenge.

Malaysian football had been reformed after a tarnished past. Its football league was suspended after 121 players and 41 referees were charged with corruption. They were now looking forward with unrestrained excitement to Asia's first World Cup. Asked whether the massive following of David Beckham, Michael Owen and English teams in general might lead to split loyalties from the supporters of Korea, Japan and China (the Asian teams who qualified) they replied, unequivocally, 'Not on your life.'

27. THAILAND

Your first feeling is a wild desire to plant a flag in the sand and claim the place for your own. I wanted to take off all my clothes and run straight into the crystal-clear turquoise waters. Sensational sunsets, golden sands, palm trees, hammocks, huts and no worries. Welcome to Thailand. The stresses and strains of making things happen were put on hold as we revelled for two weeks in this playground of a country.

Everything was so easy. The people were friendly, the place was cheap, the islands were beautiful and your every need was catered for in triplicate by a huge number of people chanting 'same same'. It is a Buddhist country and, traditionally, visitors are viewed as being sent from God.

On 26 December 2004, however, a terrible tsunami ravaged Thailand's west coast. Tidal waves beat in on unsuspecting locals and tourists alike, causing widespread destruction and enormous loss of life. It was an unprecedented tragedy. Many of the places that appeared on the news were towns or islands on which we had enjoyed the renowned hospitality of the locals and it is with a heavy heart that this paragraph has been added. But the country will recover, and visitors will return. Thailand has too much natural beauty and grace for them not to; and when they do come they will be blessed, as if sent from God.

Two overnight trains, a minibus, a tuk-tuk, a boat, a taxi, another boat and we landed on the sandy shores of Ko Pha-Ngan at 10 p.m., the night of the full moon party, and stumbled straight into Orpen, ginger goatee attached. There were some 5,000 people there that night but he was the first person I met. That's the sort of place it is. I have never thought of Orpen as being sent from God, but boy did we have a good night.

It was possibly the slowest start to a home straight yet. We were meant to be on the final charge to Korea and Japan but were pissing away our budget in the Thai sunshine, snorkelling over the stunning coral reefs and drinking beer (which could not be exported to England because the manufacturer could only pinpoint its alcoholic content to being 'above 6 per cent'). I assure you not a moment was wasted. Then, for the first time in eight months, I became separated from the table.

I had landed a job interview back home that I simply could not refuse. Hasty arrangements were made for a flying visit back to the UK. It was an expensive, budget-shattering move but my excitement had left me with no other choice and I was confident of landing some sponsorship to cover our time in Japan. So I booked a ticket and twelve hours later was back in Blighty, a frightening demonstration of precisely how small our world is today.

In my absence, my brother assumed charge of the table. Through Steve Flynn of the AFC I had been given the contact details of Peter Withe, the Thailand Manager, and had a good word put in on our behalf, but now it was down to Malc to see it through. It would be a good test. He would become exposed to the highs and lows of a lone table crusader. He would struggle with the weight of the table, camera, tripod, film and the never-ending internal monologue questioning, 'Why the hell am I doing this?' But he was also about to experience single-handedly the delight of people he would meet, their willingness to help and the snowballing success of opening doors of authority. Summed up in Malc's own words: 'After three months of travelling with my elder brother I needed a break.'

He did well. He did very well. The table graced the national stadium of Thailand in Bangkok, a meeting with our first England international player, and a training session with the Cambodian national team.

The Thais' enthusiasm for football is such that teams like Manchester United and Liverpool visit the country on pre-season tours, sell out stadiums for training sessions, and have, sadly, even prompted suicides from distraught fans who were left without tickets.

Thrown out of the Thai national stadium under suspicion of filming a commercial, Malc was due to meet Peter Withe, the Thailand Manager, in a coffee house in the centre of Bangkok. Unsure of what he looked like he searched the web and found his man on the rather unflattering site of www.uglyfootballers.com. A legend for Aston Villa after scoring the winning goal in the 1982 European Cup final, and capped by England, he was probably a rather smug 'ugly footballer'.

He was also good enough to sign the table and explain that if World Cup qualification was judged on passion alone, the Thai team would probably have been on their way to Korea and Japan. Unfortunately it tends to require eleven world-class players. 'We're working on it,' he said, smiling.

The Thai national team have had some interesting matches. In the 1998 South East Asian 'Tiger Cup' competition, the Indonesian goalkeeper deliberately scored an own goal in Indonesia's final group match against Thailand to avoid a semi-final against tournament favourites Vietnam and line up a game against underdogs Singapore. According to match reports both teams played to avoid winning, with defenders tackling their own players and strikers running away from the ball. All did not go according to plan though: the keeper was subsequently banned for life and, ironically, Singapore beat Indonesia and went on to win the tournament, their greatest-ever achievement.

Malc carried the table on to Cambodia. Its borders had

opened up just five years before after years of horrific civil war. Having been hammered by American bombers for siding with Hanoi during the Vietnam War, Cambodia was then subjected to the murderous leadership of Pol Pot and the Khmer Rouge, who did their best to ruin the country. In four years, a fifth of the population had died or fled. For safety reasons, travel was still largely limited to the breathtaking temples of Angkor Wat and the country's capital Phnom Penh.

Malc had no problems, but then he went with a football table, not weapons of war. At Angkor Wat the multitude of desperate children pawing for change or selling trinkets were silenced and distracted by the game. Their woes were temporarily forgotten as, watched by their elders, monks who will proudly tell you they starred in the Hollywood film *Tomb Raider*, they played and played. Tourists in Cambodia are generally safe – if they stick to the right areas they will come to no harm. Cows on the other hand should beware. A few enterprising Cambodians have found a way to make money out of the alarming stockpile of weapons left over from the war. For two hundred US dollars you can take out a live cow with a rocket launcher.

'We used to be the glory team of Asia,' recalled the General Secretary of the Cambodian Football Association. He was a proud man. The building was very small and due to the locals' complete ignorance of its existence it took Malc two days to find it, but Cambodia does have its own Football Association – manned by an overweight man in a dirty vest. Its officials were better dressed and were more than happy to get involved on the world stage through the medium of our football table.

Cambodia had been the whipping boys of the continent. 'We lost 7–0 to Yemen, 8–0 to Indonesia, and 6–0 to Uzbekistan,' said a wincing general secretary. However, things were changing. 'Now against them we draw, sometimes win. We still have a lot to do but we can see improvement.' The President, Mr H.E. Khek Ravy, was also Head of Commerce for the country. He was a powerful man, but made time to greet my brother, who welcomed the chance to say hello. He admitted that the Cambodian football team was famous for the wrong reason, conceding goals, but explained that their hope is pinned on the country's youth. A staggering 60 per cent of the Cambodian population is under twenty. They have developed football by tying it to education, and strongly feel that within five years they could be back within the top five South East Asian teams. On the suggestion of them possibly winning the World Cup, he laughed. 'Of course it's a dream. It has to be a dream for the President of every FA, but sadly it is an unreachable goal for me.' The twinkle that passed across his dark Cambodian eyes as he said this betrayed the fact that, despite the odds, the dream still remained.

Cambodia is a very poor country and desperately lacking in facilities. It must be gut-wrenching when your star player is forced to quit because he cannot afford to play and is needed to provide for his family through another vocation. The national side were resigned to training on concrete tennis courts, as there were no floodlit pitches in the country.

'I love football because it is like living in society,' said the President. 'You have to fight. You have to learn to win and to lose also. It's a game that requires you to understand a whole team. Strategy, teamwork, mental attitude, the fight, whether you win or lose, and then we do it again, next time, learning from the last.' Under floodlights on a tennis court somewhere in Phnom Penh, Malc introduced the Cambodian national football team to the table.

Their German coach was insisting on taking his Cambodian players back to basics and coached them purely in English. 'Football is one of the best tools of education,' he said. 'If they don't learn, they won't play, and if they don't play they have little future.'

As in so many countries throughout the world, football offered an exciting addition to the daily hardships of a poverty-stricken existence. Perhaps, someday, the players who told Malc their dreams of World Cup qualification will see them come true. If San Marino can score international football's fastest goal against England, then surely anything is possible.

At 6 a.m., as the sun rose over Angkor Wat, one of the world's great wonders, an American traveller rubbed his eyes and, within earshot of Malc, who was standing silently to one side with the camera, said: 'Gee, I thought I'd seen it all but this tops everything. Either I'm still wasted from last night or I really am seeing a football table on top of Angkor Wat.'

I touched back down in Bangkok shaken but not stirred. The interview had revealed my lack of preparation, the tests had been hard and my mind had been too firmly fixed on the table adventures to justify a place but I was now back on the trail of the table and England's first World Cup victory since 1966.

I was also reunited with Matt. He had survived the mountains but had a number of staggering stories. Having walked back to Jiri by himself, he had met a Frenchman who, walking around Lukla after dark, foolishly ignoring the curfew, had been dragged off the street into a house, bundled into a bedroom, told to shut up and locked in a cupboard. Standing in complete darkness, he waited nervously.

A few minutes later a huge explosion rocked the house. The door was unlocked and he was thrown back outside. While blowing up Lukla airport the Maoists had been trying to ensure they did not knock off any tourists. The same hapless Frenchman strayed into a gunfight between police and the Maoists at Shivalaya just days later and was again rescued off the street by a concerned local.

Amazed at how it was possible to stumble into such situations, Matt went for a stroll with a local lodge owner. Acting as his guide, the lodge owner took a short cut he knew, across a field, towards a police checkpoint. Halfway across the open ground the police spotted them and started shouting frantically. The lodge owner turned to Matt, said he thought it would be better if they took the road instead, and apologised. 'Sorry, I forgot; landmines.'

While Malc and I were ditching our thermals for shorts in

Singapore, Matt successfully made it to Annapurna base camp. The weather was bad and, as darkness fell, the lodge door burst open. Amid a cloud of snow, a haggard Belgian tumbled inside, lips bleeding and face chapped from the raging elements. He had grave news. An avalanche had wiped out a party of three Germans and their Nepali guide. They had all died instantly, blown off the trail by the devastating slide. It was a sobering moment for the inhabitants of the lodge, left to a night's reflection and fear for their own safety as avalanches around the base camp continued. They set out at 5.30 a.m. the next morning intent to escape from the bowl-shaped 'sanctuary' before any more lives were lost.

A moving one-minute silence was held at the site of the tragedy from the previous day. Struggling to justify such a sad and arbitrary event, each person took away with them a new lease on life, a greater appreciation of just how small we really are, and a sense of privilege at surviving to witness such majestic surroundings.

Listening to Matt recount these dramatic events was sobering. It was a timely reminder that we should take nothing for granted. Our lives are held by a thread in a world in which many such threads slip through the fingers of our guardian angels. In Buddhist terms it is known as the suffering of change. Nothing can stay perfect forever. We cannot control what we have, which is why we should treasure it while we can, but let it pass once it is gone.

Compounding the sadness of this tale, I have since met a trekker who was in the same area when the avalanches occurred. Those that died included a father who had returned to the Annapurna region to find the body of his son, who had been swept away by avalanche the year before. Nature had dealt a cruel hand indeed for those relatives left behind.

Having told his tales, and satisfied me of his own safety and well being, Matt lingered in Thailand to greet a holidaying friend, while I set off alone in pursuit of my younger brother and the table that was driving our dreams.

28. VIETNAM

Vietnam lived up to its postcard image yet delivered an added punch. Conical Vietnamese hats, palm-lined paddy fields and an array of strikingly lush greens litter the landscape while bicycles weave around you at every turn.

It is a poor country, devastated by the war with the Americans in the 60s and 70s, but generally clean, tidy and proudly kept. Although the gruesome memories are but a generation old, in my experience the Vietnamese are a forgiving and friendly people and many American war veterans have returned to set up restaurants and hotels. The boom in tourism since the country opened its doors to the outside world again in 1989 makes travel very easy but at the expense of being separated from daily local life. Malc, however, had a slightly different experience. Before I caught up with him he was travelling with a Canadian and noted that often the American accent was not welcome. Indeed on several occasions he was rather uncomfortably told to 'Go home'.

Vietnam is not like India where you make do like the locals. The re-emerging Vietnam is very commercially minded and those travellers we met who attempted to venture off the beaten track of separate, regular, tourist buses were led merry dances into the highlands then relieved of huge sums of money in exchange for a safe return. There was a persistence and an intent in the number of touts and sellers that could easily spoil a visit to the country if patient smiles could not be maintained.

My historical knowledge of Vietnam was previously based purely on Hollywood blockbusters and TV episodes of *M*A*S*H*. I have since learned that *M*A*S*H* was set in Korea. I knew less than I thought.

Reunited with the table in the narrow, leafy streets of old-town Hanoi, I hatched a plan with my brother for the next leg of our journey.

During his last few days alone, Malc had hit the Vietnamese FA and met a few characters. 'What's it like being the Head of Referees in Vietnam?' he had asked his last target. 'You enjoy?'

'Not enjoy, very headache!' came the humorous reply, accompanied by a loud burst of laughter. His name was Vint Nguyen Ngoc meaning 'victory'. It was not name enough to win him a game on the table, though, and his headache continued.

The Vietnamese FA had been hard to track down and, initially, deserted. Like most of its South East Asian counterparts, it was lacking in funding. Once inside, the employees were very nervous about the video camera but suspicions were dropped once the table was up and active. Malc had succeeded in sneaking into the national stadium earlier in the day but was thrown out shortly after producing the camera.

Under a Communist regime where people can, and do, disappear for minor wrongs, you can hardly blame the officials for their tetchiness. With the camera turned off and no evidence recorded, the authorities transformed and would happily take you wherever you wanted to go, as Malc found out. Trying to carry a football table while perched on the back of a motorbike, zigzagging through throngs of pedestrians, cyclists and other traffic is just something you have to pick up on the way.

The clock was ticking. Only two months remained until kick-off in Korea and Japan yet we still had to weave our way through the South East Asian backwater of Laos, journey the length of China and cross the sea to Korea.

Our building excitement was dramatically shattered by the news that David Beckham had broken a bone in his foot. He was out of the World Cup. It was a devastating blow. All those dreams smashed by a sinking realisation of England's capabilities. Stripped of our talismanic captain, and with a team blighted by a lack of imagination and general international crapness, we realised we had been kidding ourselves all along. The bubble of hype that had carried us so far had burst two months too soon.

We had already had a scare the fortnight before when, watching Manchester United in the Champions League, Beckham went down injured and was carried off in obvious pain. As one of the reporting websites wrote: 'Finding out the next day that Becks had recovered sufficiently to be able to walk onto the plane home was like discovering your girlfriend kissing a strange man only to find out it was her long-lost gay friend Simon.'

Unfortunately, this time, it was for real. He had broken his metatarsal, an anagram of which is 'alarm state', or more amusingly, 'a tart's lame'. That evening, sitting on a street corner after a traditional bowl of noodles, we sank a number of pints of local brew, reflecting on our chances. At 8p a pint it hardly broke the bank and in the process Malc met a Scottish girl who lived in Japan and generously offered to put us up for a month; but England were in trouble, and that bothered me.

29. LAOS

To shit yourself in your sleep is not recommended. To do so on a bus heading for the remote border of Laos, six hours into a 24-hour journey, even less so. Fortunately, it wasn't me. Unfortunately, it was the poor fellow behind me. He didn't know a thing about it. One moment he was asleep, the next the driver was prodding him awake, pointing his flashlight, yelling and shouting; excrement was seeping out through the lad's trousers, across the seat. I cannot even begin to imagine what must have gone through his mind.

Laos was the perfect place to escape the memories of such a journey. While it lacks spectacular monuments, dramatic mountains and postcard beaches, it offers something more, an appeal to rival any seven wonders. It oozes serenity and is described perfectly by the insightful *Asia Overland* travel guide: 'Sleepy mountains hug sleepy mountain villages and hidden caves and lush river views murmur timeless charms.'

Waiting in line near the border-crossing during the early hours of the morning was an insight into Asian smuggling. Along the last mile or so to the border, goods were being hastily rearranged, trunks strapped underneath cars, sacks stashed away on passenger buses and people emerged from the hills carrying various bits of equipment from fridges to TVs.

Driving down from the hilly perch of the border, we descended into Laos with our eyes set on FA number 23. I had originally written 23 letters but owing to the success of the trip and the numerous diversions, we had visited additional countries and were on course to pass through some 26 in total by the end of the journey. The number 23 still held a special significance though, and Laos was not about to disappoint.

Laos was years behind its neighbours. Far less developed, and notably lacking the impressive irrigation that kept Vietnam so lush, its countryside held our wonder as we rode the last ten hours into its capital on the roof of our third, final and laughably overcrowded bus.

The journalists of the Indo-China war labelled Laos the 'land of a million irrelevants', but after nearly three hundred years of war with Annam, Burma, China, Siam, France and America, the country is only now, finally, enjoying peace. America handed it the dubious distinction of being the most heavily bombed nation per capita in the history of warfare. In 1960 US aircraft dropped more bombs on Laos than they dropped altogether during World War II.

We were bombed with water. Not just water, but flour, dye, and berries. It was the Buddhist Lunar New Year and the laid-back capital, Vientiane, went absolutely bananas. There are only 4.5 million people in the whole of Laos and, with 80 per cent living rurally, the capital is the least frenetic Asian city you will experience, until New Year that is. On our pungent bus journey from Vietnam we had met three English guys, Dave, Jim and Ben, and two Danes, Alex and Morten. Regressing dramatically in age we all revelled in the most spectacular water fight I have ever seen.

Originally started with the aim of cleansing the soul of the people, it is now an excuse for a three-day party, in between temple visits to pay respect and dousing Buddhas in scented water and flowers. Outside the temple walls, anyone is fair game.

In between attacks, armed with our buckets for protection, we walked straight into the Laos national stadium. It was also home to the Laos FA but no one was around. Through a gap in the stands we walked out onto the hallowed turf. It was a pitch that Barry Town would have been embarrassed by, but it was their equivalent of Wembley, and the same psychology applies: at Wembley the ball never bobbles.

The Danes, Alex and Morten, were also heading to the World Cup, combining it with a South East Asian tour. In the centre circle of the Laos national stadium, kitted out in our respective national kits, we soundly beat them on the table. Unfortunately, having subsequently produced our football they then soundly beat us on penalties, as is the way with the English.

During the shoot out a security guard appeared, patrolling the perimeter, atop the stands, but, to our disbelief, seemed completely unperturbed by the fact that five foreigners were hacking divots in the national pitch.

The climax of the Lao security was the appearance of a very fat man from one of the stands, naked but for his pants. He stood, hands on hips, either side of his briefs, and waved. He gestured and shouted something in Lao but took no further action as we momentarily stopped our game and gawped at him before carrying on. It was quite a sight. The people of Laos are strong believers in 'face' and I can only suppose that, dressed only in his pants, he just could not bring himself to impose his authority further.

Into the unique world of the table stumbled a young Australian, Macca. Soaked from the battle outside, homesick and not inspired by the sight of his new room for the night (with a fan that sounded like a helicopter, peeling walls, peeling floors, ants and cockroaches) he opted to join us and added his own football contribution to the tales.

Iran had qualified for the 1998 World Cup by beating Australia in a two-legged playoff. After a goalless draw in Iran, the Australians squandered a 2–0 lead at home to lose on the away goals rule to the underdogs. It had just happened again, this time against Uruguay. Australia had failed to qualify once more. Macca was devastated. 'It was the worst day of the year ... I think I cried,' he said. 'Now I know what it must be like to be Welsh.'

With Macca and the Danes we travelled into the heart of Laos to the beautiful towns of Vang Vieng and Luang Prabang. The dry landscape was dotted with dramatic tree-clad limestone karsts, riddled with caves and waterfalls. The battered bus ride along the newly tarmacked road was quite an experience. The locals so rarely travel that when they do they are badly sick. Despite the country's Buddhist following, animal rights are another rarity. I cannot begin to describe the horrors of the noise emitted by a pig that is being carried by its tail and ears.

With only 44 days to go until the start of the World Cup, England had a friendly against Paraguay. Technology's sprawl has reached far, to the extent of enabling us to watch satellite TV in a remote village in Laos. It was a chance to see England perform without Beckham in surreal surroundings. A last test before the end of the league season and the team's trip out to join us in the Far East, it was just the tonic. Four goals later we had forgotten about Beckham and our charge for World Cup victory was back on target.

The next day we took the table out on a tuk-tuk to a jaw-dropping, multi-tiered waterfall. Climbing up its side through the jungle, we discovered a beautiful pool, hidden from below, where, in bizarre fashion, we found a number of Buddhist monks practising somersaults, smoking and posing for photographs of each other. They were thrilled by the table, which, set up under this higher section of the waterfall, made a magical sight surrounded by the orange robes above the glorious blue of the hidden pool with water crashing down around it.

Our enjoyment came to an abrupt and brutal end in the form of a portion of chicken fried rice. The vomiting started at 1.30 a.m. and by dawn I was reduced to continual dry retches, while the rear was in full flow. It was not until three days later that I finally rejoined the land of the living.

The trip so far had dealt me several bouts of diarrhoea, but this was by far the worst. My brother, who had also shared in the mistaken delight of the same dish, was in the same boat. We both lost over a stone in weight but were rescued by Macca who took patient care of us, brokered the difficult timeshare of the room's only toilet, and did not complain once about sharing the room with us, our sickness and the many accompanying smells and noises.

It put paid to our stay in Laos as we had chewed through the rest of our visa and were forced to press on into China. However, this was not before the gods smiled on our recovery and led me into the path of an entertaining Dutch advertising executive called Stefan whose best mate just so happened to be a personal adviser to the Dutch footballing legend Johan Cruyff. We swapped emails and he promised to put in a word about our trip.

One of the world's greatest players, Cruyff would almost certainly be at the World Cup doing commentary for a TV station and Stefan was sure that his mate would guide him to us. It was another moment of intense excitement, but like so many others, after weeks of emails to various people and authorities, it failed to come off.

Throughout the trip I was on the internet sending emails whenever I could. Despite the remote locations to which we travelled the modern world was always closer than you thought and the internet was everywhere. TV companies, contacts, friends back home who might be able to help, anybody who we thought might enable us to slip a bit further into the world of football got an email. As the saying goes, you make your own luck. The harder I tried the luckier I got.

Heading north into China, we parted company with Macca and the Danes. They had been worthy companions and we hoped to see the latter again in Japan. Alex and Morten were big football fans and fiercely Danish. They only had tickets for Denmark's group stage matches in Korea but nothing was going to stop them finding a way to get more if Denmark progressed.

They had not counted, however, on Mother Nature turning against them. In Vang Vieng, Alex ran straight over a Green Mamba (one of the most poisonous snakes in the world). It lunged at him, he felt a brush against his leg and, somehow, the fatal fangs missed their target. Alex survived this dramatic scrape with death but several weeks later was horrifically struck by lightning.

Morten had been with him in those agonising moments. They had travelled down into Thailand and were partying on Ko Pha-Ngan when the skies struck Alex down with one of the fiercest forces known to man. He had sensed it coming, screaming out before the bolt shattered down out of the heavens. Morten could but watch his struggles as the force ravaged his body.

'You cannot imagine the pain and fear,' ran the email – one of the most gripping I have ever read. I sat at my computer in shock, unable to remove my eyes from the screen, a hundred questions racing through my mind, a quiet prayer on my lips.

'I lay fighting for my life, electricity running through my body, thinking whether I could survive. I thought it was the end of me. My mind was still working but it was impossible to move. My eyes were closed and my body locked in position on the floor, the muscles cramping again and again.' Alex had survived.

'After some time the electricity stopped and I fell into a dark hole,' he wrote. Morten had tried to help, but on going close was given a shock himself. He could but stand and watch his best friend fight for his life. Alex stopped breathing. Lying, eyes closed, rigid, he grew bluer and bluer. Those five minutes were the longest of his life. 'Suddenly I started thinking again. I thought I was back in bed, then on the deck of a ship. I got quick flashes of all sorts of things round my head. I started to spit. I didn't know why, and I was trying to stop, but I kept on spitting. Then slowly, I heard people talking and I thought to myself that I should be careful not to spit on them.'

He awoke abruptly with a huge intake of breath, just like in the movies, bursting back into consciousness as if escaping from a deep, underwater prison. 'I couldn't understand what was going on and had no idea where I was. People were gathered round trying to help but I couldn't move and could only utter a few words.' Later, in hospital, the doctor told him that he knew of only two other people who had been struck by lightning. Neither had survived.

The road to China was deserted. Even the driver of the bus to the border had not bothered to turn up. Our only option was to squeeze into the back of a truck for a bone-jarring five-hour journey along a rutted mud road to a place called Luan Tham Pu where we managed to catch a Chinese bus to the border at Boten. Arriving too late to make a crossing, we spent our final night in Laos playing football volleyball with the rather relaxed border guards as the sun turned the brick-coloured sand of the pitch redder and redder and the mosquitoes finally drove us to our beds to dream about pot noodles and communism with a football table.

On the road to Japan with a Football table

30. CHINA

'China is a sleeping giant. Let her lie and sleep, for when she awakens she will astonish the world.' Napoleon was probably right. China had just qualified for her first World Cup. The giant was stirring.

Better known as the land of the little red book and the large red tape, China opened its gates and we rode across the border on a wave of expectation. The transition did not disappoint. China was clearly on the move. There was a buzz of development, construction wherever you turned and a general frenzy of commercial activity that contrasted starkly with the contentedly slow pace of life in Laos.

Kunming was the closest city to the border but, to give a little idea of the scale of China, it took us some 24 hours to get there.

Chinese sleeper buses are not designed for Western physiques. Your average Chinaman is substantially shorter than your average Englishman. However, despite the 5-foot bed, it felt like luxury after the many horrible nights we had spent trying to sleep on their conventional non-sleeper cousins. The standard of driving though was no better than the rest of Asia, sleeper or no.

Kunming is essentially a big Western city, part of the new China, and in stark contrast to the poverty-strewn rural areas. Splashed among new office blocks were remnants of traditional colourful buildings with magnificent arches. In the parks, concrete tables abounded next to ponds and pagodas, and the game of choice on every one of them was Mah-jong, played out at speed by the elderly community while music was piped from hidden speakers, laced with communist announcements and carefully selected guidance. Just in case we were distracted in the cool heat of our afternoon in Kunming from the destination of our travels, one of the elderly enthusiasts sported a panama hat adorned with a ribbon that said, 'FIFA World Cup 2002'.

Our next stop was a mere thirty-hour train ride away. Yangshuo is a beautiful little town nestled among the sensational lime-stone karsts of the Guilin region. It was the perfect place to rest up and recover from the stomach warfare suffered in Laos and to wait for the reappearance of Matt.

As mentioned, Matt had been waylaid in Thailand. He claims that cheap booze, beaches and racy women had nothing to do with it. It was good to see him again. He even had a confession to make. 'It's funny,' he said, pointing at the table, nestled in its bag, resting quietly against the wall, 'but I've actually missed that bastard.'

I knew what he meant. We had been eating, sleeping and journeying with the table for so long now that it was one of us. On several occasions it had been recognised by other travellers from its TV and newspaper coverage, and it now had a whole persona of its own. I had been toying with the idea of hurling it off a cliff in Japan at the end of it all, but the more I thought about it, the more I realised I could never bring myself to do it. It was one of the boys.

Pot noodles were everywhere on the train. People next to us, above us, walking past us, were slurping them down. Each carriage, as well as having its own guard, had its own boiler to offer a continuous supply of free hot water with which to bring alive the extensive range either on sale or brought along for the journey. After thirty hours I almost felt I was one.

We were becoming used to the inquisitiveness of the Chinese and the ceaseless stares that accompanied our every step. The impenetrable Chinese script, however, was harder to overcome. In almost every other country we had been to, travel had been surprisingly easy. Either signs had alternatives in English, or an English-speaking local was never too far away. One quarter of the world's population can speak English to some degree so we are blessed in our language of birth. Unfortunately, most of the three quarters that make up the non-speaking part live in China.

The Chinese do not have holidays from work as we do. They have national holidays. Everybody (bar the transport and services sectors) holidays at once. As we stumbled into Yangshuo at the start of the May week holiday there was not one bus, train or plane ticket available for us to leave. We were stuck there for seven days. The flip side was that Yangshuo was the perfect place to get stuck in and banished the horrors of our last week in Laos.

Beer is cheaper than water in China. All too soon we discovered the reason why and started paying substantially more. Your thirty-pence bottle of Chinese brew contains formaldehyde – better known for being the chemical used to pickle and preserve dead bodies, such as the former Chinese leader, Chairman Mao, still on display in a mausoleum in Beijing.

In another sublime stroke of luck, having recovered from our hangovers, not only did we meet the grandson of Compo from *Last of the Summer Wine*, but, having found our way up one of the many karsts overlooking the town, we met another tourist, an Englishman, who happened to work for the BBC and was a colleague of the producer of the show *They Think It's All Over*. Slapping my forehead in disbelief, I told him about our random meetings in Ireland and India with Nick Hancock and David Gower. In an attempt to facilitate the hat-trick of presenters and hook up with Gary Lineker, who would undoubtedly be in Japan, he readily handed over his colleague's email address. Yet again a chance meeting had been thrown our way, but then had we not made the effort to climb the hill it would never have happened. We now firmly believed we could make our own luck.

As Labour week began and the Chinese tourists arrived in droves, we spotted our first Chinese hooligan. Shirt off, downing drinks, two-pint pitcher on one arm, other raised in song, oblivious to the attempted conversation of those around him, he was on the rampage and loving every minute of it. Exposure to foreign drinking habits and loutishness had eroded centuries of tradition. Had they heck. He was Australian.

As Labour week drew to a close, another thirty hours of train travel took us out of the mountainous green of the south and into the industrial heartlands of China. They were grim by comparison; the misty peaks and calligraphy seemed an age away. China today is a far cry from its mythical splendours of yesteryear. While many ancient delights still remain (in part ensured by the sheer size of the country), many more were simply wiped out by Chairman Mao's 'cultural revolution', or paved over by the grey concrete of 'red capitalism'. Mao died in 1974 but his legend continues.

Wisely opting to leave the politics to others, we set our sights on something a little different: the ancient art of Kung Fu. China is home to the famous Shaolin Monks, some of whom now tour the world breaking metal bars over their heads and bending spears with their throats. In our hotel next to Zheng Zhou station they mugged Matt.

On our journey north, Malc's wallet had been stolen, cut out of his trousers while he was asleep during a short minibus journey, and since then we had increased our levels of vigilance. Hearing cries from a room down the corridor we rushed out to find Matt surrounded by a number of small but dangerous looking Chinese, practising their Kung Fu on his ribs. With the aid of a strikingly blonde American girl, who had just happened to walk past and spoke fluent Chinese, we quickly established, to our amusement and Matt's relief, that they were representatives of the Shaolin temple, attempting to attract foreign recruits in their own unique manner.

The next day we found ourselves in a car branded 'Shaolin Secular Disciples Union' on our way to the mountain where the Shaolin temple and training schools were based. Matt had always dreamed of meeting the monks and the prospect of getting them to jump Kung Fu style over the top of the table was just too good to miss. We were in a position to get behind the scenes. After much bartering, Matt's assailant had agreed to spend a day introducing us to the Shaolin school and to find monks to fly over the table. He refused to accept Matt's challenge that if he won an arm wrestle then we paid half the agreed price. He smiled, showed us his Shaolin identity card and muttered something about the fact that he would probably break Matt's arm.

In our car of monks we swept past the ticket barriers, the many tourist stalls surrounding the temple, and the temple itself, which has been spoilt by the curious circus that has sprung up around it. Winding up bumpy mud tracks, we climbed the mountain and were finally dropped at a small, simple monastery where foreign students are taught. For the sum of $1,500 you can eat, sleep and train there for an entire year.

The monks lead a very simple existence and train impossibly hard from exceptionally young ages. One of the teachers we met had been in 'iron body' training for the past ten years. In short he can punch, kick and head butt concrete pillars, break bars over his head and fall flat on his back, all without flinching. Some of the foreigners started a training session with him while we were there. They stood for forty minutes lightly punching concrete pillars. The theory is that, after months of 'conditioning', it is possible to work beyond the pain, or even feel none at all; akin to toughening up your feet by walking barefoot. Naturally, your head and fists take substantially longer to 'harden', but the principle is the same. Anything is possible when you put your mind to it. I opted to refrain from trying this exercise of mind over matter.

A group of heavily armed ten-year-olds sauntered past the monastery on their way up the mountain. As we were enchanted by their skills and flexibility, in turn the football table enchanted them. It was a moment of mutual excitement for all concerned, but the sight of Shaolin monks leaping over the table was quite something. Yet again we had achieved the seemingly impossible.

On the steps of the monastery, in front of the grand concrete archway of the entrance and the Chinese slate roof, whose ornate tips curled up to the skies, the table's latest champions held up our banner for the camera. It was a wonderful sight. Ten monks, six with palms clasped together in prayer and four beneath them, proudly holding out our Indian cloth with the Union Jack and the painted words, 'On the road to Japan with a football table'.

I can now confirm that it is possible to play tablefootball while wielding an axe. Better though was the fact that we had succeeded in engaging these youngsters in the process. Experienced martial artists they may have been, but their eyes bulged with joy when we left our football with them.

Like many capital cities, Beijing is not an accurate window on China. It does, however, contain such historic jewels as the Forbidden City, home to centuries of Chinese Emperors and their courts, into which none other than the beguiling voice of Roger Moore can now guide you. Quite how they allowed such a protector of Western capitalism to narrate the guide to the heart of Red China's national treasure is just one of the many mysteries that await travellers to this beguiling country.

With a choice of visiting the world-famous sights of the Great Wall, the Forbidden City and Tiananmen Square, we of course opted to head straight for the Chinese FA. Time was short. The World Cup was about to begin and we had a challenge to keep up with. We sensed that the end of a long road was near.

The Chinese FA proved, however, to be elusive. We found the Chinese Olympic Committee office, then the 'Sports For All Administration Centre of the State Sport General Administration of China', or SFAACSSGAC for short, but it eventually required a man in charge of Chinese golf to show us the way to the FA. He rescued the bemused security guard from my attempts to convey 'Football Association' in sign language.

The FA was tucked away on the second floor of a drab block among many other drab blocks, albeit in a leafy area. With Matt secretly filming behind me in our now well-drilled routine, I ventured inside the number that matched our address. No doubt it was well labelled in Mandarin, but our expertise lay in football tables, not Chinese characters. Random Englishmen did not appear to be frequent visitors to this part of the world, so naturally their needs were not catered for.

The FA was a badly lit warren of offices in an ageing building and, to our frustration, there was nobody there who had the authority to talk to us. Their chiefs were dotted around China organising the Chinese squad's run-in to its first-ever World Cup. We were directed instead to attend the offices of the 'China Football Industry Development Corporation' on Monday morning.

It was a blow. The clock was ticking. Our timing had been unfortunate, arriving in Beijing on a Friday, but after the successes of the past months we had reason to be confident of an immediate audience. Instead we had to stall for a further three days.

Back home, the England squad was announced and World Cup fever was sweeping the nation. With Gary Neville out injured and Jamie Carragher now also out with a knee injury, the chosen 23 were: David Seaman, Nigel Martyn, David James, Rio Ferdinand, Sol Campbell, Ashley Cole, Gareth Southgate, Wayne Bridge, Danny Mills, Wes Brown, Martin Keown, Paul Scholes, Steven Gerrard, David Beckham, Kieron Dyer, Nicky Butt, Owen Hargreaves, Joe Cole, Michael Owen, Emile Heskey, Robbie Fowler, Darius Vassell and Teddy Sheringham.

Of those 23, Beckham, Dyer and Butt were still fighting their way back from injury. The squad were off to a training camp in Dubai and then would fly to Korea for a warm-up match before journeying the final leg to Japan, playing another warm-up match against Cameroon, and finally, on 2 June, opening their World Cup campaign against Sweden.

The weekend gave us a chance to put the table in its long-dreamed-of place atop the Great Wall of China. One of the world's most famous landmarks, it stretches for anywhere between 2,500 kilometres and 6,000 kilometres, depending what you read, and is allegedly visible from space (a myth concocted by various tourist boards). It was originally begun some two thousand years ago, built by prison labour to keep out the Mongol hordes, although Genghis Khan was quick to point out, in word and deed, that 'the strength of the wall depends on the courage of those who defend it'. Any remaining defences were disarmed as the locals marvelled at the sight of the table.

A notice next to our means of departure from the top of the wall proclaimed: 'Those who suffer from high blood pressure, mental disease, horrifying of highness and liquor heads are refused.' Being 'horrified of highness' I was destined to draw the short straw and found myself hurtling off the wall with the football table on an enormous death slide across a lake to the valley below. 'Welcome to China' grinned the attendant as I swept, stunned, onto the landing pad.

'Dyer and Gerrard set to miss World Cup,' said the BBC website, '. . . pass me the revolver, I'm going for a walk in the woods'. It was devastating news, but there were more pressing dilemmas closer to home. Matt, who had been working on the assumption that the best way to organise his finances was to ignore them, telephoned his bank. It was worse than he thought. They refused to extend his loan and it looked like he was to join Dyer and Gerrard on the plane home. As if to compound his horror, he finally heard back from FIFA about his last-ditch application for tickets. 'We are sorry to inform you . . .'

He was part of the trip, a dear friend, and I was not about to sit back and let him go. In a final, desperate attempt I hit the internet and emailed production company after production company in a bid to land sponsorship that would ensure his survival. I got no reply. Matt was going home.

Of course Matt wasn't going home. We were lucky bastards. We convinced him to try his bank once more and this time he got through to his local branch and a couple of old dears whom he actually knew. He explained that he was making a film, carrying a football table on the way to the World Cup, and within minutes his Cheltenham charm had bagged a loan extension big enough to take him to the greatest sporting event on earth. 'They were so proud of me,' he said, grinning.

The Chinese police were not quite so generous. We had continued our trend of setting the table up in random squares, streets and railway stations to test the reactions of the locals. They loved it. There was always a nervous start, but then a crush of interest drew the attentions of the ever vigilant and often undercover police. Paranoid about any group gathering, the Chinese police are quick to break up any activity that is even vaguely out of the norm. The risk of a crowd championing a cause is not a risk that the system can take.

In truth we knew what could happen in the infamous Tiananmen Square, but were pushed by an irresistible urge to test the water. Under the watchful gaze of Chairman Mao's portrait, up went the table and the fun began. The police came three times. We were amazed at their concern over something so innocuous, yet there was no jest in their tone and they eyed us extremely suspiciously. We were soundly advised by a new-found friend to leave, and quickly. 'This is China,' she said, 'they won't stop to ask questions.' We took the hint, to the disappointment of the crowd.

Back in the hunt for permission to approach the Chinese FA, we tracked down the Chinese Football Industry Development Corp. Plush and new, unlike the FA, it was obviously designed in expectation of visitors. The front hall was decked out in football memorabilia including a prominent photo of none other than former England international David Batty, horizontal, in midair, in his England shirt, about to kick some poor foreigner in the head.

China might have shunned the outside world for many years, but football is now a national passion. Manchester United command a staggering 80 per cent name awareness, only surpassed by Superman. As I was unable to recall the name of the person at the Chinese FA who directed us to them and gave us the card of their customer services manager, the China Football Industry Development Corp., who manage the affairs of the Chinese FA, refused to grant us permission for an interview. We had to go back to the Chinese FA to get permission to go to the China Football Industry Development Corp. to ask for permission to get an interview with the Chinese FA.

Back at the Chinese FA we finally met a helpful young man called Dong. In an attempt to bypass the palaver of the Development Corp., he gave us the number of the Chinese national team's media officer, who was in Shenyang, with the team, in preparation for a warm-up match against Uruguay. Dong agreed to phone him on our behalf and put in a good word, as well as make a call to the Development Corp. Finally happy that we were getting somewhere, we trotted back to the Development Corp. only to be told that, sure enough, Dong had not called.

Exasperated, we headed for Beijing's International Hotel, which harbours offices for booking trains, planes and boats, and sought to arrange our imminent departure. Dong may have forgotten to get in touch with the Development Corp., but when we called him, as instructed, at 5 p.m., we found that he had called Mr Dong Hua, the media officer. It was good news. If we could make it to Shenyang in time then we could meet the squad. Amazed it could suddenly be so easy I thanked him profusely and prematurely. 'You must first get permission from the Sports Ministry,' he added. He told us they just needed to check little things like our media accreditation and visas to ensure we were not randoms without any accreditation and on tourist visas. We decided to try our luck all the same.

Dong had noted down further contacts for us, but we were fast becoming victims of one of China's rather serious problems. A quarter of the population shares just five surnames. Chinese newspapers frequently bemoan wrongful arrests, bank account errors and even the performance of unwanted surgery. The red tape seemed never ending, but we were determined.

Our attempts to find the Sports Ministry led us back to the Development Corp. It was getting farcical. The Development Corp. sent us back to the FA. This time I met a different man called Brian who worked for the sports events company that were organising the England v Cameroon friendly in Japan.

He was enthralled by the table's tale, and his first question was how we had got our camera across the border. I baulked at him, hesitated and intimated that we'd had no problem. His suspicions aroused, he asked if we had proper papers giving us permission to film. My face must have read like a book because he smiled, shook his head in disbelief and told me to be very careful. 'It is a sensitive country,' he said. 'They like to control things. You should never have got that camera across the border.' He carefully described the location of the Sports Ministry for me but, to our utter disbelief, his directions led us straight to the Development Corp., who now just started laughing each time we came through their doors.

Eventually the Sports Ministry was found and the policeman on the gate called down a man from the media section. We should have anticipated his response: we had to get approval from the Ministry of Foreign Affairs. It was never ending and we had finally reached the end of our tether and also our time in Beijing.

There was, however, a cunning short cut. 'The Czech coach [Bora Milutinovic] hates the Chinese bureaucracy,' said our latest acquaintance. 'So if you can get through to him you can bypass all the permissions. They have to keep him happy and he is good at telling them to be quiet and go away. He doesn't like the old Chinese way of doing things.'

Armed with the phone number of Mr Yu Hui Xian, the manager's interpreter, and fired up for the final time on Chinese soil, we dialled the Chinese team's base in Shenyang. There was no answer. The phone rang and rang but no one was home and there was no answer service. It was galling. We had been trailing round for days. Trying to remain positive we decided to go to Shenyang, find the team's camp and blag our way in. It was a good plan; basic, without real hope or structure; but hell, it had done us proud in the past. Shenyang was only three hours away from Beijing so we could return straight after the match and set off the next morning for Korea.

On our final day in Beijing, resigned to defeat at the hands of the red tape, we were cheered on by two entertaining girls whom we met at lunch in a colourful alleyway full of roast scorpions, grasshoppers, duck and noodles. They could easily have passed as twins, both very small with straight black hair and big eyes and filled with giggles. They were sharing our table and took the opportunity to practise their English in between impish laughter at their attempts and our replies.

Our jaws fell to the floor for the umpteenth time on our journey when we learned that one of them, Mirrir, was a football reporter. Not only was she a football reporter, she also had friends in the Chinese national team. 'You want to meet?' she asked as if it was the easiest thing in the world. Matt, Malc and I slowly looked at each other and could but laugh as we recalled all our attempts to breach the red tape, only to be presented with our prized access too late in the day, from a random lady in the street. There is always a back door; if only we had met her a day earlier.

The presence of the national team and our miraculous encounter with the girlfriend of the Chinese goalkeeper could not change the fact, however, that Shenyang was actually twelve hours away from Beijing, not three. We were bitterly disappointed; there simply was not time. Even if we flew, limited availability meant we would not make it to Jeju in time for England's friendly against Korea. Despite the lack of a guarantee of success in Shenyang, we toyed momentarily with sacrificing the England friendly for the potential excitement of getting behind the scenes with the Chinese team. As I said, it was but momentary.

In the words of Chris Patten, the former Governor of Hong Kong, 'China is neither a miracle about to be performed nor a ghastly global accident waiting to happen. But it is more than one fifth of humanity and what happens there matters to us all.' It did not matter enough for us to stay. We had travelled for eleven months to see England. We had been through blood, sweat and tears. Nothing was going to deter us now.

31. KOREA

Buoyed by the news that Wales had just beaten Germany, yet saddened by the line of dog cages whose occupants were bound for local restaurants, we stepped off the ferry. This was Korea. This was the World Cup.

It was crunch time. During the next four weeks, audited viewing figures revealed that, worldwide, 49.2 billion hours were spent watching the 2002 World Cup. We added to those figures, but from the very start our goals had been to secure tickets to watch England's charge to glory first-hand. Our work was far from complete; Malc and I were still without tickets for the final and Matt was without tickets full stop. The trip had surpassed every expectation but now it was up to us to prove that we could make the luck last, at least until 30 June, the day of the final.

'England's exotic paradise' was how the English papers had described the Korean island of Jeju. It formed a mental image that was dashed on our arrival by heavy fog. A bus to the site of the World Cup Stadium took just over an hour, looping up, over and around the central volcano that dominates the island. Trying to get our bearings in Seogwipo, on the far side of the island, we were aided by an American girl called Kristin who, seeing us wrestling with a local map, stopped, introduced herself and recommended a private room down by the Jung Bung waterfall.

Pointing at Malc's England shirt, she said, 'Should be the perfect place for you guys. It's cheaper than the youth hostel and it's right next to the Paradise Hotel where I hear your football team is coming to stay. You might even strike it lucky. Jake [the guy in charge of the room] has a friend who works there.' It seemed too good to be true.

Jake was a young Korean who worked in a tourist information shop at the top of the waterfall opposite our room. He was probably the most helpful person you could ever meet. As manager he could pretty much go where he pleased and for the next week he joined in our adventure and played a major role in taking the successes of the table to a whole new level. First stop, as soon as we had dumped our bags, was to hit the England team hotel.

Before joining Matt and me in India, my brother had made the effort to write to every England player about the table. He got a remarkable number of replies on various club-headed paper. He also maintained an immaculate 100 per cent success rate of 'sorry but . . .' The highlight came from the agents for Michael Owen:

Dear Malcolm,

Thank you for your letter addressed to Michael Owen which has been passed to me for attention.

Once Michael has joined up with the England Team for World Cup 2002 he is entirely under the jurisdiction of the Football Association. Any requests, therefore, would have to go through them. Having said that, I would make the point that Michael would not do any-thing which takes his focus off the World Cup – even for just a few minutes.

I am sorry we are unable to assist you further, and thank you for writing.

Kind regards

Marketing Director.

'Even for just a few minutes.' It was a red rag to a bull. The challenge was on. There were drawbacks to our plan, however. First, we were having a problem even getting near the England team's hotel. Second, when we finally did so our efforts proved utterly fruitless. We were stopped well up the drive and 'negotiations' began.

Having unveiled our trump card, the table, and thoroughly utilised Jake's translation skills, I was led past the blockade and down the drive. My triumphant march towards the hotel, armed with the table and the camera was short-lived, ending at a security hut with a telephone. After listening to an extended conversation in Korean, my jaunt was at an end and I was led back up to Matt and Malc who were killing themselves laughing. The England team had not yet arrived.

When they did finally arrive, I was in an ambulance on my way to hospital. Kieron Dyer had made a miraculous recovery and had rejoined the team, but I had accidentally eaten nuts again, this time hidden in an innocuous currant bun. Malc and Matt waved me off, staying put on my instructions to film the team's arrival while Jake, who looked after me spectacularly, relayed news of my progress from the hospital in fantastic fashion, bless him. As I received my life-giving adrenalin injection Jake called my brother to inform him that 'Andy is taking one from behind from the Korean nurses.'

'I think I saw Nicky Butt looking a bit bemused,' said Malc, when I saw them the next day after being discharged. The England players might not have been paying much attention but the Sky and BBC news teams had seen the table, and our banner, and asked questions. There was even a picture in the *Seoul Daily* the next day. It was the start of another media frenzy.

Jake's friend did *not* work in the Paradise Hotel but *was* a shift manager in the KAL Hotel next door, which played host to the English press pack and the England press conferences. We thus had detailed information on the movements of the England camp. This was our grand chance. In Japan, once the World Cup was under way, security would be greater and the players would be less inclined to talk. The relaxed training camp on Jeju was the biggest, and perhaps the only, window for us to get them on the table.

Walking tall, hearts thumping, acting calm, we walked straight past the burly security man and the sign requesting press accreditation to be shown and onto the large, sun-drenched veranda of the KAL Hotel. Under a small marquee, in front of various advertising hoardings, the first England press conference was under way. Sven-Goran Eriksson was ready to lead England to glory.

Talk of glory, however, was quickly usurped by questions about the injuries that were blighting preparations. 'Keown ... Beckham ... Nicky Butt ... Robbie Fowler ... Dyer ... Sol Campbell might practise, the others ... I am not sure. It is not err, the best err situation,' said Sven. It was hardly the inspiring three lions talk we had travelled thousands of miles to hear.

As I concentrated on filming the England team's Swedish mastermind, Matt and Malc were having remarkable success in the lobby. Malc had succeeded in nobbling Kieron Dyer, who had emerged from the press writers' room, and Matt had succeeded in sweet-talking the organiser of the press tour to let us on the press bus out to England's training session that afternoon.

The sheer number of eager journalists and photographers milling around meant that the FA officials ensured their charges were briskly marched between the various rooms and media obligations leaving scant opportunity for us to jump them. However, we realised that after the main press conferences Dyer had gone downstairs for some one-on-one interviews. This area was out of the way of the bustle, so down we followed, table and all. The head of security for the England team, a retired policeman, greeted us with an affable manner and queried our presence while filling the corridor down which Dyer was about to emerge. Malc's chance earlier meeting with Dyer and his minder meant we were soon on side and our way was clear. The table had its first introduction to the inky flourish of a current England international from the hand of a rather bemused Kieron Dyer.

Delighted with our day's work, we stumbled back into the shiny marble world of the KAL lobby and bumped straight into Garth Crooks who had blown us out in Munich. 'Excuse me,' said Malc sitting down next to him and interrupting his conversation, 'don't suppose you remember us from Munich do you?' Given that Malcolm and Matt weren't actually there this was a touch unfair, but Garth did recognise the table and a big smile grew across his face. 'Did I reject you then?' he chuckled, 'then I'm going to reject you now! No, how long are you around?' A time and place were set. 'They got me,' he laughed to his mate, 'they've chased me half way around the world and they've finally got me.' If only he had seen our banner. He didn't know the half of it.

Unable at the last moment to jump on the press tour bus (its occupants having paid over £11,000 for the privilege) we caught a taxi to England's first training session with our Korean lifesaver, Jake. The training ground was on a small plateau about twenty minutes away, up above the Seogwipo World Cup Stadium. Arriving at the same time as the press bus, we merged with the crowd and got in through the heavy security with ease. The guards were very excited by the table. Suddenly it took three of them to check it as they virtually took it out of its bag and had a game, granting the bewildered journalists a photo opportunity.

Almost every TV channel and newspaper was present. When the England team arrived, cameras flashed and chatter filled the air as the media hordes quickly tried to establish who was and wasn't training, before doing their piece to cameras as the England players jogged past. Everything had to be crammed into the fifteen minutes they were allowed before being evicted to enable the team to train in private.

Back at the KAL Hotel, Garth Crooks was good to his

word. It was a satisfactory 10–5 whopping, marginally aided by the fact that Garth's goalkeeper was taken over by a five-year-old Korean girl. Her parents watched on proudly in the hotel's beautiful gardens that rolled right down to the sea, and several other families wandered over to join in the fun; one child in particular stood, entranced, trying to mimic Garth's exuberant cries (and there was a lot to mimic).

Not only was the World Cup to be an insight into the world of football, it was a baptism of fire into the all-consuming media that follow it. We were to discover a rat race full of egos, interwoven with true gems and personalities as the various networks, papers and freelancers fought for prized free tickets and the scoop of the competition.

It all began with a producer for the BBC *Six O'Clock News*. Middle-aged with an immense potbelly, nervous laugh and amiable nature, he saw us with our table in the KAL Hotel lobby. In search of a story he said hello. That was our mistake. We forgot that, despite all the charm and the tales and the smiles, he was just after a story.

'So have you literally come all the way overland from England?' he asked, after seeing our card, as if we might have been lying and just touched down from Heathrow. After hearing briefly about our adventures he asked if it would be possible to do a little piece on us that they could tag onto their report about England training. Thinking on our feet, and obviously wanting to get the table onto the pitch of the Seogwipo Stadium, we said we would, if they could ensure we did it on the pitch. It was a done deal. Waving his pen, the producer sought to find a contact number for us and settled for Jake's mobile phone. While Jake read out his number, sparky from the BBC mistook it for his name. '011 . . .' said Jake, 'Ho Wan Wan' wrote the man from the Beeb.'

The stadium was everything you could dream of for a World Cup venue. With its design based on the volcano that forms the heart of Jeju Island, it had dramatic style, a beautiful location by the sea and a sunken pitch to protect play from the ocean breeze. While the *Six O'Clock News* team took the opportunity to pick up their World Cup press passes at the accreditation centre, we stumbled into Terry Butcher. Former England captain and stalwart of three World Cups, he is most famously remembered for his bloodily bandaged head in the qualifier in Sweden for the 1990 World Cup.

He was shit at tablefootball. 'I've signed some funny things in my time, but never a football table,' he said, 'and I've never been any good at it either, my kids always beat me.' While swarms of Korean school children gathered round, Terry's multiple groans of 'Oh no, not again' and 'Aargh, I don't believe that' provided ample confirmation.

Heavily armed security guards were not letting anyone through the outside gates into the stadium perimeter. Several TV crews had been turned away, but they had not come prepared with as skilful an interpreter as Jake and the ice-breaking potential of a football table. It was meant to be the other way round. The BBC were meant to be getting us in.

Once through the main checkpoint we only had one goal in mind. We were going to get onto the pitch. The BBC were less sure. With their official accreditation they were exceptionally wary of breaking any rules for fear of it being confiscated. We, on the other hand, had nothing to lose. The Korean guards were a breeze. Agitated at first, they descended upon us, but some fast-talking from Jake, a flash of the table and timely innocent grins saved the day. Working our way round the inside of the ground we eventually found an open gate leading into the stands and a path to the pitch became clear. While the Beeb faltered, we charged.

Only an hour prior to our escapade a full-scale security rehearsal had been staged in the stadium with ninja-trained riot police abseiling down from the roof of the stands, police rushing in to deal with hooligans, pitch invasions, and terrorist attacks Korean-style with as much firepower and martial arts as they could muster. This was Asia's first World Cup. Nothing, and I mean nothing, was going to go wrong for them.

They had been training for just such a moment as this but we snuck under their guard. In an impeccable bit of timing we were able to walk straight onto the pitch unchecked with our trusty companion, the table. Revelling in our freedom and the dramatic surroundings, fuelled by the taste and feel of our first-ever World Cup, and to the delight-cum-horror of our BBC compatriots, not only did we set up the table, we had a penalty competition.

With every second I expected alarms to go off or ninjas to come hurtling down from the stadium's rafters. Penalty after penalty, we played and played in utter disbelief. This was the pitch on which, the following night, England would be opening their World Cup account. Perhaps they thought we were England players. The standard of the penalties would suggest not, but the swagger and audacity to be playing on the pitch could well have suggested we had some kind of authority.

Our antics went out to over eight million viewers on the BBC *Six O'Clock News*. Friends back home finally saw what we had been up to. The producer was purring with delight. 'I'd never have risked that at their age, that was brilliant. Obviously, but for my enormous shape, I could have taken better penalties but brilliant bit of blagging by the boys.'

'There's three lots of us here,' he had told us the first time we met him; 'The *Six*, *Ten* and *One O'Clock News* teams. Despite all being BBC we're quite competitive.' He was thus delighted by our antics in sneaking onto the pitch as the *Ten O'Clock News* were running a piece on the dramatic levels of security at the stadium.

We were not yet finished though. At 2 p.m. Michael Owen, England's favourite son, was due an appearance at the KAL Hotel. David Beckham, still in a race for fitness, would not be unveiled until Japan at the earliest and Owen was captaining England in his place. It was the moment we had been waiting for and we nobbled every FA rep we could find. On hearing our tale they seemed happy to let us set up the table in the lobby and try and nab the players as they came and went. I ran into the press conference to set up the camera while Malc and Matt strove for the FA's help in bringing Owen to the table.

'Are you aware of just how famous you are in Japan and Korea?' asked one of the journalists after a flurry of activity

saw Owen whisked into the hotel under heavy supervision.
'Well, you get a rough guide from the fan mail ... most of it
comes from Scandinavia and Asia,' he replied. He played
down England's injury list and in his sensible no-nonsense
way pointed out that that is why they bring 23 players
instead of 11. 'It's part of football.'

Halfway through the press conference Matt tapped me on
the shoulder and passed me a note. It read:

> Andy,
>   Owen will
>   sign table outside
>   written pressroom.

The boys had done me proud and as a result we were nearly
responsible for one of the most bizarre injury incidents in
the history of English football. The press conference ended
more abruptly than I thought and Owen was swiftly
whisked away. Matt was on hand to grab the camera off the
tripod, charge through the doors, across the lobby and, in an
expert flanking manoeuvre, managed to get around the
marauding hordes and in front of the heavily escorted Owen
who was briskly headed for the written pressroom. In his
way was the football table and, true to his word, Paul
Newman, the FA head media officer, steered him towards it.
Malc was waiting with a ball and a pen.

The press could not believe their luck. It was a prime
photo opportunity. The sight of thirty or so richly fed,
overweight journalists stampeding towards one of
England's national treasures was not pretty. As Owen
stopped to say hello and add his inky flourish to the many
greats already to grace the table, the hordes arrived. Tables
and chairs proved no obstacle to the animal-like sea of
lenses eager to get the shot. Michael Owen was in flip-
flops. Despite England's injury crisis the unflappable young
striker stood his ground and finished the job before being
spirited away to the relative safety of the writers' press
conference while the bouncers vented their angst at the
mêlée. A true professional.

Having said that, I would make the point that Michael would not do anything which takes his focus off the World Cup – even for just a few minutes.

Once more we had slipped under the guard of the contracts, restrictions and agents. They had not counted on the pulling power of a football table. Steve McClaren, manager of Middlesbrough and assistant coach for England was soon to follow, kindly signing with a grin and a wink later that afternoon.

Our day was still far from over. At 5 p.m. the team were training at the stadium in readiness for the friendly match against South Korea, barely 24 hours away. In a masterful stroke of good fortune we managed to get on the second press tour bus to the stadium for training; masterful because the bus drove into the stadium compound and past the accreditation checkpoint. For the second time that day we had successfully snuck into the stadium.

Outside, many hopeful Korean fans were being held back by security. The majority of them were wearing Korean shirts but such is their love of England that on top of them they wore England shirts with either Beckham or Owen on the back. It was a refreshing sight compared to the loutish, violent rivalries throughout the rest of the world. The number of David Beckham haircuts, however, was worrying.

Watching the England players train, it was funny to think that only hours earlier we had been playing on the same pitch. The gap between us was closer than we thought. In one of football's more peculiar sights Beckham was bouncing up and down on a trampoline on one foot and kicking a ball with the other while Nicky Butt and Kieron Dyer were racing back to fitness on the stairs of the stands. The Korean authorities had a sense of humour, for as the England players trained, the scoreboards flashed up Korea 1 England 0.

While Matt and I got a great shot of Becks rubbing his hands together in prospective thought, Malc attempted to convince Paul Newman, the head of FA Communications, to allow us to take the table into the players' hotel. The reply was friendly, but simple: no way. He could not make any exceptions to the rule despite being entertained by our tales.

It was interesting to watch the antics of the media, hungry for their footage. Most notable was the tall ITN front man, Mark Austin, who was keen to catch Beckham running up the stairs out of the changing rooms. 'You going to try and shout something at him?' asked his cameraman. Austin hesitated, then squared his shoulders and said, 'Yeah, I will do, yeah.' As Becks emerged he leaned forward and said loudly, 'David, how's the foot, David?' But David simply kept on striding past and out onto the pitch muttering, 'Fine, thanks.'

It was striking to see first-hand the extent to which the press hang on to the players' coattails. The comparisons with bloodsucking creatures that are made about the media are not far off. I can well imagine why the players build up their walls and, to a certain extent, I have some sympathy for them; yet I confess to reading the back pages of the tabloids as avidly as the next fan. We were careful to try and distinguish ourselves from this and because of the whole story surrounding our trip I like to think we succeeded.

We had caught a few of the headlines ourselves. The *Daily Telegraph*'s Henry Winter, whom I met in Munich and had become reacquainted with at the KAL Hotel to much amusement, wrote a great piece about our exploits that day and the trip in general. 'Intrepid trio nearing end of magic table ride' read the headline and the article kicked off with the following:

> They have survived riots and bomb scares, scowls from Nicolas Anelka and charm offensives from Sepp Blatter. Iran loves them. Chinese soldiers play football with them. They have blagged their way into stadiums in 25 countries from France to here in South Korea. They are three England fans, Matt Holyfield and brothers Andy and Malcolm Sloan, and their big adventure is nearing its climax . . .

It was suitably triumphant, but we were quickly to learn about tabloid spin-offs. The day after this was published and our story had gone out on the BBC *Six O'Clock News*, the *Daily Mail*, that harbinger of truth, ran a half-page leading article with a whopping photo of Matt and me, looking miserable and carrying the table between us. According to the article we had 'travelled much of the distance on foot'. It was a shambles, but the first we knew about it was when we finally reached Japan. England fans were slapping us on the back and saying, 'Well done mate, you walked! That's amazing.'

Match day came after a sleepless night. Excitement and anticipation had seized our minds. Before heading out to the stadium, the table was required to fulfil its duty to queen and country and greet the British Ambassador. He had heard about our tale and instructed one of his minions to arrange a meeting. 'I think England will do well to win actually [against Korea],' he said. 'The World Cup is the biggest thing here since the Olympics in 1988, which in many ways was the first time Korea came to prominence on the world scene. This is seen as of the same scale.

'For the Koreans, club football is not a big thing, but the national team is hugely important . . . They've been training and playing matches for eight weeks as a team, compared to England's one. The players were not allowed to play for their club teams. Koreans look on England as the home of football so this is a very important game for them. They will play until the very last minute.' Parting ways with the Ambassador, we couldn't resist a reference to receptions and Ferrero Rocher.

'No, we don't serve them' he replied, laughing, 'but my children give them to me for Christmas every year without fail.'

Back home, some hours earlier (at 6 a.m. Korean time), Hugh Edwards, the BBC presenter, could hardly believe what he was reading. As the *Six O'Clock News* drew to a close and he finished a short story on David Beckham, he found himself stuttering to introduce our table-football table:

Now, 8,000 fans are expected to follow England's fortunes in the Far East and some of them have gone to remarkable lengths to get there. Three young England fans have spent the past year, the best part of it anyway, travelling overland to Korea carrying a t-table football game which has been signed by many famous people on the way ...

(Daniella Ralph with the report) ... The acting England captain had some extra duties today. Michael Owen became the latest name on the world's best-travelled tablefootball game, and its owners couldn't believe their luck ...

The Beeb officials back in London loved it. They even sent a courier down to my mum's house just hours before the broadcast to get some of the footage that we had posted home. Our pictures of the table up alongside Everest blew their minds. The latest story on Beckham was cut down to just twenty seconds, while we got over two minutes of prime-time coverage. The cameraman, Joan, was especially pleased with the way he had edited my wonder penalty strike onto a wonder save of Malcolm's. Younger brother had triumphed again and this time in front of an average viewing audience of eight million people.

Bum-Kun Cha is a Korean footballing legend. From the reaction of Jake and the manager of the KAL Hotel, with whose kids we had been playing football at the end of every day, we learned that he was someone very special indeed. Not only this, but his son was in the current Korean squad. Bum-Kun Cha was the Korean Kevin Keegan. He had been the first Korean to make it in Europe, playing in the Bundesliga in the 70s and 80s, and had returned home to coach the national team before carving out a career as a TV pundit. Jake was nearly beside himself and eager for us to meet him. Despite the language barrier he added his autograph to further the eclectic mix of nationalities on the table. We wished his son luck. He smiled the smile of a proud father despite his own lofty status. By the end of the World Cup he must have been beaming from ear to ear.

It was party time for the Koreans who were revelling in the unique spotlight that their country was now under. They were playing England. England! Their delightful nature made it a special occasion free from any kind of trouble. I only heard of one incident: post-match a camera crew had been sticking its camera into the faces of happily drunk England fans in a pub near the stadium in order to incite reactions. The cameraman had been duly punched.

We were the proud owners of a giant new St George's cross with 'World Cup Winners 2002' across the middle. In the four corners respectively were '3 lads' '25 countries' 'overland' 'with a football table'. With two big plastic poles on which to raise it high, we marched towards the stadium from the bus to a chorus of interest, camera flashes and songs. It took us ages to reach the ticket gates as we posed for photo after photo arm in arm with Koreans decked out in the red strip of their country, and when I finally made it through the turnstiles it was behind a spitting image of Mr Miyagi from *Karate Kid* fame. It might even have been the great man himself. On the other side of the turnstile 'anti-hooligan supporters' in big yellow sashes relieved us of our poles to put them in the 'depositary' and we set about finding our seats, calming the butterflies and preparing for the start of something special.

Walking into the crowded stands was a memorable moment. Anticipation rippled through the throng. After all the hype, all the advertising, all the talk and all the preparation, we were finally about to see some football. The 'red devils', the heart of the Korean support, were in synchronised action and voice at both ends of the stadium to dramatic effect.

From the tiers of the stands hung St George's crosses with Liverpool, Everton, Huddersfield and, more surprisingly, Eindhoven across their middles. Despite the number of Beckham shirts there was no doubt at all as to whom the Koreans were going to cheer. The relative silence during our national anthem compared to the roar that followed it made the point even clearer.

The ambassador had been doing so well in his predictions, but as we parted company he had been unable to resist forecasting a scoreline of 2–1 to England. Like deluded Englishmen the world over, despite his earlier reservations, he just could not resist calling the win. Yet when Owen slotted home in the 25th minute the reservations were, naturally, forgotten. There had been a lot of fighting talk beforehand but finally the talk was turning into goals.

Our wake-up call came early in the second half. Having failed to build on our lead, effectively fielding a B team by way of numerous substitutions, we paid the price for allowing the Koreans to come at us. It finished 1–1. A diplomatic result but not one that satisfied the dreams of eleven months on the road. The Koreans had fire in their bellies. We looked knackered and had only given our first team 45 minutes of play. As we walked out of the ground we passed a scrawled sign with a big heart drawn on it that said in shaky English 'Can we pray for you'. It was a very apt message.

We awoke the following morning to the knocks of the highest-rated TV station in Japan. They had been filming at the game, seen our flag and one of us had foolishly agreed a very optimistic time for an interview. Japan was to learn in advance of our arrival on its shores, Matt's desperate search for tickets and our table challenge to the Japanese players. At that hour of the morning the scope of our potential coverage did not quite register with us or perhaps we would have made more of an effort. Confronted with three freshly woken, semi-naked, out-of-shape Englishmen I am sure the millions watching in Japan were thrilled at our imminent arrival.

What it did do was spark a sensational number of emails through our web page. The BBC News slot back home had done the same thing. My email box took on a whole new persona. 'Better than that fridge bollocks,' said one, 'Korea fighting, England fighting,' said another.

The friendly match might have been and gone but action at the KAL Hotel was still in full flow. The England team

were not due to leave for Japan for three more days. We had
three more days of press conference opportunities. Surely
they had to wheel out Becks. They didn't.

Next up again, however, was Sven. With rumours
abounding about an affair with former-weather-girl-cum-
kiss-and-tell-specialist Ulrika Jonsson, England's very own
imported swordsman was about to come face to face with
the football table.

Security at the KAL Hotel had woken up to the prospect
of charging hordes and this time had a roped off walkway
ready. The FA let us set up the table in the middle of it as
cameras circled in expectation and my heart rate hit an all-
time high.

Sven was fashionably late. He also completely ignored the
fact that a table-football table had been set up in the middle
of his path. Striding purposefully towards his hotbed of
questions, he almost made it straight past us; I only just
managed to spring out of my chair in time. I had a card out
ready with our website on it and a few teaser words about
the trip. He signed it and handed it back. Laughing, I gave
him another and he did the same. 'No,' I cried, 'it's for you',
but by then Paul Newman had caught up with him and
pointed out the table that was now behind him. 'Ahh, the
table,' he said, as if he had spent a lifetime in its arms, then
turned and satisfied the cameras and ourselves with a few
swishes of the pen. The FA had kept their word, but Sven
seemed on autopilot, no doubt readying himself for the bar-
rage awaiting him a few yards past our position.

'Just have a look at that,' I said, handing a final card to
him by way of explanation as he finished. 'Oh, another,' he
said. It was signed and back in my hand quicker than I could
say 'Ulrika'.

'If I had acted on that second half yesterday I would have
put many more on standby,' joked Sven after revealing that
Trevor Sinclair was on the plane home (albeit in part to look
after his pregnant wife). 'If we want to win the World Cup
we have to be organised and in the second half we weren't.
It is a pity football is not like handball, basketball, where

you can bring on a player to take a free kick. We have other players who can take them, but they are not Beckham.'

We were getting into the swing of gate-crashing the England training sessions. This time the guards had upped the ante and were checking ID. But they did not know the names of the various reporters and with an array of business cards from various major newspapers in my pocket we all got in. There was good news too. Beckham was kicking the ball with both feet. It was an encouraging sight and the press boys scurried off to file their reports.

Trevor Sinclair had left on a flight to Seoul at 7 a.m. The BBC hadn't managed to get shots of him at Jeju airport. ITN didn't, so four of their crew actually bought tickets on the same flight just so they could get through into the departure lounge to get their shots and not be outdone by their rivals. As one of the BBC team had explained earlier in the week, 'If its news, they'll get it. Doesn't matter what the cost is, they want the pictures.'

With the Korean friendly over, and with just four days remaining until England's next warm-up match against Cameroon in Japan, it was decision time. To get to Japan would require a twelve-hour boat trip to Busan on mainland Korea, another twelve hours to Fukuoka on Japan's west coast and then a day on trains to Kobe. Add to that the time needed to find tickets to the match and our days on Jeju were numbered. The good news was that the *Six O'Clock News* team offered us £750 for each piece they used on us, wishing to follow us across to Japan and around the England games. It was the financial lifeline we needed to finish the trip and watch England ride to glory.

Amid rumours that Becks might be wheeled out for a press conference on the Friday we delayed our departure until Friday night. It would be tight but we could get to Kobe, the city where the friendly with Cameroon was to be played, on Sunday morning. We would not have tickets but what the hell, it had not stopped us before and where there's a will there's always a way.

It granted us one last day of opportunity. During the past week we had met nearly all the English press, our table story and antics around the hotel proving a fun distraction for them. We were fast learning the system. After the press conferences, one for the TV cameras and one for the writers, the players would go downstairs into the gardens for one-on-ones. This was our best bet to get them on the table. We had one day to do it. Nick Collins, reporting for Sky Sports, was a friendly, laid-back bloke and said he had no worries about our tagging along for a one-on-one with whoever was to come on Friday; it was just down to the FA. Paul Newman gave the nod. We were on.

'Rio Ferdinand and Gareth Southgate 2 p.m.' said the white board. No Becks, but two of the most popular members of the squad. Southgate was a seasoned international whom I watched at Crystal Palace when I was little and is perhaps, unfortunately, most famous for missing the decisive penalty against Germany in the semi-final of the 1996 European Championships. Rio was a young giant with massive lips and subject of a fat money transfer to a fat money club, Manchester United.

First up that day was a training session at 10 a.m. It had a hint of light-heartedness, as the team were to meet and greet a group of Korean school kids. In the morning sunshine we turned up early hoping to sneak in with them but ended up coaching the throng with our football outside the gates as Korean press cameras rolled.

The kids went ballistic over the table, demanded autographs from us (most of which we signed 'Andy Cole', the man who never quite made it as an England striker) and when the gates finally opened they swept us in with them. It did not take long for the FA officials to separate us, however, and send us back to the press side of the pitch. 'It wasn't us, they kidnapped the table,' joked Malc with England's head of security. 'Sure they did,' he smiled, pointing us away. But we had succeeded in one respect – Andy Cole is now a legend in Jeju.

Once we were back in the press fold, BBC Radio Five Live commentating legend Alan Green obliged us with a little piece for our camera while crouched down by the table. 'So here we are in Jeju, absolutely beautiful morning, clear blue

sky, temperature in the mid-eighties and with typical commentator's foresight I've got long trousers on. And you can
also see by my beautiful picture why I'm on Five Live and
not BBC One. Talking of long trousers I've also got boots,
and a false passport, so Sven, I am available.' He was
disarmingly friendly and, on hearing our grand plans, set
about trying to find Adam Crozier (then Chief Executive of
the FA)'s mobile number for us as a short cut to our ambitions. Regrettably we never got it.

But we did have the chance to nobble Rio and
Southgate. 'Oh no, not you guys again,' exclaimed the
head of security as he led the players down through the
hotel gardens. 'I'm going to have nightmares about you
guys and that thing,' he lamented, pointing at the table.
Southgate had finished his interviews first and with a wry
smile the security guy led him back up via us. He was keen
to play and set to with gusto. It was a good game, a long
one too, and his minders were getting itchy feet. Rio had
wandered over and was laying on his gormless look by
way of audience. At a close 2–2 security had had enough.
Southgate was having none of it though. He wanted to
win. This time it was not going to penalties.

The next goal was the decider and it was a tense couple of
minutes before it finally came. 'You can tell he's a defender,'
was Malc's contribution as the deadlock continued. I had
been on the road too long though to let the moment escape
me and with Southgate unusually sloppy at the back I
clinched the game.

Under the tropical skies in the lush green gardens of the
KAL Hotel we had succeeded in properly challenging an
England player. All the talking, all the negotiations, finally
we had been able simply to walk up and say hello. He was a
good lad and was happy to stay and chat. It was a refreshing
moment.

Rio, who had been doing his best to get Southgate to
laugh during his interview, was heavily under the watch of
the England minders. With so many injuries to the squad,
they did not want to be held responsible for another one,
however innocuous. They even jumped forward to help him

across a small stream about a foot wide. It was quite a sight. But then he is, literally, worth millions. Combined with the England shirt and the three lions on his breast I can imagine he is, and was, rather contented, despite the stupidity he has displayed since.

It was a highlight of the trip, what we had dreamed of pulling off, what we had joked about in the pub. It was what, against the odds, we had said we were going to do and we had done it. All that was left now was securing the elusive ticket to the World Cup final and a few prayers that England would beat us to it.

The final leg to Japan was to be more complicated than we had first thought though. Matt had been adamant we would not need to book the overnight ferry. Indeed, the waiting room was empty half an hour before departure, but, sure enough, the ferry was full. A phone call to the airport proved our saviour, revealing a fantastically priced ticket, not just to the mainland but also to Japan, that night, for half the price of a ferry ticket to Busan.

The reason it was so cheap was because it was fictional. 'No, I am sorry, there are no flights to Japan today ... tomorrow all are full,' said the lady at the airport upon our arrival. I mouthed the word 'but' a number of times, to no avail. We were stranded on Jeju and England's preparations would carry on without us.

Lady Luck, however, had other things in mind. England and the white cliffs had only been left with the help of one Miss Hope so it was fitting that Lady Luck should send her daughter to help us finish the job and ride on into Japan. In her hand, Katie, the beautiful, Australian, English press tour organiser had four spare tickets for the 9 a.m. flight to Osaka.

The catch was that they were FA tickets and we had to wait until morning to find out if the airline would allow us to use them, despite the fact that they would otherwise be cancelled without refund. Lacking accommodation, a late night pool hall and fifteen cans of lager helped pass the hours. A hazy incident with the police at 4 a.m. saw us flee the town and wake up on the pavement outside the airport.

According to the camera, and evidenced by several new companions, we had won some fluffy toys. Swapping concrete for marble as the airport opened, we were sound asleep when the English press corps arrived for their chartered flight to Japan. Much to their amusement we flew with them.

32. JAPAN

Proudly resting on my mantelpiece is a World Cup 2002 runners-up medal. It is not England's. Destiny had something better in store. It was to be a magnificent tournament, a fitting end to our year of dreams, and there *was* going to be a seat at the final with our name on it.

I had no idea how we were going to pull it off, but then I had no idea we would have made it this far; and had I known that I was to star on Norwegian TV, meet the greatest footballer in history, be chased by the Japanese CIA and get a free ticket for the World Cup final from an American modelling agency as escort for a number of its finest young ladies, I might just have thought I had died and gone to heaven.

In the politely crazy world of Korea and Japan, 32 of the best international football teams were to meet for the most eagerly awaited sporting event known to man. The World Cup was to bring flair, style and unbridled passion to these Far Eastern shores. Perhaps more importantly, it was also to bring the thousands of fans that follow it. In every nation, large and small, the pennies had been saved for a long awaited trip to Japan. Like many Asian countries, Japan was closed to the outside world for several centuries; now it was bracing itself for an invasion of epic proportions.

Message received via our website,
www.becauseitsfootball.com, entitled 'Welcome to
Japan'

Hello, we are Japanese fan.
We are host of FIFA World Cup Finals 2002.

Japanese rainy climate looks like Britain.
It must give England advantage.

> (people)

Most Japanese have no interest in World Cup.
Over 40 years men understand only baseball game rule.
Many people cannot understand English but kind and
gently.

> (tattoo)

If you have tattoo, never show us it.
In Japan tattoo is for Japanese Mafia, 'Yakuza'.

> (prohibit)

And you do not sing a song at public place (train, shop,
station).
Don't walk with beer bottle.
You are looked like attacking anyone by weapon when
you have can or bottle.

> (hotel)

hotel – expensive
business hotel – inexpensive
love hotel – various

The World Cup was to bring Japan face to face with one of
the most feared demons of the modern age, the English
hooligan. Like their Korean counterparts, the Japanese
police were on their highest state of alert and the general
public had been warned. One Chief Constable had even
campaigned for a temporary increase in the number of abor-
tion clinics. To the polite, gentle, discreet and honour-bound
nation of conservative Japan, we equated to animals.
Give a man a label and he is apt to play up to it, but

during the World Cup 2002 the English fans did their nation proud. Be it the effect of the remarkably accommodating hosts or the cost of a pint (let alone the airfare), the English fans that travelled halfway across the globe to cheer on their team of young lions, were exceptionally well behaved. There was still the obligatory drunkenness, nakedness and singing, but it was arm in arm with opposition fans and Japanese locals thrilled by the intoxicating effects of unbridled shamelessness and patriotism.

We were not the only ones arriving in Japan. Trevor Sinclair's air-mile account was going into overdrive. Having been called up as a late replacement to the England squad and then cut in Jeju as Dyer continued his miracle recovery, he had barely touched down in England before he was back on a plane out to the Far East. Liverpool midfielder Danny Murphy, himself a replacement for Steven Gerrard, was the latest injury victim. The replacement was being replaced. It was no surprise to find out that their shirt number, four, is Japan's equivalent of our unlucky thirteen. Its alternative meaning is death. God help poor Trevor Sinclair.

A blind eye and a friendly smile from our favourite Australian press tour organiser saw us ride on the press bus to the press corps' five-star hotel in the heart of Kobe. Japan is an economic superpower and it showed. Amid the expanse of tower blocks and industry, however, rose giant nets. Wherever there was a large enough space between an office or apartment block there was, without fail, a net towering up above its surroundings and enclosing the plot. The Japanese love their golf and the city was littered with self-contained driving ranges, targets hanging from their far walls for the businessmen to aim at during their lunchtimes.

Accommodation in Japan is extortionate. The press hotel was suitably out of our league and the England team's hotel was a £120 taxi ride away across what must be the world's most expensive bridge. We found a YMCA and started plotting.

'Go away you worm' is one of the few quotes that the media has managed to get from Japan's star footballer, Nakata.

Football in Japan, like everything else, is quite different from football back home. For the fans, supporting a team is not conditional and the lack of a critical attitude creates fantastic absurdities. If a player misses an open goal from three yards they will cheer and chant his name on the basis that at least he tried. Andy Cole would feel at home. It is very rare for fans to boo one of their own team's players. In England, of course, we are not nearly as forgiving. One slightly more comic approach existed at Reading. They had a PANTS club (Players Are Not Trying Sufficiently). If they felt a player was under-performing they would wave pants at him.

The setting up of the J-League, Japan's own commercial football league, sparked a new craze. Spin-off branding on curry, crisps, nightclubs and bikes, to name but a few, spread it far and wide. It was even voted 'word of the year'. Crazes are rife in Japan. People have a strong desire to be part of things. It makes for an amusing sight. The youth of today, for example, all want to be different from their staid, traditional elders. They all want to rebel. They all want to dye their hair and rip their jeans. So they all look the same. David Beckham is cool. They see him as different. There are a million David Beckhams in Japan.

'It is a little against the spirit of Japan,' said one of the first imported foreign coaches when asked about football. The Japanese were shocked by the swearing and yelling. The antics of players such as Hristo Stoichkov, who finished their careers with a lucrative move to the new league, were simply unheard of in Japanese football. Stoichkov's aggressive eyeball to eyeball confrontations with the referee were best described by one commentator as 'the cultural equivalent of pulling a large gun and shooting the ref in the stomach'.

Despite this, as with everything, Japan has adapted and embraced the sport. The Japanese FA only came into existence in 1921 because of the embarrassment caused when the English FA sent a replica of the FA Cup as a gift. There had been no reciprocal FA to receive it.

Football was introduced to Japan in the 1870s by the English Royal Navy. Before then Japan had cut itself off from the outside world and, while English public schools prepared to rule an empire with rugby and cricket, the sons of Japanese samurai practised the traditional arts of swordsmanship and archery (football was actually banned in England by King Edward III in 1369 because it interfered with archery). But the FA Cup found its way to their shores, an FA was founded and the long road to hosting Asia's first World Cup began.

In 2002, football was the perfect way for Japan to embrace its new generation and at the same time provide an outlet for patriotic feeling. It was a way for Japan to overcome the burden of its history and healthily engage in nationalistic displays without reviving past conflicts and the militarism that has dogged its memories. Those that knew the World Cup was on had been looking forward to this tournament for a very long time.

After fighting over the single bed in our extortionately priced YMCA room, we set about hunting tickets. First stop was a telephone box and it was Matt's turn to make the call. 'Can anyone speak English there please?' The man on the other end replied that he could not, but that he would try. It made for a long, frustrating conversation.

The man's efforts were endearing but fruitless: welcome to Japan. Like so many countries we had passed through, the locals would bend over backwards to help you; yet in Japan, if they did not know something they would not admit it, they would attempt to help you nonetheless. Often it was an amusing case of the blind leading the blind.

The table was far beyond blindness. It was legless. Somewhere between our antics on Jeju and our arrival in the land of the rising sun, we had lost a leg. It was the table's worst injury to date but a remarkable chance for the people of Japan to prove their worth. I kid you not, but within fifteen minutes of presenting myself at the reception of the Shinkobe press hotel to ask for anything vaguely similar to one of the remaining legs that I was waving, such as a bit of wood or plastic that might just prop up our pride and joy, I had a perfect metal replica cut and laid in front of me. The maintenance man was sweating profusely but he had succeeded in his task, undefeated, honour intact.

The repair came just in time for the table's next scalp. Trevor Brooking might have led the line for West Ham and England in years gone by, but on the table the result was only ever going to be one way. We managed to spring the table on him in the lobby of the press hotel the morning before the Cameroon match. Unfortunately he informed us that Gary Lineker had not made the long trip, rendering unlikely our extraordinary hat-trick of *They Think It's All Over* presenters.

More pressing, however, was that we remained ticketless for the friendly against Cameroon and, just as we thought our hopes of seeing the match could not get any slimmer, they did. On our way to the stadium, hoping to blag tickets in some way, shape or form, we were detained by police merely yards out of the railway station. 'Dangerous,' they chorused, pointing at the table, halting our progress and surrounding the offending item. Then they saw the plastic poles for our giant flag. 'Dangerous' they squealed again and insisted on us taking the poles out of the flag and carrying them separately, despite our protests that the poles would be safer holding up a flag. Frustrated, we tried to reason, but met the brick wall that is the inflexible Japanese rulebook. When they found out we were without tickets, they radioed for backup.

Eventually we had had enough. Their reinforcements were taking too long and we had tickets to find. 'You take them,' I said holding out the poles. The five-foot four-inch policewoman hesitated. 'No,' she said. Her four colleagues who had surrounded us were equally unsure about the actions of these crazed English football hooligans. 'Dangerous?' I asked, pointing at the poles. She nodded. 'So you take them.' There was nothing in the rulebook about her taking poles. They were all completely flummoxed. So off we walked with the table and the poles. There was a vague cry of 'Police, no, dangerous,' but nobody followed.

Securing a ticket for this match was possibly our best blag to date. The legions of police ready for the hooligans' first outing had sent the touts into hiding and it had looked increasingly as if we would be left empty-handed. We needed to go back to basics. It was the table that had got us this far and it was the table that would get us further.

Walking around the stadium, through the sea of fans, we found the VIP and press entrance. As we had learned from the tales of Genghis Khan, a wall is only as strong as its weakest point, and our table made a great battering ram. A series of trestle tables were lined with security. By walking in to speak with them under the guise of random questions we were able to skip past the first two before being properly detained. We then split forces to test the defences further.

While Malc and I distracted the all-too-friendly and inquisitive security personnel with the football table, Matt was able to slip out the side of the tent between tables and into the crowd *within* the ticket check barriers. His mission was to report back on any further checks before reaching the seating, but he vanished. The cheeky bastard swanned on in, flashing a BBC card to get past a final ticket check. Fortunately, my brother and I went one better.

Donning matching England polo shirts sporting the Nationwide sponsorship logo (given to us by Nationwide) we marched up to the press tent and asked for our accreditation. The man behind the counter was most embarrassed when he could not find it. Gesturing dismay and annoyance we asked what could be done. Through a combination of name-dropping, persistence, politeness, and with the helping hand of a well-orchestrated, timely intervention from Warren (one of the press tour organisers) asking if they had found our passes yet, we started to make progress. It was a long, nervous wait, but with minutes to spare the man waved us back over, apologised for the confusion and pressed two passes into our hands. I proudly signed the register, *Andy Sloan – Because its football.*

England had never lost to an African side. Despite going a goal down to Cameroon, they managed to maintain this record courtesy of a late strike by Robbie Fowler. Akin to the friendly against Korea, England had avoided defeat but failed to inspire. 'I'd have said we'd do well to get past the last sixteen,' Trevor Brooking had said of England's World Cup chances hours earlier in the Shinkobe lobby. It was a realistic prediction given the spate of injuries but, disappointingly, we were still yet to find someone with the same flicker of hope and glory in their eyes that had so fuelled our long journey.

We finally found him just moments after the players had left the pitch against Cameroon. He was Scottish, his name was Adam Crozier, he was head of the English FA and he got me in trouble with Radio Five Live. He was the first person in the entire England team and press camp who gave off the belief that we had a chance of winning the tournament.

Our press pass for the Cameroon match did not grant us access to the 'mix-zone' where, post-match, the players run a gauntlet of journalists via the relative safety of a barrier-lined walkway. Pushed away by security when I nonetheless attempted to enter the mix-zone, I turned round and, ludicrously timely, a small Japanese official pressed a mix-zone ticket into my hand.

There, outside the England changing room, on the other side of the mix-zone walkway, was Adam Crozier. I caught his attention and, leaning across the barrier, threw him one of the cards we had had made up in China. 'I believe you heard about it?' I shouted across. Picking up the card, he laughed.

'Yeah, yeah, very good. How long are you boys staying out for?'

'As long as you are,' I replied.

'So till the end of June then,' [the final being 30 June] he quipped, thumbs-up with a knowing grin on his face and a spark in his eye. The sceptical would say that he was a former advertising executive; the naïve that England could and would go all the way.

The problem with Five Live was that our conversation rendered inaudible their interview with Robbie Fowler, scorer of the last-minute equaliser. But, as a cameraman put it later, 'F*** 'em, they'd have done the same to you. If you'd had a proper camera in your hand they wouldn't have said anything. If you can blag onto a press tour bus and into these games when you're surrounded by the number one blaggers from across the UK's media then good luck to you. I think you'll just find new friends and everybody will wish you to do well with your tour, with the table.'

In our first 24 hours in Japan we also had the pleasure of tempting the legendary commentator John Motson into sharing a game and, most entertaining of all, we had done a Des.

We were fast learning about the media and our relations with the BBC were beginning to falter. The World Cup was looming, the press corps' workload was increasing and tensions were starting to arise. Our original plan had been to head straight to Tokyo, missing the warm-up game in Kobe against Cameroon. Youth hostels in Japan are at least £25 a night each and in Tokyo we had a friend with a floor. 'That's a shame,' the producer of the BBC *Six O'Clock News* had said back on Jeju, 'how about if we paid for you to go there. I'm sure we can find a spare room for you to stay in.' Our hand was swayed.

The accommodation promised to us was out on Awaji Island. Ideally placed next to the England team hotel, it was also, as previously mentioned, a taxi ride across the world's most expensive bridge and completely out of the question. The travel money was not forthcoming either and the producer was acting increasingly nervous.

Added to this was the fiasco of their replacement camera. Because the Beeb's editing equipment was running on Japanese systems and not English, they had wanted to get us another camera. I had done my research before I started the trip and ensured I had a broadcast quality camera, so, naturally, I was keen that they supplied us with the same so that our footage did not deteriorate. Considering they went to the expense of having someone buy one in Singapore and courier it to Jeju, it was perplexing that it failed to match our specific requests.

Cue an email from my girlfriend the night before the Cameroon match. A man had called her from ITV Sport and passed on a mobile number for me to call day or night. It was to be an extraordinary evening.

Nothing had been signed with the Beeb so I gave him a call. They had seen the piece on the *Six O'Clock News* and loved it. The negotiations began. Wanting to be fair to the BBC, we let them know everything that was going on and gave the producer the chance to match ITV's offer. 'Fair play, boys,' he said, 'I know you're strapped for cash. If they offer you something more then you should go for it, I know I would.' He was not amused, however, to learn of our intention to take the offer from a BBC colleague whom we had mistaken for an ITV presenter.

While Malc and I slipped cards to Sheringham, Heskey and Crozier in the mix zone after the Cameroon game, Matt was waiting outside. One of the *Six O'Clock News* team appeared and amicably relieved him of the camera they had lent us. The problem was that we forgot to take the tape of our footage out of it. We never saw it again.

The promise of money upfront (which would secure our stay until the final) clinched it. As rather symbolic dark clouds rolled across the sky and lightning crashed around the Shinkobe tower we decided we simply had to take the ITV offer. Out of courtesy, and holding to our word, Malc called the BBC producer to let him know.

His response was that he would be showing our footage from the camera on the news that night. Not realising the implications of this, Malc came back to our room a bit confused to relate the conversation. Matt and I were very alarmed. Such a deliberate airing could scupper the exclusive deal that ITV were after and we might be left with nothing.

Matt hit the phones to reason with him. He met with a hostile response. It seemed he was not nearly as pleasant as we had first thought. For someone with his journalistic experience I would have expected a slightly higher standard of integrity or at least a more varied vocabulary. The conversation was quite an eye-opener. Fortunately we took a rough record of it as soon as Matt returned, although there may have been more expletives:

Hi, it's Matt here, Malc said something about you using our footage, I don't quite understand.

What do you mean? I can do what I want with it.

But it's our footage, and we agreed with you that the deal was off.

I can do what the f*** I like. You can f*** off.

Don't speak to me like that.

What do you mean, you've embarrassed me in front of my colleagues, I'm getting shit from London, I heard that you were going around touting for business, so you can f*** off.

No, we weren't. We thought it was a man from ITV. Besides, we told you before then, as soon as we found out.

You've made me look like an idiot, so f*** you.

Don't speak to me like that. I'll lose my temper; you're really starting to piss me off. I'm trying to be civil. You didn't honour our agreement, we got f*** all what you promised, no money, no signed contract, a second-rate camera, what do you expect?

You're just three lads.

Three lads with three degrees and more than half a brain cell between us which I'm afraid I don't think you have. You really don't want to piss me off.

Are you threatening me?

No, I'm just telling you what a f***ing idiot you are.

Matt hangs up.

It was all rather fraught. The producer was getting shit from London about letting our story go. Now he had just nailed his own coffin as far as we were concerned. Some quick calls to an understanding man at ITV put our minds at rest. The deal was safe. We now had enough money to stay and see out the full month of World Cup action. The producer never did air the footage.

That night, despite the ugly turn by the producer, we were back at the press hotel. Through the easily approachable Trevor Brooking we had arranged a meeting with the legendary sheepskin-coated commentator John Motson. Malc made a call to his room from reception. The poor guy got very bemused but, good to his word, he came down and all was revealed. 'Ahh yes, I think I read about it somewhere . . . so where does it all end up then? With the World Cup final?' He took the words right out of my mouth.

'If we can get our best team on the pitch we might have a chance,' said Motty on England's prospects. 'But I just can't see it,' he mused. 'Every English person hopes we'll make it but there's just been so many disappointments,' he added. 'I've done [commentated on] eight World Cups, but I've never done England in a final. Hopefully, before it ends, I might get a chance. Wish you guys all the best; sorry I was a bit confused. So, I drew two-all there did I? Make sure you tell Trevor when you see him. Good luck. You know, you could write a fantastic tale about your experiences.'

The FA press man, Paul Newman, was doing his job well, too well. 'I think you've had quite enough from us already,' he told Malc over the telephone that evening as we made another attempt to find a way into the England camp. It seemed that ideas put forward by certain journalists had not been accepted. The table would have been a great PR exercise for the England camp as well as something to heighten spirits. Anyone can play tablefootball, injured or no. The press had proposed touting us as a shining example of the right sort of England fans. Sadly it was not meant to be. The team's heads were down and concentrating on one thing only, 2 June, and their opening match against Sweden.

Ecstatic with what we had achieved, but tired of the media circus, we made a conscious decision to break away from the England base. It was time to set up shop in Tokyo and set about blagging some World Cup tickets for Matt, and for the final for all of us.

To avoid the train fares we opted to hitchhike. Our first lift away from the dark cloud of the English media camp came after just five minutes with our thumbs out. It was a middle-aged Japanese couple whose surname was apt indeed: 'Kohei' meaning 'Justice'.

Our home in Tokyo for the month was uniquely Japanese. The traditional thin walls, sliding doors, low tables and wooden floors merged with the latest home technology. The hot water was electronically adjustable to half a degree, along with the bath. 'The temperature has just been adjusted to your every desire,' purred a voice in Japanese from the dial. It was also able to maintain bath water temperature once full. Many hours were spent in that bath as a result, soaking away the grime and aches of ten months on the road.

Unfortunately, it could not soothe away the Asian bugs in our bellies and it was to be some time after our return home before bowel movements returned to normal. Still, the toilet came with a heated seat, a built-in air dryer and a bidet (which, according to the dictionary definition, is 'a machine for washing genital and anal areas; or a small horse') with two settings, one for boys and one for girls, whichever tickled your fancy.

This good fortune stemmed from a chance meeting with a feisty Scottish lass called Jasmin whom Malc had met on a street corner in Vietnam. Twenty-eight years old, she had been living in Japan for four years and was now working in Tokyo. She invited us to stay and in one fell swoop our accommodation issues were solved. Moneywise it was manna from heaven.

Through the medium of her American flatmates and the Japanese family next door who owned the house, we were to be given a rare treat, one not afforded to the casual hotel-based visitor, an insight into life in the suburbs of modern Japan.

Mama-san was a highlight of our trip. Within hours of our arrival she had hit the kitchen and was bringing round delight after delight of Japanese food. Matt, for whom this trip had, believe it or not, given a *first-ever* taste of pasta, curry, kebabs and baked beans, was struggling to come to terms with a fresh onslaught of marginally less palatable experiences. Seaweed, raw fish and fermented soya beans did not light up his eyes, however hungry he might have been. Over the next four weeks a cultural exchange of sorts took place as Mama-san fed us an education of Japanese cuisine and we pulled her interest into the world of football.

With the table and the bags of cheap Korean rice (bought in Jeju to mitigate the expenses of Japanese living) safely stashed, our immediate concern turned to picking up our England tickets. It was a worry. We had been hearing numerous reports that thousands of tickets had gone astray. Back home people had to catch flights before their tickets had arrived. It was a fear that had been growing steadily in my mind. The prospect of everything being swept away by an administrative blunder was beyond contemplation. The FIFA assistant at the ticket office in central Tokyo, however, did his best to enhance it.

When I told him that we had been on the road for a year and had organised for the tickets to be picked up in Tokyo he pulled a pained expression. He called someone else, fidgeted through some papers and scratched his head before, finally, they were found.

The feeling as I took hold of those three prized pieces of paper was simply divine. A shivered rush of anticipation, excitement, nervousness and relief washed over me. Sweden, Argentina and Nigeria. It was the 'group of death', and only four days remained for the grim reaper to sharpen his scythe in preparation. If Matt had not been ruing his foolishness in rejecting tickets the year before, he was certainly feeling the pinch now. But as we stocked up on face paint, hair dye and clippers, a ray of hope landed in my email account.

It was a reply from Keith Cooper, FIFA director of communications. Our random stumble into the Swiss beauty Daniela in Eastern Iran had paid off. Keith had included his Japanese mobile number in his email and told us to call if we needed any help in our quest. Call we did.

After a brief exchange of pleasantries he asked after our ticket situation. On hearing of our two-sets-of-tickets-for-three-people dilemma he immediately launched into a number of possible solutions. You could hear his mind working. In a well-spoken, ponderous tone he worked through questions and possibilities before knocking me right off my feet.

'If I made an exception to my own rules because I think you deserve it, if we got you accreditation, then that would get you in and you could use the other two tickets for your mates.' I was about to get my very own World Cup press pass.

It seemed too good to be true. It was. There was a lot of administrative ground between Keith and me. As I cawed in wonder, he told me, 'You've got to go to the accreditation centre in Saitama. To get you an accreditation at this late stage you need to fill out a late accreditation form. They'll fax it to me here [in Korea] because I'm the only person who can approve these requests. I'll approve it, fax it back and they make you a badge.'

'Fantastic,' I replied.

'Well, you haven't got it yet, it's not fantastic yet,' he reminded me. They were wise words. I should have heeded them more.

No amount of help, though, could get me the pass in time for England's first match. 'I think what we have to do here,' said Keith, 'is give my colleague Nicholas a call for a normal ticket. He works as one of my press officers and will be doing the game in Saitama (England v Sweden).' Matt was made to sweat, but did rather well out of Nicholas. It all looked rather rosy.

YOU'RE MERDE AND YOU KNOW YOU ARE sang the headline on the *Sun*'s website. The World Cup had kicked off in style with a famous victory for the former French colony of Senegal over the World Cup holders, France. The favourites for the tournament had stumbled at the first hurdle. On television back home the former England midfield genius and Geordie joker, Paul Gascoigne, exclaimed, 'I've never even heard of Senegal,' to which the presenter, Des Lynam, smoothly replied, 'It's been there in West Africa for some time, Paul.'

It was quite a night in Tokyo. Among the bright lights and claustrophobic bustle we found a bar that realised the World Cup was on. With the right result and beer in our bellies we went on the rampage with newly found Japanese friends. We had them all convinced that Matt, sporting his Nationwide England polo shirt, was in fact Manchester United defender Phil Neville. He had actually been mistaken as such by some of the English press corps in Kobe. He was not amused, until the young ladies came flocking. Suddenly Phil was having a ball.

England's friendly against Cameroon had given us a glimpse of what was to come. Thousands of Japanese had filled the stadium adorned in England shirts, face paint and seemingly ready to cheer the house down, yet the atmosphere was like a snooker hall, the silence only being broken by hushed coughs and shuffles. It was a clash of cultures and traditions, but one that was slowly changing. As World Cup fever spread and more foreign fans arrived, the Japanese fans felt better able to express themselves. And when Japan won its first-ever World Cup match, boy, did they go nuts.

Mr Okada, manager of the Japanese national team that qualified for France '98, said, 'we have a bit of a complex about nationalism, and football is a way of beating this complex.' In their opening match against Belgium, on day five of the 2002 tournament, the Japanese fans were getting into the spirit of things, booing the opposition before kick-off. But they were made to wait for their first jubilant release of euphoria. Inamoto's brilliant solo goal, winning Japan their first-ever World Cup match, was ruled out. The score remained 2–2 and Japan had to settle for a draw. It only took Inamoto 51 further minutes to set the record straight, banging home the winner against Russia.

The Japanese fans went berserk. Adam, one of our American hosts, returned home from work very late that day looking shocked. 'Gee, what have you guys done to them?' he exclaimed in his Alabama drawl. 'They're like shouting and hollering and running over cars and all.' He had been down in Roppongi, the entertainment district of Tokyo, which had ground to a halt in a most unusual display of delight. World Cup fever was starting to hit home.

Even Japan's elite were catching on. When the Japanese Prime Minister was asked about the on-going negotiations with Russia concerning the territorial possession of four disputed islands he said, 'First we must beat them tonight, then we can get our islands back.' Football allowed Japan to become nationalistic once more and openly take pride in being Japanese.

33. THE GROUP OF DEATH

England's first march on the World Cup stage was to be our second on the TV screens of the Japanese nation. Akiko and the camera crew who had taken a liking to us in Korea had kept in contact. At 7.30 a.m. on the morning of England's opener against Sweden they knocked on our door and began filming our preparations.

To Akiko's horror, delight and disbelief we shaved Malc's head, leaving only the cross of St George. An alarming amount of spray paint later he sported a striking crown of white and red. Matt, meanwhile, was on the phone to Keith Cooper's media officer, Nicholas, still chasing a ticket. 'The best way is for you to get your friend's accreditation done quickly,' he said. 'For me to get you a ticket for the game to hand to you before is just mad, its just not possible. But call me later, at 3 p.m., and we'll see.'

The impressive UFO-cum-shoulder-pad-inspired stadium at Saitama, an orchard-strewn suburb of Tokyo, cost a smart £60 million to build (the new Wembley Stadium has cost approximately £757 million). But Saitama was in the middle of nowhere, nullifying any chance we had of watching the other match in England's group, Nigeria v Argentina. This is where having Japanese TV following you comes into its own. After filling out my late accreditation form to much laughter and bemusement in the accreditation centre and an entertaining live interview with Radio Five Live (past grievances forgotten) about our hopes for the Nigeria v Argentina game (5–0 to Nigeria), Akiko proposed a solution.

Ten minutes later we were inside the home of a local resident. Thrilled by the novelty factor they treated our intrusion embarrassingly well, serving us Japanese green tea, biscuits and then ice cream in return for many photos of Malc's head.

Despite a brave and worryingly proficient display by Nigeria, the Argies won 1–0. If England wanted to avoid France in the second round they had to top the group. The pressure was on. During our journey we had taken on all comers and, bar a battering on the table in Iran, had come out with victory for England. Now it was down to Becks and co.; could they follow our winning ways?

David Beckham's fitness and availability was, of course, the question everyone wanted to know the answer to. One English fan we met had a good theory. 'Apparently Sweden have the lowest number of yellow cards and I reckon they are quite a fair team. I think it'll be 1–1 but I think Becks will definitely play. Nobody's gonna stamp on his feet like the cheating Argentinians.' With Golden Balls on the field, anything was possible.

Meanwhile, Matt's faith in the FIFA rep, Nicholas, paid off. The cheeky, lazy bastard became the proud owner not just of a free World Cup ticket to England v Sweden, but a VIP one. He would watch the game in style from a VIP box with free champagne, food and many suits for company. Breaking out of his reverie he was back on cloud nine.

The final approach to the stadium was mesmerising. Thousands of fans were milling around in all states of dress and undress. There was a buzz wafting through the air tinged with trepidation. As England fans, we eternally dreamed, but our dreams were so often questioned that we just did not know what the result would be. It could easily be England's year, but for the first time fear fully gripped my heart that we could be going home in just twelve days' time. We took our seats and crossed our fingers.

My fears were echoed by the fan sitting in front of us. Like myself he had stumbled across the FIFA ticketing website over a year before and emailed all his friends in excitement. Yet he was in Japan on his own. His friends had not even believed England would qualify.

It belted home the scale of the risk we had taken setting out when we did, months before England's qualification was secured. But then again, it is risks that reap rewards, and the nail-biting events of qualification: the epic win in Munich and the last-gasp free kick against Greece – that we sweated over on our Russo-Turkish ferry – had given the trip its edge. It had been an emotional rollercoaster of the most bizarre variety; and it was about to get worse.

The game mirrored the England fans' vocal accompaniment of the national anthem. The first verse was loud, proud and well orchestrated, but they did not realise the band were going to play a second. Beckham was deemed fit enough to lead the team out and England bossed the first half, taking a 1–0 lead from a Becks corner. The Japanese, bless them, were relatively new to the whole game of football and the commentator made the fans choke on their half-time burgers and sushi by declaring that 'England lead by one point to zero.'

But then England forgot how to play football and we watched on after the break as they went off song. The Swedes rallied, scored and nearly ran away with a victory but for another vital match-winning save by David Seaman. It was worrying to watch and on the final whistle the England faithful were reacquainted once more with their question marks. Only David Seaman stayed to clap the fans. The Swedish team vigorously applauded their travelling faithful.

Matt had had a vastly different experience. The only one not dressed in a suit, he had shared a box with FIFA executives and had drinks with Adam Crozier who, since our last encounter, had been out of our reach at the opening ceremony in Korea. 'You're one of the tablefootball guys,' he said to Matt as he wandered over. Matt spoke to him about how we wanted to try and get the players on the table, that it was for a good cause, and about the trip in general. Crozier said he would speak to Paul Newman about it and hopefully email us in a few days. Rather unsurprisingly, he didn't.

Our mood was lifted threefold the following morning by the televised efforts of Akiko and her crew, our attempts to shave Matt's head, and an email from Norwegian TV.

At the peak time of 6 p.m. on Japan's largest television station our website www.becauseitsfootball.com flashed up on screen in front of the two jovial news presenters. It followed a 3 minute 20 second edit consisting of Malc's head shaving, our journey to the Sweden game and Matt getting handed his VIP ticket. Millions of Japanese witnessed my inept attempts to draw a number three on my belly to complete a shirts-up 'England 3 Sweden 0' moment and our obvious post-match disappointment.

Our hosts were gobsmacked. Both Jasmin and Mama-san shrieked with laughter and disbelief that their guests had managed to get themselves on national television. From that point on Mama-san was glued to the World Cup and, for every England game, looked out for us on the television. The anchorwoman on the show even appealed to the Japanese team, live on air, to sign the table, while our website was still displayed on screen. Akiko later proudly told us it was the highest-rated story at that time in Japan.

My email account went into overdrive. In an amazing display of support and enthusiasm I received email after email from the website. 'Hi there, I'm Japanese football fan, I watch you on TV programme, I supporting you.' There was a youthful exuberance to the messages that I found inspiring. Our tale had struck a chord.

Matt was also feeling exuberant. Things had gone rather well for him in Saitama given that he was ticketless until an hour before the game. He had been such a misery that we had jested about shaving his head if we succeeded in swinging him tickets. His exact words in jubilation upon receiving one were, 'You can do whatever you want to my hair; I don't care.' They were the precise words we had been waiting for.

A glance in the mirror later at his new Mohican and he threw a tantrum. 'I look like a German trying to be cool,' he cried. We hid the shaver with the granny next door and he was left with nothing but nail clippers. To my astonishment they proved quite effective.

Norwegian TV had somehow heard about our trip and were eager to meet up. Busy feeding footage back to Norway, they could not meet us until about 10.30 p.m. The last train home to our suburb from the centre of Tokyo was at 11.30 p.m. and taxis were now well beyond our budget, so the only way to meet them realistically involved staying out all night. When they recognised that we were skint and unable to afford the £4–£7 pints at Japanese bars, an inducement was offered. Four hours of free beer later, in the entertainment district of Roppongi, seven undercover Japanese police were trailing our magic table.

We had set the table up on the roadside and toured up and down the Roppongi strip in and out of bars full of fans of all nationalities. One bar manager was so taken when he passed us on the street that he threw a tablefootball party offering half-price drinks to anyone and everyone who came in with us. It was a crazy few hours among the bright lights, neon advertising and bustling prostitution of the area. The Irish went mental, the Mexicans loved it, and a surprising number of people recognised us from the telly.

The Japanese police were not so convinced. Our antics were clearly radioed back to base by the first poor officer we attempted to lure onto the table and, before we knew it, we were being closely monitored by special agents in suits with earpieces while uniformed officers with light-sabre-style truncheons attempted to keep us moving along.

All we wanted to do, of course, was entice onto the table the plethora of fans drinking on the strip. This led to bizarre consequences. At one point we were physically carrying the table by its two ends while a Mexican in a huge sombrero played a local in a Beckham shirt surrounded by over seven police officers whose attire distinctly resembled Hollywood's depiction of the FBI.

Fellow Mexican supporters cheered on their compatriot with trumpets and maracas as the bewildered police maintained their insistence on our continued movement. Fortunately the situation remained humorous and civil and was in no way threatening. Once we hit the junction at the end of the street, however, we could move on no further. 'Circular motions' went the cry from the Irish spectators and the baffled police were forced to watch us 'moving along' on the same spot.

Filmwise, for us and for our newly found Norwegian friends, it was a magical use of police resources. Malc was keen to test how far the police would go in following us by attempting to convince Norwegian TV to pay for us to take the table into one of the many 'hostess bars'. Apparently it was the highest-rated story in Norway that day.

For this, the final month of the tour, our ranks had swelled once more. Three had become four. Nidge was a 24-year-old backpacker from the throbbing heart of the north, Wakefield. He had staggered across the table adventures in Thailand and was reunited with us once again. Timing his arrival well, he was able to revel in the generosity of the Norwegians. Reviewing the footage of that night still brings tears to my eyes. It suddenly goes black. It remains black for a good few minutes. 'Neil, Neil,' you hear me cry. 'You've got the lens cap on.'

'Ahh, I wondered why it was so dark,' come his slurred northern tones, 'I've been wandering around trying to find some light.'

In the second big upset of the tournament the USA beat Portugal 3–2. The mere thought and reality of it trebled our hangovers. In twenty years time the country that hosts the World Series baseball championship, consisting purely of American and Japanese teams, will probably be attempting the same with football, to the exclusion of everyone else. To make matters worse, news came through that my application for accreditation had been rejected.

With only two days remaining until the titanic clash of the tournament, the much-awaited revenge match between England and Argentina, Matt's hopes of getting a ticket were not looking good. I hit the phone to Keith. Perhaps he had had a change of heart? Perhaps he could not bend the rules for us? Perhaps he was just too busy? Perhaps our luck had run out?

No. My application for a World Cup press pass had been rejected because of the Chinese. The red tape had caught up with us. A dramatic influx of last-minute applications by a swarm of dubious Chinese journalists had been hurled straight into the bin. Sadly, it seemed that mine was in among them. With only hours to go until our overnight train left for Sapporo in Japan's northernmost isle we found ourselves back at the Saitama accreditation centre and filling out another form.

In the nicest possible way they seemed completely incompetent and, once completed, I did not want to let my form go. Perhaps to them it was just a football match. It would be hard to comprehend the feelings generated by 23 years of indoctrination into the hopes and dreams of the England football team. But this was England v Argentina. I had a ticket, my brother had a ticket, Nidge had a ticket, but Matt did not and it just would not be the same without him. It was a simple case of all for one and one for all. Writing in big letters 'As agreed with Keith Cooper and for his immediate attention', and underneath, 'Tablefootball', just in case, I closed my eyes, took a big breath, put my faith in their eager smiles and handed it over.

The Japanese rail system was a revelation. Sapporo was over twelve hours and nine hundred kilometres away. Two changes with a turnaround time of five minutes each went like clockwork. Welcome to Japan. We covered three quarters of the distance in a quarter of the time on the bullet train, travelling at 300 kilometres per hour. The rest of the journey was a little slower but brought dramatic views of

sea and mountains as we left behind the industrialised eastern swathe of the country.

There was no press pass waiting on arrival. Like a space
age tank the Sapporo dome was an intriguing sight, but any
magic captured in its dramatic design was quickly dispelled
by the blank stares of the staff at the accreditation desk.
Embarrassed to keep plaguing Keith, and aware that our
goodwill could run out at any moment, I called him once
more from our hostel. This time there were no Chinese
involved. It was good news. He had received and approved
my application but it had to go via the main FIFA centre in
Japan first before being sent to Sapporo.

The accreditation centre back at the stadium had other
ideas. According to them I had to fill in another additional
form to be sent to head office and approved and '. . . it could
take some time'. My heart sank. There were only thirty
hours left until kick-off. It took twenty minutes.

Covered in World Cup logos, bar codes and holograms,
it was one of the most beautiful things I had seen all
year:

There was my name and the tag of our trip, a culmination of twelve months of hope, adventure and a breathtaking chain of events. I could but stand and stare, my photo grinning back in confirmation of this latest achievement thanks to the spirited goodness of Keith. It was valid for every single World Cup match. I was in heaven. My goal was complete. The table had worked its magic and opened the door to a childhood dream. I had a ticket for the World Cup final.

Or did I? 'This pass does not get you into any of the matches,' ventured a nervous voice. My reverie was shattered. 'Pardon?'

'This pass is not like a ticket. The tickets for press were all allocated by a ballot in January.' Heaven had become a very ordinary place on earth. 'But . . .' I began. To be this close, to achieve the unachievable only to find it worthless, was testing every fibre of my being. Scarlett, the Ferrari, Spurs and the Premiership, likewise it was all a figment of my overactive imagination. Did I really think I could be that successful? Did I honestly believe that a few ordinary fans could break in behind the system solely on the back of goodness and adventurous endeavour? The fears, which had haunted every step in the back of my mind for so long, came rushing to the fore.

'But what you can do is put your name on the waiting list for each game.' A lifeline had been thrown. My woe had been too hasty. 'For every match there is a list to which you can sign up the day before at the stadium. This list goes to FIFA who tick those they think should get in. The names are then announced and the tickets handed out an hour before the game. Normally everybody on the list gets a ticket.' It sounded too good to be true. 'Whom at FIFA does the list get sent to?' I asked. 'Keith Cooper,' was the reply.

The true value of the press pass is its ability to access all that surrounds the match. We had wrestled our way past many sets of security on our travels so it was joyously that I strolled through seven sets of security hassle-free and out onto the pitch of the Sapporo dome. I was not alone. The England team were moments behind, about to be put through their paces one final time before the vital clash.

Henry Winter's jaw dropped when I walked past. 'You again!' he exclaimed. 'You'll be playing by next week.' The boots were, admittedly, on standby. Walking around, despite having a pass swinging from my neck, I still felt like an impostor. With each set of security I hurried my step, half expecting a shout, a clamour of recognition from someone, anyone, announcing my real status, and challenging my right to be there. I had every right in the world, perhaps more than some of the nonchalant hacks, but the fear of confrontation, of a scene, kept me shuffling back and forth out of view. There were a number of matches to go and I didn't want to blow anything now.

My pass granted me access not only to the press centre, but also to its computers. Every statistic imaginable was at my fingertips, and free to print out, along with quotes from press conferences, the post-match mix-zones and the latest news on the teams. On the Sweden game, Sven was quoted as saying, 'I think it is a fair result. We didn't win, we didn't lose.' But the reality of only gaining a point, not three, was clear. 'We know it's two finals we have to play if we want to go on playing in the World Cup. Hopefully we will play for more than 45 minutes against Argentina.' Hopefully? Hopefully?! What on earth did that mean?

On fire with anticipation, none of us could sleep in our 'Japanese style' hostel room in Sapporo. 'Japanese style', it seemed, meant that there weren't any beds. Provided with a duvet and a pillow each, we slept on the floor of the empty square room.

With three hours to kick-off Matt did not have a ticket. The excitement all around was reaching tempestuous levels and he simply could not risk my non-appearance on the press waiting list. I had signed up as instructed but did not expect my name to attract the vital tick. 'Because it's football' was sandwiched between the *New York Times* and the BBC. The hunt for the touts began among the carnival scenes of milling fans on the green spaces of the city centre.

There were tickets everywhere, it just depended how much you were prepared to pay for them.

As Matt haggled, I bumped into Jason, last seen in Munich setting off to the World Cup the other way round the world. Amid hugs and cheers he told me he had been in Argentina when the draw was made. 'They didn't even bat an eyelid,' he said. 'They are convinced they are going to beat us.' In Colombia his bus got hijacked and he was robbed with a gun to his head. 'What don't kill you makes you stronger, and if England win tonight I'm going to be in those fountains. We wouldn't be here if we didn't think we were going to win it,' he reflected, smiling widely in the afternoon sunshine.

And with that Matt landed his ticket. It cost him a whopping 50,000 yen (£300) but it was a ticket to England v Argentina and behind it was another story. He only had 40,000. Two passing England fans, Dave Mitchell and John Smith, who had heard of our tale in the papers, each gave him 5,000 yen to keep the dream alive. It makes you proud to be English. He returned beaming. Despite all his consternation and cash problems it was worth every penny.

Fairly drunk, in my England shirt, camera wobbling all over the place, I had to fight through a crowd of anxious journalists to see if my name was on the list. To my shock and wonder, Keith had kept his word and our trip had been recognised above those claiming a ticket by right of a plane ride and a pen. It was a triumphant moment.

It did not go to waste. Matt had his ticket off a tout and Malc and Nidge and I were already sorted, so I pressed it into the hand of a BBC cameraman I recognised from our press tour days on Jeju. Hopefully it would smooth over any bad feeling that might have spread after the antics of his producer. I asked if he needed a ticket. He nodded his head, and was stunned when I produced one. He was surprised to see me in there at all. I left him mouthing 'How?' and, buzzing from beer and the adrenalin, ran to take my seat next to my little brother for the pinnacle of the year so far.

England's daunting task of slaying the Argentinian beast was not going to be easy. 'Pace, ambition and class' was FIFA's summary of the Argentine side. In the words of the Colombian national coach: 'It is hell playing against Argentina.' He was right; it was hell.

In France 1998 there had been an early exchange of penalties then Owen's wonder goal and an equaliser from the Argies before David Beckham's fateful lunge that resulted in a red card. The ten men of England held on like heroes for over an hour and, in extra time, Sol Campbell headed the winning golden goal but it was disallowed and the game went to penalties. We lost. I remember it like yesterday.

When the World Cup finally came to the civilised time zone of France I was, as luck would have it, working at a school in New Zealand. I saw the game at 5 a.m. in an Australian backpackers' bar during the school holidays. We were devastated, but there, in Australia, with the morning sun climbing into the deep blue sky and perfect waves rolling onto a glorious beach, despair had a get-out clause: 'Fancy a surf?' This time it was different. This time we were in Japan, at the tournament, at the game.

With bated breath we watched in the Sapporo Dome as Owen weaved his way into the Argentine box. After the draw with Sweden, Owen had said, 'I had chances, it was frustrating and hard, but I'll be much better for the Argentina game.' He was. He went down. All eyes turned to the referee and the world stood still for what seemed like eternity. The crowd around me yelled, screamed, waved, prayed, hugged and exclaimed. There was no doubt, and, for once, the referee agreed: penalty.

The stage was set for the fairytale recovery to become complete. Up stepped David Beckham. 'I didn't have a choice,' said Owen, the nominated penalty-taker; 'he was going to take it, simple as that.' 35,927 breaths were held inside the stadium as the run-up began. The rest is history. An explosion of emotion rocked the dome as if we had won the World Cup itself. So much anger, bitterness and regret was banished in a split second of that euphoric 44th minute.

The remaining 46 were the longest I have ever watched.

My heart was in my mouth every time a blue shirt picked up the ball, which, with eleven shots and nine corners to their credit in the second half, was quite often. We walked a knife-edge of terror as if afraid to believe we might actually do it. An unbearable tension fuelled the crowd's shouts and choruses, and when the whistle finally came the cheer was almost bigger than for the goal itself. It had been a long bloody road but we had beaten the Argies. It was an even longer night.

'As a footballing nation we've been waiting a long time for this victory,' said Beckham when interviewed after the game. 'A lot has been said about my last World Cup against Argentina, and I think it's nice that finally I can lay it to rest.' The newspapers back home were a little more aggressive in their response to the victory. UP YOURS SENORS roared the *Sun*, Beckham's grin beaming out from the page.

We now needed just a draw against Nigeria to qualify from the group. A diplomatic 0–0 five days later in the humid heat of Osaka saw a noble exit from the tournament for Nigeria and a berth in the second round for England. The group stages, so easily a ticket home, had been successfully negotiated. Now we could really sit back and enjoy the tournament.

On our arrival at Osaka station, I had been able to take advantage of my press pass and get a free bus ride out to the stadium where I had the delight of sitting in the press enclosure, watching Nigeria train, while on the TV in front of me was Denmark v France. In faith to our Danish friends, I had put £10 on the Danes to win. They did not let me down, scoring two, knocking out the French (who had not even scored a single goal in the tournament) and securing a second round tie against England. We would see our friends again.

Continuing the Danish connection, I had kept in touch with Jan, the Danish stadium manager from Basel, Switzerland. Sadly he was not working for the Germans, but he was at the World Cup and keen for a rematch on the table. Somehow he had wound up organising a tour party of English fans. 'If you need any help with tickets then give me a call, I might be able to do something,' he said when I rang his mobile from the Osaka press centre. 'Of course, it depends on the result of the rematch,' he added with a chuckle.

Explaining that neither Matt nor Nidge had tickets, but that I could hopefully get one via the press waiting list, as I had for the Argentina game, I asked how he could lay his hands on more. 'I guess having travelled so far and had so many experiences and coincidences you will not be too surprised,' he said. 'I am working for David Beckham's parents.' Our paths had finally crossed.

The table had missed out on the first two of England's World Cup matches, but for England v Nigeria it enjoyed a starring role, set up among the milling crowds to much acclaim. It was stunning the number of people who had seen us in the news and were eager for a game.

Jan, meanwhile, had spoken to Beckham's mum and dad and told them about the trip. It was a staggering touch and possibly the best chance of getting their star son onto the table.

Months earlier, my girlfriend, Em, had been a star and written to David Beckham on our behalf. His press secretary had taken the time to call her up, but with the news that David would be unable to join in the table adventure.

We had subsequently tried his agents, his sponsors, his club and the English FA. But considering the nature of our trip, this was all wrong. It was about a human touch, not moneymen or contract-conscious agents. It was about an appeal to people's sense of humour and love of the game. What nicer way than to share our tale with the parents of England's captain marvel. Proud parents, their son is quick to sing their praises in return. 'My parents have been there for me,' Becks once told a newspaper, '... ever since I was about seven.' Bless him. Bless them. To my amazement they came up with a ticket for us.

Jan showed up for our rematch in time for the press cameras that were circling the crowd. In a teaser for the second round clash of England v Denmark (which, at that time, was but a prospect), Jan and I locked horns once more. It was a spirited challenge and Jan took a 2–0 lead, but the months on the road and the hundreds of games I had played paid off. England remained triumphant.

Amid the celebrations I was tapped on the shoulder by one of the most beautiful girls of the year, a friend from my hometown who was backpacking with her younger brother. It seemed so long since I had seen my girlfriend, or someone from home, that her timely presence blew my mind. It was a surreal day. I was even late for kick-off.

I missed the national anthems and the first ten minutes of a match I had travelled for twelve months and over ten thousand miles to see. The press waiting list was meant to have been announced at least an hour before the match but dissolved into chaos as, with ten minutes to go until kick-off, a man with only four envelopes finally appeared; the fight began.

A name was read out and the FIFA rep insisted on finding that person before moving onto the next envelope. He was a Spanish journalist. There was outrage that a Spaniard should top the list for an Anglo-Nigerian clash. Blood, it seemed, was about to be spilt. Jostling with the thirty or so irate journalists I could make out a list on the front desk. My name was there, but it was not one of those highlighted. I fled. Even if my name had been chosen I would probably have been set upon in rage. It was bad news for Matt, but he did not miss much. England's run of scoring in ten straight FIFA World Cup final competition matches came to a dire end.

It could not dampen the party spirit of the supporters though. With our friends from home, Hayley and Andy, we hit the town for what turned out to be a mammoth night. We even succeeded in passing Andy off as David Beckham's younger brother to some kids on the tube. They could see my pass, and the camera, so we acted as if we were following Andy, as if he was someone special, until they started to ask questions. Before he really knew what was happening, he was mobbed, only escaping after agreeing to many, many signatures. It made everybody very happy although Andy Beckham had a somewhat longer and more expensive night

than the rest of us. Having lost us late on, he not only got on
the wrong train home and accidentally fell asleep, but he got
on a bullet train and woke up in Tokyo, hundreds of kilometres away. It cost him £85 to get back. Efficiency has its
drawbacks.

Argentina and France crashed out in the group stages. The
two teams most favoured by our many table opponents on
the trip so far were out of the 2002 World Cup at the first
hurdle. The Argentinians were philosophical: 'WELL, WHAT
DO YOU KNOW, GOD ISN'T AN ARGENTINIAN,' said one South
American tabloid. The French were in a sulk. They now had
the ignominious title of being the first-ever defending champions to fall at the first hurdle without scoring a goal. After
all the money spent, it was an especially costly exit for the
French advertising industry. Va Va Voom anyone?

With Italy, Spain and Germany all on the other side of the
draw and struggling, Brazil were the only major team
between England and the World Cup final, a World Cup
final we all fancied we could win. First up though was the
minor matter of Denmark.

Despite our confidence, the finality of the day sparked a
nervous feeling. It was the knock-out stage. Someone would
be going home. We may have claimed the scalp of the
favourites, Argentina, but we had yet to shine. We needed a
kick-start, a bit of luck to spur us into action, and what better kick-start could there be than when the opposition
keeper slings the ball into his own net.

The pre-match beers were joyous as we successfully met
up with Alex and Morten who had arrived in Japan following Denmark's mighty win over the French in Korea. They
were impressively bedecked in Danish colours and were too
keen to remind us of their penalty victories in Laos. In order
to save money on accommodation we travelled up to
Niigata from Tokyo on the morning of the match and journeyed light, without the table. Retrieving it from the Osaka
press centre after the Nigeria game had taken hours.
Combined with the stress of sorting tickets for the others
beforehand it had been quite a day. I had decided that the

Denmark match was going to be solely about the football. No hassles, no media and plenty of beer.

Matt's lucky streak had continued. He had not decided to cast off his layers, but via the generosity of another England fan, a friend of Jason, he had a ticket for the match at face value. Had the gunmen in Colombia had a bad day and taken Jason's life, not just his wallet, Matt would have missed one hell of a party.

God, it seems, is not Danish either. Among the misty mountains of the Niigata region, on a steamy, rain-strewn night, England were 3–0 up by half-time and the congas began. A huge, potbellied bear of an England fan near us picked up the small Japanese steward in front of him in delight. The poor steward was terrified. He spent the second half staring up at this beast of a man, who was lovingly resting his hands on the steward's shoulders as the jubilant congas circled all around.

The Danes were devastated. To their credit they had cheered throughout. Using the zoom on our camera we could pick out Alex and Morten still waving their flags, but it was with resignation amid heavy sighs. Their favourite chant, 'I'd rather be a Viking than a Brit', now sounded a little hollow.

It was a cruel exit for them, especially after the high of whopping the French. In 1992 they had failed to qualify for the European Championships but, after the expulsion of the former Yugoslavia, they were recalled from their holidays and went on to win. Ten years on they honestly believed they had stumbled into the same kind of fortune. Unhappily, this time, it wasn't meant to be. England, and the table, had a date with destiny and nothing was going to get in the way.

'Saw you on telly mate, well done, that's f***ing brilliant.' The recognitions were becoming numerous and, as the alcohol flowed at the all-night 'Samurai party' in town (intelligently thrown by the local council to mop the revellers off the streets), they were getting more raucous.

Part of what made the evening's celebrations so special was the enthusiasm of the Japanese. They were hooked on the novelty of English clowns singing and drinking their way around the streets, and the English fans were hooked on the celebrity of it all.

The majority of tickets for the World Cup had been sold to the host nations. To overcome their neutrality, and to boost the representation of the smaller participating nations, each Japanese applicant was allotted a nationality with their ticket. They embraced it in spectacular fashion, dressing up, buying flags and shirts and merging in where they could with the travelling fans of that nation. It was a special sight. I cannot imagine it happening in any other country. The Japanese added their own touch to the 2002 World Cup, which surely will be remembered as one of the friendliest and most trouble-free in the history of football. Why throw pints at the Germans when a) they cost £7 and b) you can spend your time posing for photos with young Japanese women?

Our Danish friends had shared the same hotel in Niigata as the conquering England team. I could not believe it. Possibly our last and greatest chance had passed right under our noses. Of course the hotel management are going to block Englishmen with football tables coming into an England team hotel, but if you are a valid guest, booked in with a Danish family, then . . .

The Danes had to check out for the night of the match itself but checked in again the next day with me in tow. I had woken up on the 8 a.m. train to Tokyo well past the suburb to which they had been relocated and where I had intended to disembark. Unsure of my location, I got off at the next stop to investigate and in my hungover daze was promptly left stranded, alone on the platform, as my sleeping companions sped on to Tokyo. It took me some time to get back to Niigata and it turned out that I had only been some twenty minutes outside of Tokyo. So there I was, with the Danes, checking back into the England hotel in Niigata in front of the families and girlfriends of the England team. The team itself had left at 9 a.m. but, frankly, I was too hungover to care.

I did, however, get to watch Ireland's cruel exit to Spain

on penalties with Michael Owen's parents in a pub nearby later that day. Of course, I did not know this at the time, and neither did the Englishman sitting next to them who banged on about how Owen had dived to get the penalty against Argentina. He was mortified when, after they had left, a fellow Englishman informed us. Ireland had battled hard but, like myself on stumbling into the England team hotel, simply had not been prepared enough to take the chances presented to them. The difference between us was that, while they were packing their suitcases, we had a date with Brazil.

34. ENGLAND v BRAZIL

The tournament was really starting to sizzle. After the excitement of group stage qualification and the thrashing of Denmark we now had a week off to repair livers and watch every game we could. Each day we would get up late, play football in the park, get thrown out by the university officials who owned it, then settle down with Mama-san and Ryugo (her thirty-year-old son) to follow South Korea's spirited progress.

The South Koreans, co-hosts of the tournament, displayed astonishing levels of support for their young team, and were repaid handsomely with some mighty upsets. They had fire in their bellies. In their last group match they played Portugal. Portugal had to win to qualify for the second round unless the USA lost by two clear goals in the other group match against Poland. As news filtered through that the USA were 2–0 down it looked like the Portugal v Korea match might be tamely played out for a convenient draw, sending both teams through. In front of their home crowd the Koreans were having none of it.

In a display of passion, throwing away a second place spot in the group, which would have secured an easier second round match against Mexico, they took the game to Portugal and scored, topping the group and lining up a match with the now joint favourites, Italy. The Portuguese, dumped unceremoniously out of the tournament, were stunned. The Korean nation was beside itself with ecstasy.

The Italians were the next to fall. In our Japanese living room Mama-san shrieked with glee. History was being made. In the 4th minute Korea won a penalty, and missed. Italy, as expected, then took the lead. The Korean dream had faltered, but it was only for an instant. Their opposition, spoilt with the trappings of fame, simply could not contain the will of the Koreans. They were unknowns, playing on the biggest stage of their lives, roared on by an entire stadium of red shirts who carried their team forward in unrelenting waves of emotion. With just two minutes of the match remaining, Korea equalised. In our room, let alone a stadium filled with sixty thousand Koreans, the buzz was electric.

The Korean David was holding his own against the Italian Goliath. They needed luck, an Italian goal was disallowed and Totti was gloriously sent off for diving, but it was luck that they had earned with their character. Our table had been unable to slip behind the defences of the Italian FA in Rome, but in extra time the Korean number 19, Ahn Jung-Hwan, who actually played his club football in Italy for Perugia, became immortal.

'That man will never set foot inside this club again,' cried the Perugia President. The 1.76 million Koreans gathered on the streets of Seoul watching the match on giant screens could not care less what he said. Neither could Ahn Jung-Hwan. He had just scored the goal of his life, a 'golden goal' in extra time. Korea were through and Italy were on the next plane home.

The quarter-finals brought Spain and, as I had learned in Barcelona, Spain always lose in the quarter-finals. The Koreans, however, after Herculean efforts in their previous matches, looked tired and Spain scored twice. Yet the Koreans were on a roll and, as we had found in our surge with the table across the globe, when you are on a roll, everything seems to go your way. Both goals were disallowed. The game went to penalties. Korea won.

If Korea could reach the semi-finals then surely England could too. After the confident display against Denmark our nervousness had abated and we were starting to swim in the joyful waters of belief.

Comparing our record of qualifying for the World Cup with that of Brazil, however, gave some sort of idea as to what we were up against. The 2002 World Cup was England's second consecutive appearance in a World Cup tournament (we failed to qualify in 1994). This was on a par with other giants of the modern game such as Tunisia, Paraguay and Costa Rica. Even Saudi Arabia ploughed ahead of England on this statistic. By contrast, it was Brazil's seventeenth straight World Cup. Four times World Champions, they were in a league of their own.

The winning goal was, how shall we say, unfortunate. Our goalkeeper, despite so many past, pivotal saves, lacked agility in the crucial moment, and we all watched on in horror as the ball passed him by, curling into the net, condemning us to defeat.

It would have been hard to swallow but for the fact that the rules had been changed. Our loss to the Brazilians was a blow, but not a fatal one. For the first time in its history the World Cup format in the latter stages had been altered. Knockout stages were a thing of the past and a new round-robin (all play all) champion's league style format had been put in place. We were robbed of a World Cup winners' medal by goal difference alone. The slip against Brazil proved decisive and we had to settle for the runners-up spot on a rain-soaked pitch outside of Tokyo.

Had it not been for my brother's fateful loss of footing, the fans' World Cup five-a-side tournament would have been ours. While Matt stayed in bed, the 'Matt Licks Windows' team consisting of myself, Malc, Nidge and three new crusaders – Raj, Mike and Ben, in full England kit courtesy of T-Mobile – had momentarily carried the hopes of the nation. At the presentation ceremony, organised by the England Supporters Association, we proudly accepted our runners-up medals in their velvet-covered boxes.

Destiny had had one last masterstroke in store, for on the inside of my box were not the words 'Runner-up' but 'World Cup 2002 Winner'. And it was true. Whatever happened in the official England v Brazil match, the trip had been a success. We had broken down more barriers than had been humanly thought possible, far exceeded the expectations of our friends and, more importantly, we had done what we said we were going to do.

The official match in Shizuoka on Friday 21 June could have been so different. It was a scorcher of a day and Matt, of course, was without a ticket. This time he was rescued by the fact that I was an 'England fans' member. After scandalously turning down one thousand extra tickets from FIFA for the game with Denmark, the FA had finally come to their senses and were releasing extra tickets for the Brazil match to England fans members. Quite how these tickets had remained unsold until this point was one of the scandals of the summer. Hitting redial solidly for fifty minutes, Matt's waning persistence paid off and *voila*, he had a face-value ticket for what was being touted as the World Cup final itself.

In those final days leading up to the match, sleep was hard to come by. Whoever won our quarter-final would be favourites to lift the famous trophy. They would face a semi-final against either Senegal or Turkey and, in the other half of the draw, which would provide the opposition finalist, there only remained the USA, South Korea, Spain and Germany. We had beaten Spain 3–0 in a friendly some months before and had to fancy ourselves as victors over the inexperienced USA and the tiring Koreans. As for the Germans, taken apart 5–1 by us back in Munich, their former player and coach Franz Beckenbauer was to say of their quarter-final performance against the USA, which they sneaked 1–0, that 'If you put all the outfield German players in a sack, shake it about and punch it, whoever you hit would deserve it.'

As England and Brazil walked out into the belting Shizuoka sunshine I was running with my football table.

There may have been some expletives. On account of trailing out to find the pickup point for Matt's ticket and the massed queue for buses to the stadium we, to my anguish, horror and rage, were late. I could see the stadium, I could hear the roar, but my legs simply could not go any faster.

Where the earlier matches had been potential banana skins or marred by the mathematics of qualification, this had a touch of magic, the magic contained in a clash between a Brazilian team that are so wonderful to watch, and the blind hope and worldwide following of England, the home of football.

It was also the latter stages of the tournament. As with anything else in the world, the bigger it is the more the excitement will grow. The Brazilian broadcaster TV Globo's coverage of the match attracted 46 million viewers, an impressive audience for a broadcast that took place at 3.30 a.m. local time. No one wanted to miss a thing.

In the 23rd minute my head was buried into the bosom of the supporter next to me. A slip by the Brazilian defender, Lucio, an ice-cool finish, and Michael Owen had taken us to the Promised Land. Adrenalin coursed through my body as England fans all around me threw their arms to the skies in jubilant choruses of thanks to the heavens. England were 1–0 up against the Brazilians. After days of grey clouds and ominous horizons, the rays in Shizuoka blew away the shadows and, led by Owen, highlighted clear as the blue above that the tournament was England's for the taking.

Yet the fans never sang of glory. 'We're not going home, we're not going home,' was their choice of verse. The Brazilians on the other hand believed they could, should and would win, and the quality behind that belief burst the English bubble on the stroke of half-time. The buck-toothed wonder we had laughed at in Paris, Ronaldinho, made a surging run straight through the heart of the English midfield. Making a mockery of Ashley Cole, he then laid the ball off to the World Footballer of the Year, Rivaldo. He did not miss.

If Owen's goal had been fortuitous, then now was the time for England to show that they deserved to regain the lead. They passed, hassled, harried and engineered, but lacked the magic of the current masters. We watched on, painfully, as their demise unfolded in front of us.

I should not have cheered as much as I did all those moons ago in Esfahan. I had delighted in the misfortune of the Yazd team at the freak cross-cum-shot that had drifted over the keeper's head and sealed Esfahan's victory. In the 50th minute Brazil won a free kick on the right wing. Seaman flapped, we fell to our knees, and Ronaldinho peeled away in celebration as his free-kick nestled into the England net. In five minutes of play the lead had been reversed: it was England 1 Brazil 2. What goes around comes around and now it was England's turn to taste the bittersweet fortune of another team. The dream was over.

'I think we could have done better,' said Sven in one of the understatements of the tournament. 'We were chasing, chasing and I do not believe we had one shot on goal.' He was wrong. They did; but it came from Danny Mills, a statement in itself.

England had been thrown a lifeline seven minutes after Ronaldinho's goal when the plucky scorer was sent off, yet failed to seize it. Against ten men for 33 minutes they generated that single shot from a defender, Mills. The Hindu jungle masters had done what they could but as our Buddhist friends from Nepal had said, 'A goal can never be reached through force or by aspiration and ambition alone.' We thought we were destined to win the World Cup, almost by right. The Brazilians played for it, pure and simple, and their compassionate desire stemmed beyond the world of football. 'I want to say my last words to the people of Brazil,' said their coach after the game. 'Believe. Believe, because we can do much more. Not only football, I want to say all the nation can do more.'

Until next time, England were out. I was forced finally to confront my biggest, inevitable fear. The trip was over. The magic seemed at an end, fading with the sunlight as the shadows drew across the empty Shizuoka pitch. I was the last fan to leave the stadium.

The feeling was a numbness creeping through my body and mind. I could not clap. I just stood and watched. Watched as others raged, applauded, sang and cried. The players exchanged shirts and Beckham led them on a circuit to thank the fans. For some of the team this acknowledgement seemed too much. They trailed round, eyes distant, which upset me more. It was emotional, but on a scale of emotion their triumphs and woes can never really match those of a fan, for it is the fans who make the game and who sacrifice so much to support their heroes. '*Con el socio todo, sin el socio nada*': with the fan everything, without the fan, nothing. For some, this journey, this tournament and this match would be the pinnacle of their lives and incomparably superior to their daily life and work. Yet some of the players could not find the energy to applaud them.

The Japanese have a strong tradition of honour. It extends to failure, for there can be honour in defeat. The idea of 'noble failure' originates from the story of a legendary Japanese Samurai who was betrayed and surrounded. Outnumbered, with no hope of survival, he calmly met his fate by the strength of his own hand, by *seppuku*', kneeling and then falling onto his sword. He would commit suicide rather than surrender. This idea of noble failure is massive in Japan.

The drama of David Beckham overcoming his personal demons adorned the covers of even the baseball-orientated daily papers. It was an inspiring tale and a memorable victory, which meant that, come the 94th minute in the quarter-final, when the whistle went and England lost, he had still triumphed. His team of warriors had taken a lead against the best in the world and gone down still coming forward. As he raised his arms to the fans the Japanese praised his nobleness. As an Englishman, the defeat was still hard to swallow.

Twenty-one days earlier, when the World Cup had finally kicked off after our months of travel to reach it, a sickening feeling had begun to grow in my stomach. England's elimination would spell the end of the adventure. The planning, the expectation, the stories, the hope, the longing, the excitement and the fantastic rollercoaster that we had ridden for the previous ten months would stop, abruptly and without thought for our dreams.

In Shizuoka, as I stood there in the stands, I felt as if it had been cut short, as if I had stumbled rounding the home straight. The next day was even worse; I was a million miles away from home in Tokyo, for no reason. My reason had vanished. The players would be on their pre-organised flight back to England, leaving their faithful followers to cope on their own. I was miserable. Inconsolable. Our long tour, after so many omens and fateful signs, had failed to end as we had so hoped it might.

35. THE GRAND FINALE

It was the Koreans who pointed out my mistake. Desperately hunting for the next flight home I watched them take on Spain in their quarter-final. They were lucky, but the penalties in which they triumphed set my blood racing once more. Unperturbed by the spectre of defeat they had fought to the end, securing success against the odds.

Our reason had not gone. The table, which was the champion of our journey, and our goal, the World Cup final, were still there and in my hands I had a World Cup press pass. The tour was far from over. Its biggest challenges, a ticket for the World Cup final and the touch of the greatest footballer on earth, were still to be met. England would not be there, but more than purely the success of our national team, it was the competition that had drawn us this far and the challenge of attempting to work our way into its legendary culmination, the final.

Just twelve hours later, Nidge and Malc's immediate decision to depart inadvertently swayed mine to stay. Any temptation to wallow in the easy option of disappointment was given the boot by a blinding night-out in Tokyo to say farewell to them. While I was unable to convince them to remain, that last night saw a re-ignition of my dream of capturing a ticket for the World Cup final. Who had I been kidding? I couldn't give up now, days away from our initial goal. I might never be in such a position again. We had a story. Despite England's elimination the table was on a roll; we could not bail now. The trip had only one end date and that was 1 July, the day after the final. Matt was in agreement. We were in it for the duration.

I awoke on the Tokyo metro. My head was pounding, my stomach felt decidedly unstable and the early morning commuters were wisely giving me a wide berth. In my hand was a business card. The memories came flooding back. An American modelling agency was in town. Stumbling into a club called 'The Lexington' with our camera, and with more than a few beers inside us, we had talked our way, courtesy of the owner, into the VIP section, which was filled with some of America's finest young ladies, free drinks and tickets to the World Cup final.

Yet again, it was too good to be true. I met a guy called Chris Rosaasen, who was with them and had his own clothing line in the U.S. He had seven tickets put aside for him to entertain some of the girls and on hearing our tale offered to include Matt and me. While maddened that tickets to the world's greatest sporting event should be dished out in this manner to such indifferent recipients, we were quick to capitalise on our good fortune.

What a climax it might have been. Unfortunately, as I said, it was too good to be true. After the exchange of a number of emails I heard no more. Fortunately, in the meantime, I took a gamble on the press waiting list and was richly rewarded. Brazil carved up Turkey 1–0 in their semi-final and I was there. I got a seat sitting behind former Arsenal and England striker Alan Smith and next to a comedy journalist from Pakistan who, after ten minutes, tapped me on the shoulder and asked what colour Brazil were playing in.

The day before I had made the trip out to Saitama Stadium, yet again, to sign up and test whether Keith would continue to tick my box. He did, and this time I collected my ticket in more extravagant fashion. 'Andy Sloan, Because it's football,' said the FIFA official. In front of a crowded room of journalists, my name was read out third. A number of

Burberry-clad English journalists choked on their coffees. 'Because it's what?' I heard one guy say to his mate as I strode forward, '. . . the cheeky bastard'.

Not only did I get to see Brazil step up another gear and simply outclass the Turks, I found a form for World Cup final accreditation. Accreditation for the final was not allocated until the two finalists were confirmed. Could it be possible that Keith would bend his rules enough to grant me a place? I could but try.

When Keith had initially heard about us from his colleague Daniel Rupf, whose cousin we met in Iran, I had cheekily asked via email if he could grant us press passes. Despite his willingness to help, this, he replied, was out of the question. Yet over the next few months I continued to send updates of our travels and he warmed to the table. He had learned its rough progress from the cauldron of Iran v Iraq, surviving riots in India, to high altitude in the Himalayas, and was so impressed by our 'extraordinary initiative' and how the table had become our passport across the globe that he was prepared to bend the rules that bit further for us. After all the contact, and his fantastic generosity in sorting me out with a press pass, it was time to meet him.

'Now, our final stop this morning is to introduce these two young men over here, Andy and Matt.' On the morning of the final, the last day of the tournament, Keith introduced us to the world in the closing press conference of the 2002 World Cup. After a video about FIFA's dope-testing throughout the competition, which revealed that Ronaldinho (sent off in the England v Brazil game) and Danny Mills (who caused Ronaldinho to be sent off) were both 'randomly selected' post-match and had to share a room, he turned to us. 'These two guys, since September, have been hitchhiking on buses and trains and God knows what else on a very modest budget. We said if they made it to the final that we would give them a couple of tickets, so we are keeping that promise. Their passport through these 26 countries was the tablefootball game in front of you. Andy, do you want to come up here and tell us all a bit about it . . .'

My head swam. Walking up to the podium to take a seat

in front of the microphone I blushed with pride. In J.R.R. Tolkien's *Lord of the Rings*, Sam turns to Frodo and says: 'Perhaps one day, Mr Frodo, people will write about us. They'll sing songs and tell tales, and we'll be there to laugh with them.' Sam gauged it as a form of success, of acceptance of something remarkable, and it wasn't until now that I was finally able to let myself relax and look back on our journey with a sense of achievement.

The dream of seeing England lift the World Cup may not have come around this time but Daniella Ralph had wound up her *Six O'Clock News* piece on us perfectly:

> ... They draw a crowd wherever they play, they're treated like celebrities. A map and a game have brought them their own kind of World Cup success.

And Keith more than kept his word. He had personally ensured the completion of our year-long quest. Both Matt and I had tickets for the World Cup final. He had also gone one step further. On the day of the final, Keith had arranged a fitting finale for the table.

In person, Keith was even more accommodating than on the phone. His mind was clearly racing when we met him and, considering his position, he had a million things for it to race about. Despite this, his gentle easy-going manner seemed to generate time within the bustle, and when he approached us after a long wait we felt embarrassed for the inroads we were making into his last few hours of organisation. It was then that he revealed he had been running around trying to organise a rather special audience for the table – the greatest footballer of all time: Pele. Mr Keith Cooper is one remarkable man.

Pele, on the other hand, was late. In a hotel in central Tokyo we were carefully vetted, checked and double-checked by his security team. The great man's movements were choreographed to the minute but he succeeded in infuriating them by taking time out for the table. Pele, three times World Cup winner, lived up to his billing. As he was marched by his entourage across the lobby towards us, already late and with the limousine engine already running outside, our chance seemed to be fading fast. Yet he stopped, said hello, dallied and posed for pictures; he just could not resist. Halfway out the door he came back for more.

As regards donning a Brazilian shirt and challenging England to a rematch on the table, he hesitated. 'Sorry, sorry, I am late, it is late, we must all go.' He dithered but then made the dash to his car. Even once placed in his limousine, and having driven out of the hotel, he returned to ensure a little Japanese girl, who had missed out on a photo as he had driven off, got all the shots she wanted.

Matt looked at his watch. 'Shit, he's right, look at the time.' Whereas Pele was chauffeur-driven to the Yokohama stadium we had a ten-minute run, three tubes, an hour-long train journey and a bus ride. My proposal that there might be just enough room in the limo for three men and a football table had not been accepted on the grounds that the main security man was around 7-foot tall and almost as wide. At least we had the greatest possible excuse for being late to a World Cup final: an audience with Pele.

The World Cup final is an event of staggering proportions, the most viewed occasion in the world; a match composed of football's hottest talent, the finest technique, the greatest finishing . . . and the Germans. Mama-san had predicted it. Asked why she thought they would beat the Koreans in the semi-final her reason was clear, firm and perfectly logical. 'I . . . like . . . white.' In an ideal world England would have been there, but the man upstairs had a sense of humour and had sent the Germans through. The last laugh though was ours. Brazil, spearheaded by the rejuvenated Ronaldo, set the stage alight with two goals to seal a record-breaking fifth World Cup title.

There were actually two finals taking place that day. Bhutan had played a role in the table's encounters and, at the death, was not to be forgotten. In what was hailed as 'The Other World Cup Final', Bhutan (ranked 202nd out of 203 in the world by FIFA) were playing Montserrat (ranked 203rd) to decide the worst international team in world football. Ghinley, the monk we met in Bodhgaya whose cousin played in goal for Bhutan and was coached for a spell by the American we met in Kathmandu, must have been on cloud nine, especially when it was revealed that the match was to be played in Bhutan, at altitude. Bhutan won 4–0.

And so it had been done. The trip ended in the Yokohama Stadium, Japan, some 342 days after it began, on a magical night indeed. The match itself was a good one by previous final standards but it was not until the famous trophy was presented that my heart truly leaped. As thousands of cameras flashed like so many blinding stars, the Brazilians hugged and wept on the pitch, the crowd cheered the result and the anticipation built while the presentation stage was erected. This was where the magic lay. The most celebrated and photographed moment, the moment beyond scoring the winning goal to which every little boy aspires: the thrusting aloft of the beautiful trophy.

The ground seemed to shake with joy as the prayers of so many were answered in a single moment. Everyone around me was filled with an irresistible euphoria and the well-behaved press area in which I was sitting erupted with a mixture of delight and amazement at the moment. It was impossible not to be touched by awe.

To receive the trophy, Cafu, the Brazilian captain, was helped aloft a small pillar on the stage and handed the globe-topped prize. He raised it in triumph as over three million multi-coloured origami cranes fell from the skies over the sixty-thousand-strong crowd and the sound system erupted with the climax of the World Cup theme tune. It was a feeling I will never forget. I cannot imagine what it must have been like to be Brazilian, let alone on the pitch. Words simply fail, for when something has been driven for with body, heart and soul, success is sweeter than anything in the world.

'Nothing could ever be as rewarding as winning the World Cup,' said Ronaldo in an attempt to explain a fraction of what he was feeling. 'It's not that sex isn't great, just that the World Cup is only every four years.' Worldwide, a record 1.1 billion people downed tools and watched on as another never to be forgotten moment of football history was etched into their memories, Cafu raising the ultimate prize to the heavens.

Only in this moment of euphoric climax did I finally notice a small sticker that capped off our year. There it was attached to the back of my seat. Beyond our wildest imaginations this was something we could never have foretold. 'Because it's football,' read the label. We had a seat with our name on it. There is a God and he plays tablefootball.

The day after the night before, I was standing on the same spot with the table, a last final pitch invasion. Now empty, the stadium still resounded with the magic of the previous evening as I gave my final piece to camera across the companion that, although inanimate, had brought such life to our journey.

During the match I had seen a number of people from throughout the trip. Their reactions on seeing us there, accredited in the World Cup final, were worth all the effort. There was Henry Winter, first met in Munich, Emmet Malone from Iran's match in the UAE, Jake from the offices of 'FootballAsia' in Singapore and Daniella Ralph from the BBC. The emotion of the final had lingered and, tinged with my own feelings as the curtain fell on our year, I was sad to leave. Matt had stayed in bed. No matter how far you travel, what you see or do, some things never change.

Within hours the table commenced its retirement and we boarded our plane home, exhausted but content. Beckham had eluded us but then perhaps it was better that way. He remained an image on the television, a poster on the wall, a fiction, clear of the imperfections of real life. We had had our taste of the football world. With the nonsense of the football table, goodwill had triumphed over the commercially shrouded new era of football, but there should always be something more that remains uncovered, untouched, enabling fairytales to build and legends to grow, because without them we would not have dreams to aspire to; and if we changed our minds? Well, we were already counting the days until Germany 2006.

The tablefootball quest had been hailed as 'brilliant', a 'stroke of genius' and a 'great idea' during the course of our journey. Yet it was simply a drunken moment. The only 'brilliance' came from the fact that we had carried it out. That was it. We had dared to dream, dared to take the first initial step, and from there the adventure unfolded. The table was our key to the numerous challenges that befell us and surpassed our expectations as a remarkable passport all of its own. Our year on the road had treated us well and blessed us, and the many characters we met, with countless memorable experiences. As the master storyteller Tolkien wrote, 'Step out your door and who knows where you'll be swept off to.'

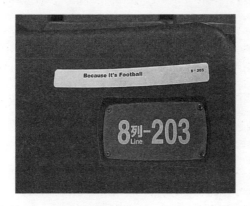

THE END

INDEX